The Option for the Poor in Christian Theology

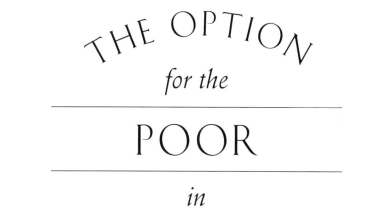

THE OPTION

for the

POOR

in

CHRISTIAN THEOLOGY

edited by

DANIEL G. GROODY

University of Notre Dame Press
Notre Dame, Indiana

Library of Congress Cataloging-in-Publication Data

The option for the poor in Christian theology / edited by Daniel G. Groody.
p.   cm.
Includes index.
ISBN-13: 978-0-268-02971-5 (pbk. : alk. paper)
ISBN-10: 0-268-02971-7 (pbk. : alk. paper)
1. Poverty—Religious aspects—Catholic Church—Congresses.
2. Liberation theology—Congresses.   I. Groody, Daniel G., 1964–
BX2347.8.P66O77   2007
261.8'325—dc22

2006039789

∞ *The paper in this book meets the guidelines for permanence
and durability of the Committee on Production Guidelines for Book Longevity of
the Council on Library Resources.*

To Gustavo Gutiérrez

and

Virgilio Elizondo

Witnesses to the God of Life and the Journey of Hope

CONTENTS

PART SIX. POVERTY, RACE, AND GENDER

PART SEVEN. POVERTY, LITURGY,
AND POPULAR RELIGIOSITY

PART EIGHT. POVERTY, RELIGIONS, AND IDENTITY

INTRODUCTION

DANIEL G. GROODY

In the spring of 2000, Virgilio Elizondo and I attended a meeting in Paris, France. While we were there, he asked me if I wanted to get together with a good friend of his named Gustavo Gutiérrez. I was grateful for the invitation because for many years I had been greatly influenced by Gutiérrez's writings and welcomed the chance to meet him in person. The three of us went out to lunch together and spent hours talking about many things, not the least of which was the option for the poor in Christian theology and where it stood as an issue within the church and the academy today.

This lunch in Paris was particularly timely. It was becoming less clear where this topic of the poor fit within the discipline of academic theology. Undoubtedly, many today recognize how Gutiérrez has pioneered a new area in the discipline and has put this whole notion of the preferential option for the poor on the theological map. But as I looked at the current state of the question, I wondered if, at least in theology, the theme was receding into the background.

There were various reasons why the preferential option for the poor seemed at low ebb. One was the inevitable development of the theme and its transformation into new expressions, accelerated in particular by

1

changes brought about by globalization. While Gustavo's groundbreaking work *A Theology of Liberation* in 1973 reflected on the preferential option from the perspective of those who faced dire economic poverty, in the years that followed it became evident that this option had to include not just those who were marginalized economically but also those who were poor because of gender, race, culture, and other reasons.[1] As the idea developed, this central notion of God's preference for the poor extended to all who are vulnerable. The notion has not disappeared; whereas in previous generations most areas did not show even a trace of reflection on the subject, today almost every area of theology shows its influence.

At the same time I realized that the notion of the option for the poor could be understood so broadly as to lose much of its meaning. Saying "We are all poor" takes the edge off the challenge of the option and makes the notion so commonplace that it is hollow and empty. Such a perspective also preempts the conversion process that is inevitably a part of this option. Further, it can reduce the task of theology to an abstract exercise rooted in peripheral questions rather than a concrete exercise of faith seeking understanding within the particular social challenges of our contemporary context. Partially because our understanding of poverty has become more and more complex, and also partially because the option for the poor has become so watered down that it can apply to everyone and mean little, many theologians now believe that the liberation theology of the late 1960s through the 1990s has made its contribution and run its course. Some might even say the river has dried up. Given that fewer people seem to be interested in the topic, it looks almost as if this topic has been somewhat of a theological fad that has come and gone. The fire that ignited such passion a few decades ago has burned low, and as the coals of liberation begin to lose their heat some wonder whether it will simply die out all together or be just an occasional spark here and there. As Gutiérrez, Elizondo, and I ate lunch, I thought much about these questions, so it seemed particularly urgent to throw some more socioeconomic wood on the theological fire.

POVERTY: AN ANCIENT PROBLEM, A CONTEMPORARY THEOLOGICAL CHALLENGE

Since Elizondo, Gutiérrez, and others began writing about poverty and liberation in the 1960s, in many respects the situation of the poor today has gotten worse, not better. While there is good news that more than half the world is experiencing economic progress because of globalization, the bad news is that the other half still does not have even one foot on the development ladder.[2] More than half of the planet still lives on less than two dollars a day, and the current course of globalization has only further widened the gap between the rich and the poor. The income disparities between the richest and the poorest have deteriorated at a rate never before witnessed in human history.[3] The economic difference between the richest and poorest countries was 3:1 in 1820, 11:1 in 1913, 35:1 in 1950, 44:1 in 1973, and 72:1 in 1992.[4] Research in the new millennium indicates that this gap continues to widen and worsen.[5] The critical condition of the poor in our times makes the concept of the option for the poor not less but more important than ever. And the task of thinking critically and academically in the face of the current, complex social reality of poverty is one of the great theological challenges, if not the central theological challenge, of our times. This volume seeks to address that challenge as well as examine the ways it is being reconceived and renegotiated in light of today's global realities.

Gutiérrez, Elizondo, and others like them did not invent the notion of the preferential option for the poor but rather drew it out of the Christian tradition. They sought to read current social problems in light of the Gospel, as did the first Christians. From the earliest days of the church, the reality of poverty has made an explicit demand on Christian conscience.[6]

The preferential option for the poor is in fact one of the oldest and most central themes of Scripture. Amidst the doctrinal controversies of the early church, when many dimensions of the faith were being debated by Paul and theological doctrine was still up for grabs, the one thing that was clear to all of them—whatever their doctrinal differences—was "to be mindful of the poor" (Gal. 2:10). This is no less true today. Whatever doctrinal and ecclesiastical controversies the church faces, the one central issue of Christian faith that all can agree on is commitment to the poor. What does theology say to the countless people still subjected to high infant mortality, inadequate housing, health problems, starvation wages, unemployment and underemployment, malnutrition, job uncertainty, compulsory mass migration, and many other problems?

While theologians have made many important contributions over the last decades and liberationist themes have permeated various disciplines, the issue of the poor more and more appears to sit on the sidelines of Christian theology rather than be one of the central players on the theological field. Whatever else theology says or wherever else it takes us, the preferential option for the poor is at the heart of Christian theology. Without it, theology can become useless or irrelevant. But how does one make this option and do Christian theology in a globalized world and even a theological discipline that has become more and more complex? To me this is one of the great challenges that lie ahead, and it has been one of the great moments to build a community of reflection where a team of theologians could work together to reflect on how our theological task could be enriched when done from the perspective of the least of our brothers and sisters.

When Gutiérrez, Elizondo, and I came to the University of Notre Dame in the fall of 2000, I believed that one of the important places to begin this community of dialogue would be a conference on the preferential option for the poor. I believed such an event could bring together a group of senior theologians and honor the foundational work of Gutiérrez and Elizondo but also bring together from around the world younger theologians like myself who were interested in this same theme and could begin to advance the topic in the decades ahead. I also felt that the conference could bring together not only scholars but church leaders, activists, and other pastoral workers who work with the poor on the grassroots level. This gathering, I believed, could facilitate a rich dialogue on the option for the poor, engage a broad cross section of experience, and forge new networks of relationships that could bear fruit in new projects that would advance some of the pioneering work Gutiérrez and Elizondo had begun.

In the fall of 2002, this dream became a reality, and we sponsored a conference at Notre Dame entitled "The Option for the Poor in Christian Theology." We invited men and women from around the world to come together for three days to reflect on the reality of poverty, the biblical and patristic foundations of the option for the poor, and specific themes relating to culture, gender, race, and other issues. These presentations were the beginning of this edited volume. We also invited other scholars from different parts of the world to add essays to those we had from the conference, and the eventual result was this present collection. Through its essays we came to see how the preferential option for the poor has now extended to other areas like gender, race, and culture in a way that it has enriched many different areas of theology.

The Option for the Poor as a Theological Concept

Since the publication of Gutiérrez's groundbreaking work *A Theology of Liberation* in 1973, much has been written on the preferential option for the poor and liberation theology. Arguably, it has been one of the most important theological developments of the twentieth century. It has also been one of the most controversial. The option for the poor in Christian theology seeks to respond to the question: How can one live a Christian life in a world of destitution?[7] The starting point for Gutiérrez's work and for many theologians since then has always been the reality of poverty. That is, theological reflection begins from the perspective of those who are poor, those who are marginalized from mainstream society, who have no influence or voice in the socioeconomic and political processes that so profoundly shape their lives and condemn them to dehumanizing misery.

Though an accurate grasp of social reality is an important foundation to this book, we are concerned here with the option for the poor not simply as a socioeconomic problem or even a compassionate gesture but most of all as a theological concept. The option for the poor finds its meaning and purpose not simply in logical reasoning and humanitarian virtue—although it includes these—but in the very life of God.[8] One can speak about a preferential option for the poor because the Judeo-Christian Scriptures reveal first of all a God of life who opted for the poor in the past and continues to opt for the poor in the present. The whole ethical foundation for Israel rests not in an arbitrary commandment from God but in the memory of how God acted on behalf of Israel in her insignificance: "For, remember, you were once slaves in Egypt, and the LORD, your God, ransomed you from there; that is why I command you to observe this rule" (Deut. 24:18). In other words, the heart of Yahweh reveals a God who says, "Because you were poor and I had mercy on you, you too must also have mercy on those who are poor in your midst." In this sense, Israel's liberation from Egypt—a paradigm for all people oppressed in bondage in any form and called to live in the freedom of the Children of God—is both a gift and a demand. Because of God's option for Israel in her insignificance, Israel is called in faith to respond to others in the same way, especially to the widow, the orphan, and the stranger (Deut. 24).

While liberation theology has always begun with the reality of poverty, in recent decades much more has been written about how to understand the complex reality of poverty and its many dimensions. This volume begins, then, not with doctrine or Scripture or the experience of the early church but with the experience of poor people today. Gutiérrez's essay gives us a social and theological framework for understanding the multi-dimensionality of poverty. Elsewhere he notes that in some ways poverty is like Noah's ark: when we look inside, we see a poverty animal of every kind—spiritual poverty, racial poverty, gender poverty, and many other species. As Gutiérrez notes, "To be poor means to be insignificant." It does not mean only that one does not have money, although this is certainly a big part of it and one of the primary roots of the problem. To be poor means that one does not have options, that one does not have opportunities, that one dies before one's time. The poor undergo death on many different levels—sickness, fatigue, hunger, the violation of human rights—and they suffer dehumanization and the negation of life in many other ways. Though this volume looks at many different kinds of poverty, its essays are unified around the theme that poverty is contrary to the will of the God of life.

But this book is not just another work on the complexity of poverty and its many dimensions. Fundamentally, as noted above, it is about how to understand this reality from a faith perspective. Moreover, it is about how to do a faith reading of reality. If one may even put this forth modestly but directly, it is an attempt to ask, What does God say about this reality? What demands does this reality make on human conscience? How, in the face of the reality of poverty, can one live out an authentic response of discipleship? These are some of the fundamental questions that *The Option for the Poor in Christian Theology* seeks to address.

Following Gutiérrez's initial essay on the multidimensionality of poverty, we look at some of the foundational sources that shape our reflection on this topic. Among these, the principal sources are the Judeo-Christian Scriptures, as the essays by Elsa Tamez and by Hugh R. Page Jr. give us ample opportunity to realize. Tamez brings out how this option for the poor is not only the option of the God of Israel or the option of Jesus Christ but the option to which all Christians are called. In this respect, the word *option* can easily distort the theological meaning of the concept. *Option* does not mean that those who profess Christian faith can choose to work for the liberation of the poor or not, as if it were a matter of buying a red car or blue car. From the perspective of fidelity to the Gospel, the option for the poor is not "optional," as if one can say "no" to the option and still call oneself a Christian. Rather, *option* here means that there is a choice and that the choice entails making the poor central to one's vision of life, as they were for Jesus: "The Spirit of the Lord is upon me, because he has anointed me to bring glad tidings to the poor. He has sent me to proclaim liberty to captives and recovery of sight to the blind, to let the oppressed go free, and to proclaim a year acceptable to the Lord" (Luke 4:18–19). As Tamez says, "We can affirm that precisely because the love of God is universal, God opts for the poor so that there may no longer be excluded persons in society."

In a similar vein, Hugh Page explores what this option looks like from the vantage point of African Americans living in the United States. He presents the experience of the poor as the hermeneutical starting point for reading the Scriptures and shows how the Scriptures not only give us an account of the poor in Israel but offer marginalized groups like African Americans a new way of imagining one's life before God and before the powers that be. They subvert the existing power structure and offer hope to all who are oppressed: in other words, they give us a new way of imagining one's place in the world created by God.

The second major theological foundation for the option for the poor is explored in the essays by Brian E. Daley and Jon Sobrino, which show how, in addition to the Scriptures, the writings of the church fathers help us understand the early church's approach to issues of faith, poverty, and even martyrdom. The power of reading these church fathers, and looking at them in light of the current social challenges, is that of hearing them speak from their own generation an enduring and liberating truth for all generations. The patristic foundation offers a way of reading the present, and attentiveness to the present reality gives a new way of understanding the church fathers and their times. Daley looks at some of the anthropological and moral issues raised by the Cappadocian fathers— Basil of Caesarea, his brother Gregory of Nyssa, and their friend Gregory of Nazianzus—in the context of poverty of their own day and age, and he brings out how one of their major contributions was their Christological understanding and the philosophical tradition that anchored it. As much as these theologians dealt with formulating abstract theological language about the mystery of God as a Trinity, they "shared an urgent concern to draw the attention of their contemporaries to the plight of the poor, the diseased, the marginalized, the 'insignificant' . . . precisely as a challenge to faith in the transforming work of an incarnate, self-communicating God."

Jon Sobrino, who many know was a member of the house of the Jesuits in El Salvador who were murdered by death squads in 1989, speaks about how martyrs are witnesses not only of the ancient church but also of the contemporary church. Grounding his reflections on "the crucified peoples of today," he speaks of those who have chosen to opt for the God of life and challenge unjust structures—a varied group including peasants, workers, students, lawyers, doctors, teachers, intellectuals, journalists, catechists, priests, religious, bishops, and archbishops, only a few of whom are publicly recognized. He argues that the problem with the current state of the world is not atheism but idolatry, not a matter of if one believes in God but what God one believes in. His essay is a stark reflection on reality as it is defined by the poor, the defense of the poor as it reaches its maximum expression in the martyrs, and the martyrs as they bear witness to the undying love of God. Sobrino notes that "without a willingness to get involved in the conflict of reality, to shoulder its weight, and to pay some price, the church will not bring salvation. Nor will it have credibility."

While theological reflection on the option for the poor is thoroughly grounded in social reality and thoroughly oriented toward creating a more just and humane social order in this world, Christian hope also looks to the future as it looks for the fulfillment of justice. David Tracy and J. Matthew Ashley give us ways of looking at the option for the poor not only from the perspective of the past and the present but also from the perspective of the future as revealed in apocalyptic thought.

According to Tracy, the central problem is not about believing in God in a world of modern science but about believing in a personal God in an age when the poor are considered by the reigning elites as nonpersons. Just as the poor themselves are marginalized in society, the notion of the preferential option has been marginalized in much of theological scholarship. Nonetheless, the poor remain central to faith seeking understanding. An accurate grasp of this faith entails not only attention to the prophetic dimension of the option for poor but also attention to its intrinsic mystical dimension. Part of this mystical dimension affirms not only that Christ came in the flesh and concretely opted for the poor but that this same Christ will come again. Thus Tracy argues that to the great Christological symbols of Incarnation, Cross, and Resurrection we must add Second Coming, with its "Come, Lord Jesus!" Only through the integration of the apocalyptic dimension into the theological framework of believers can the church move from its comfort zone and temptation to domesticate the Gospel and truly discover its calling to working for a more just and humane society that will reach its fulfillment when Christ comes again.

Ashley's essay also reiterates that the option for the poor in Christian theology needs to turn to apocalyptic thinking to develop an adequate Christology, one that signals not only the negative dimension of "not yet" but also the positive in-breaking of God's reign in history. He brings out how part of this apocalyptic mentality, especially in the Gospel of Matthew, is revealed now in the "radical praxis of feeding the hungry, giving drink to the thirsty, clothing the naked, welcoming the stranger, caring for the sick, visiting the imprisoned." What is necessary to ground this vision of Christian discipleship is not only a theology of liberation but a spirituality of liberation that leads to transformed lives. In the process, one comes to see the importance of context in theological reflection and the hermeneutical privilege of the poor in understanding Christian hope. Ashley adds that the option for the poor is so pregnant a theological concept that generations will be needed to discover all the ways it adds to our understanding of God's saving self-disclosure in Jesus Christ.

Another important development in analyzing the multidimensionality of poverty and reflecting on its theological implications is attention to the area of culture. The essays of Virgilio Elizondo and Patrick A. Kalilombe give us powerful reflections on doing a cultural reading of the Gospels and a Gospel reading of culture. They bring out how important social location is in the doing of theology, and how, whether one admits it or not, all theology is culturally conditioned. Elizondo's essay begins with a declaration of his rootedness in the Mexican American culture of San Antonio, Texas. Kalilombe, on the other hand, locates his reflection within his experience of himself and the church in Malawi, Africa.

Elizondo's essay elaborates on the multidimensionality of a poverty that cuts across all socioeconomic lines: material poverty, psychological poverty, spiritual poverty, and existential poverty, which—at its root—is a cultural poverty that distorts how human beings come to understand themselves, define themselves, and relate to each other. This issue of culture also brings us face to face with how we deal with differences, especially cultural differences. Elizondo's essay reflects on how one encounters "the other," that is, someone who is fundamentally different from oneself. He notes that "the most injurious crime of the conquest of Latin America, and there were many horrible things about it, was that the white European *conquistadores* imposed a deep sense of shame of being an *indio,* mestizo, mulatto." Elizondo refers to it as a "branding of the soul." The ultimate meaning of the option for the poor can be found only in the reading of Jesus of Nazareth, who offers us new insight into what it means to be human, beyond the degrading stereotypes imposed on the poor by the sin of society.

Patrick Kalilombe's essay explores the successes and failures of the building of Christian communities in Malawi, Africa. His reflections are rooted in his experience in Africa, where the social order is breaking down and people wonder what their sense of purpose is. People's experiences of being dominated, subjugated, disempowered, oppressed, and exploited have led to poverty, insecurity, and the loss of hope for any meaningful development. Kalilombe notes that this is the antithesis of the kingdom of God. He clarifies that the proclamation of the Gospel is not about preaching salvation in the afterlife. Rather, what is needed is a comprehensive message of hope in this life, a hope that life will change for the better and that the poor will someday achieve "real freedom, joy, dignity, and power worthy of God's children."

M. Shawn Copeland looks at the experience of African Americans and brings out how many people in the world are multiply oppressed: because of their economic poverty, their culture, and their skin color. For these, poverty is not a concept but a way of life. As she graphically describes, "the poor are children who cannot breathe because of vermin-induced asthma. The poor are mothers who chain-smoke to stave off hunger. The poor are fathers who weep in shame because they cannot protect their families. They stand and wait in lines—to fill out forms, to eat soup, to bathe, to sleep. The poor are brought to resignation; they have no options." Copeland points out that the option for the poor in Christian theology is an option to stand in solidarity with those who suffer, an option for integrity with the God of life who stands with them.

María Pilar Aquino takes this point further in bringing out how the issue of the option for the poor relates particularly to the experience of women. She notes that "theological discourse that begins from and speaks about the crucified majorities, the suffering peoples, the great masses, or the poor is insufficient if it does not specify that these majorities are women." Likewise, Mary Catherine Hilkert points out how this issue must be addressed not only within the society at large but even within the church itself. Her essay is also a challenge to reflect more generally on all structures of oppression because oppression cuts across all boundaries of gender and brings out the fundamental human need for conversion.

Luis Maldonado and Casiano Floristán offer a view of the option for the poor from the perspective of popular religiosity in general and the Eucharist in particular. Maldonado's reflection on Christology comes "from the ground up." That is, the starting point for his reflections is not simply abstract doctrine, or even the experience of poverty, but the faith expressions of the people of his native Spain. Drawing on the life of the towns, villages, and cities of his country, he reflects on the integral relationship between community and Christology and the suffering of the people, and he describes the God of hope who emerges in a tradition uniquely their own. He brings out how the kingdom of God expresses itself in the profound act of table fellowship, a fellowship that has as its basis the sharing of a meal in which all people—and especially the excluded—are called to participate. The basis of the eucharistic celebration is the communal meal, a meal in which the rich and the poor share in solidarity with each other in the "dangerous and unsettling memory of Jesus."

Finally, although the option for the poor is at the heart of Christian theology, Michael A. Signer and Aloysius Pieris bring out how this issue is at the heart of other religious traditions as well. Signer gives us a glimpse of what care for the poor means within Judaism. He shows how the Jewish tradition, through its daily prayers, the Hebrew Bible, and the rabbis, gives the Jewish people "a vision of moral grandeur that requires each generation to be linked to courage and audacity of spirit." He reminds us that the option for the poor is a reflection on God's justice, which ultimately expresses itself in caring for widows, orphans, and the poor. Pieris looks to how an "identity crisis" in the early church can shed light on a similar identity crisis in the church today and especially on the challenge of preaching the Gospel in the context of Asia, where the majority are non-Christians and where there are many social, economic, and theological challenges on the horizon. However these challenges are answered, it is clear in all the essays above that the poor can and must continue to hold a privileged and central place in the ongoing task of theological reflection.

THE OPTION FOR THE POOR AND
FUTURE THEOLOGICAL REFLECTION

While the notion of the option for the poor has changed and developed much in recent decades, the depth of this theological concept is just beginning to be explored. At the end of the conference at Notre Dame, after the senior generation of scholars like those mentioned above had presented their papers, we gathered fifteen young, emerging scholars from ten countries to present the current trajectories of their research. They came from Africa, Asia, Europe, Latin America, and North America to form a community of friends who were interested in a common theme and capable of working on common projects together. These were people like Jacques Haers from Belgium (Christology/liberation theology); Clemens Sedmak from Austria (philosophy/theology/culture); Carlos Mendoza from Mexico (fundamental theology), Mary Doak from the United States (political theology), LaReine Mosely from the United States (black theology), Renata Furst from Canada (biblical theology), Michael Lee from the United States (Ignacio Ellacuría/liberation theology), Paul Kollman from the United States (Africa/missiology), María José Caram from Argentina (Latin America/ feminist theology), Gioacchino Campese from Italy (migration), Jude Fernando from Sri Lanka (Asian liberation theology), John Markey from the United States (American philosophy/liberation theology), and Sr. Therese Tinkasimire from Africa (pastoral theology). This moment of the conference marked an important beginning and an important transition. It was a time to express gratitude to those who had opened up new perspectives in theology, a time to found a new community of reflection, and a time to embrace new theological challenges in light of the pressing social questions of today. At the conference, each young theologian had a chance to speak about the particular context and his or her research trajectory, and afterwards, fittingly, Gutiérrez gave each young theologian a cross (handmade by Edilberto Mérida, the artist who made the cross of the "passionate Christ" on the cover of *A Theology of Liberation*). Gutiérrez put a cross in the hand of each and said, "Go forth and do theology according to the image of the crucified." It is my hope that this publication will contribute to this effort in some small way.

I would like to thank all those who helped bring out this book, in particular those individuals and constituencies from the University of Notre Dame, including the Department of Theology, the Institute for Latino Studies, the Henkels Lectures, the Institute for Scholarship in the Liberal Arts (ISLA), the Kellogg Institute for International Studies, the Mendoza College of Business, the College of Arts and Letters, the Graduate School, the Law School, the Institute for Church Life, the Center for Social Concerns, the Department of Art, Art History, and Design, the Center for Continuing Education, the Congregation of Holy Cross, Moreau Seminary, the

Program of Liberal Studies, the Holy Cross Family Ministries, the Office of Campus Ministry, the Office of the President, the Office of the Provost, the Daniel B. Fitzpatrick Family Fund of the Community Foundation of St. Joseph County, and the United States Conference of Catholic Bishops/ Secretariat for the Church in Latin America. Most especially, I would like to thank John Cavadini, Gilberto Cárdenas, Allert Brown-Gort, and Mary Doak for their constant support and guidance in this project. Many generous individuals supported our efforts, and I would like to thank in particular Mike and Liz LaFortune, George Dilli and family, Eugene and Denise Desimone, Robert Van Kirk, Mark Nishan, Chad and Paula Tiedemann, Macrina and Ed Hjerpe, Daniel B. Fitzpatrick, and Jim and Colleen Ryan. I am also grateful to all the individuals who were instrumental in translating, proofreading, and helping prepare this manuscript, especially Natalia Imperatori, Michael Lee, Sr. Rosa María Icaza, and Betsy Station. The dedicated, patient efforts of Terry Garza, Marisa Marquez, Claudia Ramírez, and Elisabeth Magnus helped refine and complete this project and added much to this final version. I am also grateful to Mary Miller, whose attention to detail, precise editorial skills, and quality work greatly contributed to completing this book. Finally, and above all, I would like to thank Virgilio Elizondo and Gustavo Gutiérrez, whose decades of work have inspired this book and whose graced friendship and committed scholarship have not only made this work possible but sowed the seeds of liberation for generations to come.

NOTES

1. Gustavo Gutiérrez, *A Theology of Liberation,* rev. ed. (Maryknoll, NY: Orbis Books, 1988).

2. Jeffrey Sachs, *The End of Poverty: Economic Possibilities for Our Time* (New York: Penguin Press, 2005), 19.

3. As noted in the 2005 Human Development Report, "On average, people in developing countries are healthier, better educated and less impoverished—and they are more likely to live in a multiparty democracy. Since 1990 life expectancy in developing countries has increased by 2 years. There are 3 million fewer child deaths annually and 30 million fewer out of school. More than 130 million people have escaped extreme poverty. These human developments should not be underestimated." At the same time the report says these advances should not be

exaggerated, since 10.7 million children never reach their first birthday, more than one billion live on $1 a day, and the HIV/AIDS pandemic has claimed three million lives and left five million infected, leaving millions of orphans in its wake. United Nations Development Programme, *Human Development Report 2005: International Cooperation at a Crossroads* (New York: Oxford University Press, 2005), 16–17.

4. Angus Maddison, *Monitoring the World Economy: 1820–1992* (Paris: Organisation for Economic Cooperation and Development, Development Centre, 1995), and *The World Economy: A Millennial Perspective* (Paris: Organisation for Economic Cooperation and Development, 2001).

5. See World Bank, *World Development Report 2006: Equity and Development,* (New York: Oxford University Press, 2005); Branko Milanovic, *Worlds Apart: Measuring International and Global Inequality* (Princeton: Princeton University Press, 2005); and Glen Firebaugh, *The New Geography of Global Income Inequality* (Cambridge, MA: Harvard University Press, 2006).

6. Justo L. González, *Faith and Wealth* (San Francisco: Harper and Row, 1990).

7. For a good introduction that examines this question in more depth, see Leonardo Boff, *Introducing Liberation Theology* (Maryknoll, NY: Orbis Books, 1987).

8. Gustavo Gutiérrez, *The God of Life* (Maryknoll, NY: Orbis Books, 1991).

Part One

THE MULTIDIMENSIONAL
REALITY OF POVERTY

Chapter 1

MEMORY AND PROPHECY

GUSTAVO GUTIÉRREZ

On the eve of the Second Vatican Council, September 1962, John XXIII would suggest an innovative pastoral and theological perspective when he spoke of the church of the poor. "Before the underdeveloped countries," he said in an oft-cited text, "the church is, and wants to be, the church of all people and especially the church of the poor." If this proposition had few immediate repercussions, the intuition behind it did have an impact in the following years.

It expressed a sensibility to the new questions humanity was asking itself and a willingness to listen to what God is telling us throughout history. That is, it suggested a reading of the "signs of the times," an invitation to adopt a view that was perceptive, critical, and at the same time hopeful, sensitive to the positive elements of the historical moment—regardless of how difficult that moment might seem—but also alert to the dark clouds on the horizon.

It is significant that at the fortieth anniversary of the pope's statement and of the opening of the council we find ourselves reflecting theologically on the paths that were opened on that occasion and through which the Christian community in Latin America's life and understanding of faith took shape. The perspective that John XXIII articulated manifests itself in the prioritized commitment to the least of society, which is formulated as the preferential option for the poor.

In the summer of 1967, I was welcomed to the University of Notre Dame by Fr. Theodore Hesburgh, C.S.C., and other friends, and I began work on the biblical significance of poverty and of the poor. In July of 1968 I taught a class at the University of Montreal and began writing on what we would later call the theology of liberation.

The expression *preferential option for the poor* was constructed piece by piece, starting from the experience of many people who belonged to many different Christian communities, as well as lay movements, in solidarity with the poor around the years when the episcopal conference at Medellín took place. The focus was later picked up by the Puebla conference, giving the phrase the recognition we know currently in many different areas of the Christian churches and indeed outside them as well.

The preferential option for the poor is not merely a phrase. It is a style of life that has inspired much commitment on three diverse but interrelated levels: the pastoral level, perhaps the most visible; the theological level, as a point of view for doing theology; and, as the basis of all this, the spiritual level, pertaining to the following of Jesus.

In this chapter, I emphasize the second of these levels, namely how the option for the poor relates to theological reflection. However, the option for the poor has a theological dimension because it is situated between the proclamation of the Gospel and the *secuela Christi,* or spirituality. What I find interesting is the theological challenge that comes from the situation of the poor, as well as the place and scope of the option within the theological task. Thus I am not merely mentioning one aspect of this option but rather going to the heart of it: it is a theocentric option, centered on the gratuitousness of God's love. Because God's love is universal, nothing and no one lies outside it; at the same time, God gives priority attention to the insignificant and the oppressed. The term *preference* in the phrase *preferential option for the poor* recalls both dimensions of God's love: universality and preference. By going to the root of these concepts we can understand the meaning of the option for the poor.

The preferential option for the poor was manifested with precision and beauty by a person who knew how to be in solidarity with the indigenous peoples of the lands that are today known as the Americas. I am referring to the Dominican missionary Bartolomé de las Casas, who in the sixteenth century said of the foundation of his defense of Indians' rights (and later of the rights of Africans, who were violently incorporated into the history of this continent): "God has a very vivid and recent memory of the smallest and the most forgotten."[1]

This text shall inspire three reflections. First we will consider the memory of God as the foundation of the option for the poor. We will then ask who the poor are and how we understand poverty. We will conclude with some perspectives on the tasks that lie ahead of us.

THE MEMORY OF GOD

The understanding of faith begins, historically speaking, from the location of the human person and the location in which believers profess their faith. From there they reflect, inspired by the memory of God, which is a "central concept in the biblical understanding of God."[2] Their own memory of the initiative of God's love is always present. This is the framework for the faith life of the follower of Jesus, which is also that of a "faith seeking understanding."

The Present of Our Past

In the Bible, memory is not principally, or exclusively, related to the past; its primary link is with a present that projects into the future. The past is there, but to give depth and fullness to the present moment of the believer. To phrase it another way, precisely and briefly, as Augustine did: "Memory is the present of the past."[3] If it evokes a previous event, it is because of the relevance of that event to the present. In both the First (Old) and Second (New) Testaments, expressions abound that say that God is at work in the world today and that consequently God's followers must make decisions in the present moment. Memory in the Bible goes beyond the conceptual; it points toward a conduct, a practice designed to transform reality. To remember is to have in mind, or care for, someone or something. One remembers in order to act. Without this, memory lacks meaning; it is limited to being a kind of intellectual gymnastics.

This is a memory that grasps time, subverts whatever cynicism and indifference have accumulated there over the years regarding the least ones of history, and converts it into a permanent, exigent, and creative present of the way to God, of commitment to the poor and struggle for the construction of a just and friendly world. This view presupposes a particular sensitivity to the time in which our lives take place and in which the reign of God begins to unfold, the coming of which we request in the fundamental Christian prayer.

Time acquires, in this way, an urgent, salvific, and human density. Far from being an abstract category, or from being limited to a tiresome chronological succession, time becomes, thanks to memory, a space where we encounter the face of Jesus, the Son of God made flesh, and a space for encounter with others. In time are rooted two liberties, God's free self-revelation in the gratuitousness of love and the human freedom to accept this gift; the first calls forth and constitutes the second.

The present of the past takes us back to the importance that the Bible gives to the present moment. The present is about the here and now of the salvific presence of God, which biblical texts like Deuteronomy insist upon—"The Lord has concluded this alliance with us here today" (Deut. 5:3)—as well as Luke's Gospel: "This scripture is fulfilled today" (Luke 4:21). Historical events constitute a challenge to commitment and reflection. It is necessary to live the moment with force and creativity. In our age, we find ourselves before uncertain and particularly challenging signs. They invite us to a discernment that will allow us to get to the essential without getting wrapped up in what is secondary or tangential, the trees that hide the forest. They call us to situate ourselves before the future, starting from the present.

For these and other reasons, biblical studies insist on the difference between history and memory.[4] The connections are clear but subtle; memory is not history, if we understand history as a simple narrative of past events, and memory is more than an actualization of what happened. It is a present that has its fount in the always active and ever-faithful love of God. This is a key to comprehension that makes "of history a theophany,"[5] a revelation of the God who calls us to life and rejects any form of unjust death. It places us, at all times, before the alternative that we find in Deuteronomy, a book that brings with it a rich theology of memory: "See, today I put before you life and good, evil and death . . . blessing and curse. Choose life, so that you and your descendants may live" (Deut. 30:15, 19).[6]

The God of the Bible is a God who remembers, a God who does not forget the covenant established with his people. A number of texts in Scripture allude to this. For example, "God remembers his covenant, his given word, for a thousand generations," says Psalm 105:8–9 at the beginning of a listing of all God has done for Israel in the past, the reason for giving thanks today and always. We are here before an evocation that is permeated with tenderness, despite the fact that many times the people turn away from the received precepts (see Ps. 106:45, the twin of Ps. 105).[7] Human beings' love for God has its roots in divine liberty and gratitude and not in the behavior of those God loves: "He has remembered his loyalty and fidelity to the house of Israel" (Ps. 98:3). It is, in effect, about the loyalty and fidelity of God.

Loyalty (Hebrew: *emunah,* firmness) gives meaning and strength to the established covenant. This is what makes God trustworthy, demanding and at the same time willing to forgive. Although it seems paradoxical, God forgets the people's faults because he is a God who remembers: he remembers the promise of love and the covenant (see Wisd. 11:23–24). Indeed, the prayer of the believer is frequently directed to this divine memory: "Remember, Yahweh, that your compassion and loyalty are eternal" (Ps. 25:6, see also Ps. 74:2; 89:51, 119:49). God's mercy and capacity for love go beyond even the Jewish people; this is what Jonah learns, though at great personal cost, according to the short text, one of the jewels of the First Testament, that tells us his story. Sent to Nineveh to announce the punishment that its conduct deserves, Jonah seeks to shirk his assignment out of fear that the warning will give the inhabitants, who have humiliated and oppressed his own people, the chance to repent and that Yahweh will then forgive them. In the end, however, Jonah is compelled to deliver the message that results in the city's being spared.

Making God's Memory Our Own

In the First Testament, whenever a pact was made, two wills were represented. Because of this, in the Bible, God's memory fosters the memory of the people who believe in him. Deuteronomy is a clear witness to this connection between God's memory and the behavior of the believer.[8] The giving of the law and the norms of conduct begins with "Remember that you were slaves in Egypt and that Yahweh your God led you out of there" and similar phrases (Deut. 5:15, 15:15, 16:12). The liberating act of Yahweh provides the meaning and the model for social life within Israel but also toward the stranger and the immigrant (Deut. 24:18).[9] The way God treats his people is the paradigm for how those who believe in Yahweh should act.

In the Second Testament, we find the same perspective. "Love one another as I have loved you" (John 13:34) is the new commandment of Jesus
to his disciples and in them to us. The free and gratuitous love of God,
the heart of biblical revelation, is the model of action for the believer. It is
the most important content of the memory that indicates the path for the
community of Jesus's disciples, whose commitment is, precisely, to be a
sign of that love in history.

Care for the poor is expressed, therefore, in a central theme of the
Bible: Jubilee. In a very concrete way, the celebration of the Jubilee gives
norms for the social relations of those who recognize Yahweh as their God.
These norms of justice and rights are expressed in a primary way by solidarity with and care for the most vulnerable. The Jubilee takes place in history as an event that points constantly toward the return of society to its
roots and to faithfulness to God's will for life: a society of equals in which
justice and rights are established. Believers do not place themselves in a
dark corner of human history to watch it go by; they are present in it, not
spectators but participants in the historical process.

Therefore, the Bible invites us to make God's memory our own. One
of the essential components of this memory is the priority of the oppressed
and forgotten ones. Let us take a particularly meaningful text, one that is
alluded to in the Gospels, as an example: Deuteronomy 15:1–11.

The fundamental assertion is "There should be no poor among you"
(Deut. 15:4). The goal toward which Israel should be directed in its practice of Yahweh's precepts appears with total clarity. It is a rejection, without concessions, of poverty—not only as an economic condition but as
a global condition of insignificance and of premature and unjust death.
To overcome poverty, to propose to oneself the construction of a society
without poverty, is to recognize, in practice, the gift of life that comes from
God. Thus this is a matter of great complexity, for in it lies the reason for
being the people of God.

To this statement the text, in a more realist mode, adds conditionally:
"If there are poor among your siblings . . . do not harden your heart or
close your hand to your poor sibling, but open your hand and lend what
he needs to remedy his poverty" (Deut. 15:7–8). The obstacles to reaching what is proposed do not negate the imperative of giving primary attention to persons in need; even less can they be the motive for a cynical
desire to leave things as they are. On the contrary, proper conduct is dictated, precisely and exigently, by the proposed goal: to open one's hand
to the sibling in need in the effort to forge a nation without poverty.[10]

One cannot deny the persistence of poverty in human history. Thus the text goes one step further and a few verses later affirms what was previously expressed conditionally: "The poor will always be with you" (Deut. 15:11).[11] This statement does not invalidate the search for a society without poverty; rather, it provides an additional reason to reiterate the attitude we have already seen: "Open your hand to your sibling, to the poor, the destitute in your land" (Deut. 15:11).[12] The ideal, what we should strive for, is that there be no poor; if there must be some, the conduct of the believer should be that of opening one's heart and one's hand to the poor.

"In Memory of Me"

At the beginning of the church an important encounter took place in Jerusalem among those largely responsible for the proclamation of the Gospel. It was resolved that a kind of division of labor would be undertaken: some would continue to proclaim the Gospel to the Jewish world where it arose, and others would take the good news to the Gentile world. It was not easy, as Paul testified, to see the universal character of the message of Jesus. At the end of this meeting, the pillars of the church at Jerusalem, James, Peter, and John, recognized the meaning of Paul's work. As they accepted his task they told him, and the others, that they should "remember the poor."[13] This was a point on which they all agreed, as various texts of that epoch attest (the Acts of the Apostles, the epistles of James and Paul). Paul claims simply and firmly, "It is something we have tried to do with all our effort" (Gal. 2:1–10). The recognition of this dimension of the church's mission happened early on; the meeting at Jerusalem is believed to have occurred circa AD 40 or 50, and the epistle to the Galatians was composed soon after that.

The text has frequently been interpreted as a direct—almost unique—reference to the help offered to the Christian community in Jerusalem. Some indications point in that direction. For example, in many places the texts speak of Paul's preoccupation with the organization of a collection to benefit the mother church (see Rom. 15:25–29; 1 Cor. 16:1–4; 2 Cor. 8:1–15; 9; Heb. 11:29–30). It would be tangential to analyze these texts here.[14] In them one can perceive a connection between the realization of the collection and what is affirmed in Galatians. But even the passage that asserts this connection most clearly, Romans 15, specifies that it is about "the poor *among* the saints of Jerusalem" (v. 26, my emphasis), a group that must not be identified, therefore, with all the Christians of that community.[15]

Furthermore, in Galatians 2:10 there is no direct reference to almsgiving, which was valued at the time as a manifestation of justice and solidarity with the poor. Of course, neither is almsgiving rejected. Thus the application of the phrase "Remember the poor" may be broader and more permanent, and it cannot be excluded that Paul may have considered this concern as an integral part of the apostolic task.[16] The importance of remembering the poor is especially upheld if we place the recommendation made by the pillars of the church in the greater context of what Paul has discussed about the meaning of what he calls "the truth of the Gospel" in the same letter to the Galatians (1:11–2:14).[17] Consequently, we find ourselves, it seems, before an intrinsic dimension of the work of evangelization.

This aspect of the proclamation of the reign of God is understood as a demand—"Do this in memory of me"—in Paul and Luke's accounts of the Last Supper of the Lord. It is a remembrance that goes beyond ritual, or, to be more precise, it is situated in the context of the basic understanding of cult in the Bible: it implies the memory of all of Jesus's teachings (cf. Matt. 28:20) through "his actions and words."[18] The memory of this joining of the testimony of the Lord seals the universality of the mission of his followers, who have been charged to take the good news "to all nations" (Matt. 28:19) and "to the ends of the earth" (Acts 1:8).

The eucharistic celebration, the central act of the life of the church, synthesizes the fundamental aspects of Christian life: the loving memory of God as expressed in the life, death, and resurrection of Jesus, the love for all, and the preference for the most insignificant and forgotten come together. The memory of the ways one should proclaim the good news and be faithful to the design of God's life and to solidarity with others is also included.[19]

It should not appear strange, then, that theologians and Bible scholars have pointed to how the God of the Bible is associated with the reign with the poor and the insignificant ones. We shall take the testimony of two of them, neither of whom is Latin American. Most clearly, Karl Barth maintains: "God always places himself unconditionally and passionately on the side of the poorest and only on that side: against the proud, always in favor of the humble, against those who possess and defend their rights, and on the side of those to whom those rights are denied."[20] For Joachim

Jeremias, in an audacious sentence, the "essential characteristic" of the reign of God is expressed in the first beatitude, in Matthew and in Luke, which should be read as "The reign belongs *only to the poor,*" keeping in mind that "the Semitic tongues frequently omit the restrictive adverb 'only.'" This is good news that cannot but scandalize the privileged of the time.[21]

The Poor and Poverty

Recently a series of historical events and new approaches to the analysis of historical reality have prompted an important change in how we understand the reality of poverty. For a long time poverty was considered a natural fact independent of human will: one was born either rich or poor. But poverty is not a fate; it is a condition, not a destiny; an injustice, not a misfortune.

A New Perception

Various factors led to a different understanding of poverty. The visibility of the misery and marginalization of many people, the appearance of movements in defense of workers and of those who have no access to work, the demands for the respect of the human dignity and human rights of each person, the demand to create a just social order, and the contribution of social sciences—subject to critical examination—for a better knowledge of the socioeconomic mechanisms involved all had a decisive role in the change. The growing awareness that poor peoples of the world took from their situation, their abilities, and their culture had a crucial function in this process.

It became clear that poverty is the result of the way society has been organized, in its diverse manifestations. Thus poverty results from human decisions that create social structures and give birth to racial, cultural, and gender prejudices that have accumulated throughout history. Consequently, the notion that the transformation of society is out of our hands gained ground. This perspective points to a collective responsibility, with an emphasis on who in society has the most power and privilege. It is that simple and that revolutionary. Since it was first proposed, the understanding of the complex reality that is encompassed by the word *poverty* has changed radically, leading to the rethinking, not the abandonment, of the classical forms of attending to the condition of need (such as direct and personal help and social assistance in cases of extreme poverty).

Despite the evidence, we cannot say that the new perspective—which centrally takes into account the causes of poverty—has become a generally accepted opinion in today's world, especially in Christian contexts. The inertia of the old ways of facing this condition and the resistance to a point of view that is undoubtedly questioning, if not conflictive, impedes this acceptance.[22] Furthermore, in our days we are witnessing an insistent and concerted effort to return to one of the most tired reasons that has been trotted out in the past to explain poverty: the poor themselves are responsible for the situation in which they live. If at other times in history it has been said that poverty was a punishment for moral failings,[23] now it is said that poverty is the responsibility of the poor due to their incompetence, negligence, or laziness.[24] This understanding gives excuses for not facing the current situation head on but does not prevent an analysis of poverty's structural causes.

A Complex and Planetary Reality

Poverty is a complex reality that is not limited to its economic aspect, however important that may be. From the beginning of its reflection on poverty, liberation theology perceived this diversity because the reality of multicultural and multiracial countries (as are the majority in Latin America) offered a direct and inevitable experience of it and because the Bible represents the poor in diverse ways.[25] This complexity of poverty was affirmed from the beginning, despite the later deepening of its particulars, in what today international agencies have begun to term multidimensionality. The early expressions *nonpersons* and *insignificant ones* used in liberation theology for speaking of the poor pointed to this complexity. They were used to bring to mind all those who were not recognized in their full human dignity.[26] Such nonrecognition occurs for various reasons, especially economic but also racial, gender based, and cultural.[27] All these can mark human conditions that the dominant mentality of our societies does not value. This judgment depends on mental categories and on social structures that remain under our control to change. Naturally, recognizing the multidimensionality of poverty leads us to see the delicate and conflictive nature of the issue, which is why many seek to obscure the variety of these causes. Discussing them, though, is demanded by honesty and is the only way we can get beyond an inhuman situation.

Additionally, the planetary dimensions of the situation in which the majority of humanity finds itself are being increasingly perceived. This pertains to all the aspects of poverty, but in terms of its economic aspect—the easiest to perceive—in the past persons would recognize only poverty that was near their homes or, at most, in their countries. Their responsiveness was limited to what they had before their eyes and within their reach. The conditions of life did not permit them to have a sufficient understanding of the state of things.[28] This situation has changed qualitatively because of the ease with which information can be gathered. What used to be distant and remote has become proximate and common. Furthermore, the studies on mass poverty carried out by countless organizations have multiplied the information available and the various methodological approaches to the complex reality of poverty.

Another element that has modified our approach to the subject of poverty is the deepening of poverty worldwide and the growth of the gap between rich and poor individuals and countries. This gap, according to certain economists, is leading to what has been called neodualism: the world's population is increasingly found at the two ends of the socioeconomic spectrum. Culture, race, and gender do much to determine placement on one side or the other of the divide. The effect of gender has led to justified talk about the feminization of poverty. Women constitute the sector of society most affected by poverty and discrimination, especially if they belong to oppressed cultures or ethnicities.[29] The gap between rich and poor has been widening for decades but has now reached scandalous proportions.[30]

Today we can no longer be ignorant of the causes of poverty or unaware of its complexity, extent, and depth, whether or not we have a direct experience of it. All of this information should be crucial in determining how we can manifest the human and Christian quality of solidarity with the poor.

Poverty as a Negation of Life

Life, a gift from God, is also the first human right. The poverty and insignificance in which many people live violates that right.[31] In effect, poverty means death, both physical death that is early and unjust, due to lack of the most basic necessities for life, and cultural death, as expressed in oppression and discrimination for reasons of race, culture, or gender. Theologically speaking, poverty is the negation of the significance of creation.[32]

It is contrary to the will-to-life of the Creator-God. To go to the root of the problem theologically is not to obviate its economic and social dimensions or the mechanisms of oppression and marginalization that produce it but merely to grasp poverty's cruel and deep meaning: its radical rejection of life, the gift of God, as this life is manifested in the narrative of creation.

Therefore, we find in Scripture the repudiation of poverty but along with this the *denunciation* of those responsible for this situation, who are frequently driven by selfishness and indifference toward other members of society. These are attitudes that, in a faith-based analysis, we call sin: the negation of the love of God and neighbor, which the Bible also calls death. Poverty is tied to injustice. The difficult biblical texts of prophets like Amos, Micah, Isaiah, and, of course, of other biblical authors on the subject are well known. The guilty ones are openly named. The Second Testament condemns, likewise, the abuse and violence suffered by the poor and contrasts their situation with that of the rich and powerful, of whom they are many times the victims. The Gospel of Luke and the terms used in the epistle of James are clear testimonies to this way of seeing things, but of course they are not the only ones. In various places this view is presented by what has been called the "messianic inversion," the insistence—expressed in various ways—that "the last shall be first." All these texts will later inspire various writings in defense of the poor from those known as the fathers of the church.

A Theological Matter

The condition of the poor, because it is deeply tied to inhumanity, is a radical and global challenge to the human and Christian conscience. No one— no matter their geographical or social location, their culture or religion— can pretend that they are not gripped by it. To perceive the condition of the poor, it is necessary to see poverty in all its depth and breadth. It is a challenge that extends beyond the social field, becoming a demand to think about how we proclaim the Gospel in our day and how we might present the themes of the Christian message in new ways. Poverty, in all its complexity and multidimensionality, is the negation of God's will-to-life; it is a situation that wounds, in many regards, the very heart of the good news of Jesus. The Christian is a witness to the resurrection, the definitive victory over all forms of death.[33]

We stand, then, before an issue that is fully a part of the context of theological reflection. Nevertheless, a good part of academic theology still has difficulty in recognizing this problem. Some insist on pigeonholing poverty in the category of social or economic problems without noting that this is only an aspect, albeit an important one, of a complex phenomenon of insignificance and exclusion. For this reason, they suggest that reflections that come from the situation of the poor and marginalized find their proper place in the frame of the social teachings of the Christian churches, which is undoubtedly important, but this position reveals only a partial understanding of the problem. Or, in the best cases, such reflections are considered contextual theologies, as if all theologies, including European or, more generally, North American theologies, were not contextual. A noncontextual theology, and there are those that claim to be such, would be so abstract as to be useless for the life of a community seeking to witness in history to the God-made-human.[34]

The questioning that comes from the least ones of society does not remain at the margins of the theological task. The issue has an impact on long-debated themes, and it takes theological reflection down new roads. For example, in the years around the time of the council, the concern for building society was seen as not only different but separate from the task of evangelization, or, more favorably, as merely an important part of pre-evangelization. Certain progressive theologies of the time went a step further, valuing the Christian commitment to social justice but still hesitating with regard to its evangelizing status.

The state of the matter today is quite different. Theological reflections, including those of Latin America, ecclesial events such as the Medellín conference, and other factors have led to a more comprehensive and precise language that is being assumed, bit by bit, in various instances by the ecclesial magisterium.[35] As John Paul II noted in December 2001 in an address to the Honduran bishops, "We should not forget that the preoccupation for that which is social is part of the evangelizing mission of the Church and that promotion of the human is part of evangelization, for this leads to the integral liberation of the person." This is why, the pope continued, the church should be attentive to the cries of the needy and insist on the "preferential option for the poor."[36] These are the same affirmations that thirty years ago were accused of reducing evangelization to the construction of a just society in the temporal realm.

Without Memory There Is No Prophecy

To conclude, I will consider future tasks for the church with regard to the three realms in which a commitment to the option for the poor can be situated: the proclamation of the social and pastoral Gospel, theological reflection, and spiritual life. We shall do this, furthermore, with an eye toward future tasks.

Against the Grain

The term *option* in the phrase *preferential option for the poor* can be properly understood only if we go to its roots, namely the sense it was given by Latin American theology in the mid-1960s, which would later be expressed at Medellín, of a Christian commitment to the poor. According to this focus, the commitment has two intimately linked aspects: solidarity with the poor and protest against the inhuman situation of poverty in which they live. The option for the poor has to do with a lifestyle and not with sporadic acts of proximity or assistance to the poor. That option is a perspective on human history that sets in motion our own lives and enables us to understand the Christian message.

It is urgent, as Walter Benjamin said, to read history against the grain, to consider events from the underside of history, regarding not only the problems that affect the poor most immediately but also other situations in which humanity is involved and other matters of Christian faith. Moreover, this perspective can open up unexplored ways to perceive faith as a wellspring of Easter joy; even though it must travel through a period of stripping and death, but in the final instance it is an affirmation of life as a whole, material and spiritual. Thus it seems good to take up again in present terms what the challenge of poverty signifies for a faith seeking understanding. A perspective from the underside of history, from the experience of the "crucified peoples," as Ignacio Ellacuría called them, invites us to make our own the memory of the God of Jesus. In the hungry and the thirsty, the ragged and the marginalized of history, we should recognize the face of Christ. Only in this way will the proclamation of the good news manifest its prophetic dimensions.

This point of departure should include the sufferings but also the joys and the hopes of the poor. To keep in mind the ills of those who suffer mistreatment and exclusion is extremely important, but to recognize only this is to see only one aspect of a broad and complex reality. The situation of the poor does not make them less human, and all human beings experience moments of authentic joy and laughter, no matter how humble, fragile, or transitory these may seem to those who view them from afar. It is precisely these moments that sustain them as human beings. Similarly, all people have plans and hopes of their own, many times anchored in cultural values and in religious faith, even people who must fight against resigning themselves to a status quo that claims to be inevitable.

Recognition of these aspects of the condition of the poor is not meant to downplay their victimization or the systematic violation of their most fundamental human rights. It is part of remembering their humanity: the fact that they are not simply objects to pity or help but, above all, persons destined to be the subjects of their own destiny and history. The theological reflection that begins from these people takes into account all these elements and does not pretend to be—as is said many times with goodwill that we are all aware of—"the voice of the voiceless," except in very special cases. Instead, the option for the poor is a contribution that empowers them to take ownership of their own voice by proclaiming the Gospel's challenge to remember their human dignity as daughters and sons of God.

Theology as a Hermeneutic of Hope

To give an account of our hope is an essential part of the Christian witness (see 1 Pet. 3:15). Theology situates itself in this context. It is always an interpretation of the motives we have for hoping. In this consists its prophetic nature, that which makes it always alert to the signs of the times.

Hope is, first of all, a gift from God. It pertains to God's plans for us. Jeremiah remembers this as he transmits the message of the Lord: "I know the plans I have for you, plans for welfare [shalom] and not for evil, to give you a future and a hope" (Jer. 29:11). It was not an easy hope for the prophet. His nation, the next to fall under the domination of an enemy power, was devastated and imprisoned by despair. Jeremiah suffered with his people. However, a family's offer to sell some land, at a time when no one expected anything from the future of his nation, made him understand that God wanted him to accept the proposal in order to express, with this concrete and, under the circumstances, incomprehensible act, that even in the midst of hardship it is possible to hope for better times.

The witness of Jeremiah is exemplary. The times we are living in are not easy, particularly for those who are most vulnerable in society. We have already mentioned the huge and still growing social, cultural, and knowledge gaps that separate individuals and peoples. Further, a formidable campaign is being waged to convince everyone, especially the poor, that we are living in a radically new time with little, if any, historical relationship to the period immediately preceding it. In this view nothing, or almost nothing, that we have lived before this day should be relevant in the future. We are at a new beginning in an era that is "post-" everything we have ever known: a postmodern, postindustrial, postcapitalist, postcolonial, and post-socialist society. We stand before the deaths of philosophy, metaphysics, ideologies, and utopias. It has even been affirmed, with unintended humor, that we are at the end of history.

We cannot deny the huge changes that have occurred in our time, and we can find important values in several of the trends described above. However, it is one thing to recognize the unexplored extent or complexity of what is opening up before our eyes today and a very different thing to be blinded by the novelty of the moment. It is true that we must reevaluate many things: many of the analyses, categories, and propositions enunciated in recent years have become obsolete. But to advance these ideas in absolute, a-critical terms could lead to the erasing of the historical memory of the poor and could generate a certain skepticism regarding the possibility of changing the status quo, with consequences that range from passivity to desperation. Globalization is a fact, and there is no sense in talking about turning the clock back; what is at issue here is how it will be implemented. To be against globalization as such is like being against electricity. However, this cannot lead us to resign ourselves to the present order of things because globalization as it is now being carried out exacerbates the unjust inequalities among different sectors of humanity and the social, economic, political, and cultural exclusion of a good portion of the world's population. New forms of exclusion reinforce, for their part, the condition of insignificance of the poor.

In the complexity of the current hour, with its novelties and its burdens, we are called to live and witness to the Gospel of Jesus. Called to live the memory of God in our time, we can also perceive new and promising ways of living in society, living the life of faith, and embracing the gift of hope vividly and creatively. Theology, insofar as it is a hermeneutic of hope, has an important role to play. Our theology, inspired by examples like Jeremiah, should encourage us to "take possession of the land" so that we may affirm and construct a new future.

The Following of Jesus

Liberation theology understands theological discourse as critical reflection on practice in the light of faith, which is the same as saying that it is a reflection from the perspective of following Jesus. In this profound conviction I have been influenced by my longtime contact with the person and work of Marie-Dominique Chenu, who saw following Jesus as the foundation of theology. "Definitively," said this great teacher, "theological systems are nothing but the expression of spiritualities. In this consists their interest and their greatness." From there he offers a luminous definition of discourse about the faith: "A theology worthy of the name is a spirituality that has found rational instruments adequate to its religious experience."[37] This is truly the understanding of faith. Spirituality is its axis. Spirituality gives theology its most profound meaning.

A text from the Gospels in a way summarizes many of the points we have explored: the story known as the anointing at Bethany. I will draw on the version in Mark 14:3–9 because it seems particularly meaningful. But the story is found in all four Gospels, an indication of the impression it left in the memories of Jesus's followers.

When an anonymous woman overturns a jar of perfume on Jesus, those present—perhaps the disciples themselves—criticize her for the waste of money in the act of service she has performed. The argument they use against her attempts to conform to the teaching of Jesus: "The perfume could have been sold for more than three hundred denarii, which could have been given to the poor." But Jesus defends the woman, replying, "She has done a good deed for me." The word we have translated as "good" is *kalos,* which also means "beautiful." The woman has performed a beautiful act, with everything that word presupposes of gratuitousness, of something not immediately useful. Jesus adds, responding to the murmurs of those present, "The poor you will always have with you; but you will not always have me" (Matt. 26:11).[38] The responsibility toward the poor is a daily one; our solidarity with them and the search for justice is ongoing. A few lines later, Jesus specifies the nature of the woman's act: "She has done what she can. She has anticipated my embalming for burial." Jesus, on the eve of his imprisonment and execution, is vulnerable; he can do nothing before the powers of his day that have already condemned him to death. He is a victim who cannot delay the threat that hangs over him. He is at a unique and unrepeatable moment in his life. Neither can the woman do anything; she is insignificant, being a woman and being anonymous, except for expressing her affection and wishing him life with her beautiful gesture, without expecting any results.

We stand now before the two great dimensions of Christian life, namely gratuitousness and justice: gratitude for the initial love of God, which reminds us that all love is at root gratuitous, and the practice of justice, the recognition of the rights of all, especially the poorest ones. From there are derived two ways of speaking about God, which is theology; the contemplative language of mysticism and the prophetic language of justice, which we distinguish but do not separate, are mutually enriching and ultimately become one. We find them both in the text from Mark. Jesus keeps his attention on, and solidarity with, the poor, an inescapable daily task of the Christian that Jesus's witness demonstrates clearly. For her part, the anonymous woman expresses an unconditional affection in her gratuitous act, a desire—without immediate results—for life and a pure friendship. Without such gratuitousness there is no true solidarity with the poor, since they not only have material necessities but also seek to be treated with dignity as equal persons, to be accepted and understood. This is why they are so sensitive to disinterested acts of friendship.

In this context, we can understand and even measure the impact of Jesus's final words in this episode: "I assure you, wherever the Gospel is preached in the whole world, what she has done will also be told in memory of her."[39] What is less understood, or perhaps it is understood, is how little has really been said of her throughout the two thousand years of the proclamation of the good news.

NOTES

1. Bartolomé de las Casas, "Carta al Consejo de Indias" (1531), in *Obras escogidas,* ed. Juan Pérez de Tudela (Madrid: BAE, 1958), 5:44b.

2. O. Michel, "Mimmnéskomai," in *Theological Dictionary of the New Testament,* ed. Gerhard Kittel, Gerhard Friedrich, and Geoffrey W. Bromiley (Grand Rapids, MI: Eerdmans, 1986), 4:678.

3. Augustine, *Confessions,* 10.20.29, trans. Vernon J. Bourke (New York: Fathers of the Church, 1953), 289–90.

4. These studies have multiplied in recent years. Brevard S. Childs, *Memory and Tradition in Israel* (Chatham: W. and J. Mackay, 1962), and Willy Schottroff, *"Gedenken" im Alten Orient und im Alten Testament* (Neukirchen-Vluyn: Neukirchener Verlag, 1964), are two classics on this theme.

5. Yosef Hayim Yerushalmi, *Zakhor: Jewish History and Jewish Memory* (Seattle: University of Washington Press, 1982), 13. The author insists on the difference between memory and history: "The biblical call to remember has little to do with curiosity about the past" (10).

6. This text is part of the so-called "Testament of Moses." See also Deut. 11:26–28; a similar option is presented in Mark 3:1–6.

7. Both psalms "present history as a 'history of covenant.'" Norbert Lohfink, Erich Zenger, and Everett R. Kalin, *The God of Israel and the Nations: Studies in Isaiah and the Psalms* (Collegeville, MN: Michael Glazier, 2000), 186.

8. This connection is the center of the interpretation of the text presented by Walter Brueggemann in *Deuteronomy* (Nashville, TN: Abingdon, 2001).

9. The question of the immigrant is increasingly important in our day; in it the situation of the poor takes on new, unseen conditions and possibilities. See Daniel Groody, *Border of Death, Valley of Life: An Immigrant Journey of Heart and Spirit* (New York: Rowman and Littlefield, 2002).

10. Jeffries Hamilton considers that the expression "open your hand" is a call to constitute a society in which no one is dependent upon and oppressed by others. This is directed with urgency to those who have some type of power to achieve the necessary changes. Jeffries Hamilton, *Social Justice and Deuteronomy: The Case of Deuteronomy 15* (Atlanta: Scholars Press, 1992), 13–19.

11. This phrase is cited in the Gospels and often used blatantly out of context to discount the meaning and possibility of solidarity with the poor.

12. See especially the chapter on Deuteronomy in M. Díaz Mateos, "Tu hermano pobre (Dt 15:7)," *Paginas* 121 (June 1993): 63–75.

13. The term used here for the poor is *ptojoi* (beggars, destitute ones), the most common term of the Second Testament.

14. We will limit ourselves to a mention made by Paul to ground the generosity that should be the impetus for the collection: "[Christ,] who was rich, made himself poor [literally, "he impoverished himself" (with the verb corresponding to *ptojós*)], so that you could become rich from his poverty" (2 Cor. 8:9). The text is frequently cited as an expression of the material poverty of Jesus. Nevertheless, Paul's expression does not seem to point to this, at least not at first. More than a reference to a social state—just as "rich" is not a socioeconomic situation alone—the passage has a theological significance bearing on the Incarnation that we find in Philippians 2:6–11. Being God, he became one of us; to become poor in this case would be equivalent to becoming a human being. Nevertheless, the metaphor is meaningful also for our theme: the solidarity of Jesus with the poor made him care about their destiny and ultimately took him to the cross.

15. Some authors interpreted the term *poor* to designate the church. For them, the passage from Galatians and the other texts alluded to referred, then, not to

the needy, but to the "saints," to all the members of the Jerusalem Church. The appearance on the scene of the Qumran manuscripts gave new life to this theory years later, as the subject is frequently discussed in commentaries on these texts. But, as L. E. Keck (from whom we take this information) has proven, there is no solid basis for affirming the synonymous nature of the poor and the saints (the Christian community). L. E. Keck, "The Poor among the Saints in the New Testament," *Zeitschrift für die Neutetamentliche Wissenschaft* 1–2 (1966): 54–78.

16. This is the opinion of M. R. Gornik. See "The Rich and the Poor in Pauline Theology," *Urban Mission* 9, no. 1 (1991): 15–25, esp. 21–23.

17. This is the conclusion, after a careful analysis of the debate in Jerusalem, of Fern K. T. Clarke's "Remembering the Poor: Does Galatians 2:10 Allude to the Collection?" *Scripture Bulletin* 1 (January 2001): 20–28.

18. Paul VI, "Dei verbum," November 18, 1965, no. 2, www.vatican.va/archive/hist_councils/ii_vatican_council/documents/vat-ii_const_19651118_dei-verbum_en.html (accessed August 9, 2006).

19. In this sense we have said that "the first task of the Church is to celebrate . . . the Eucharist: memorial and thanksgiving." Gustavo Gutiérrez, *A Theology of Liberation: History, Politics, and Salvation* (Maryknoll, NY: Orbis Books, 1971), 325.

20. Karl Barth, *Dogmatics,* 2.1–2 (Geneva: Labor et Fides, 1957), 135. A few lines further down, he adds: "It is necessary to understand, from the start, that the justice of God, the action by which he is loyal to himself—which is manifested as help and liberation, as a saving intervention on behalf of persons—is directed to the poor, the miserable, and the abandoned as such and to them alone; it has absolutely nothing to do with the rich, the satisfied and their security" (136).

21. Joachim Jeremias, *New Testament Theology* (New York: Scribner, 1971), 133 and 142–44 (emphasis in original), quoted in Jon Sobrino, *Jesus the Liberator: A Historical-Theological Reading of Jesus of Nazareth* (Maryknoll, NY: Orbis Books, 1994), 143.

22. Dom Helder Camara's phrase is well known: "If I talk about the poor, people tell me that I'm a saint; if I talk about the causes of poverty, they tell me I'm a communist."

23. About this mentality, from the beginning of modernity, see the comments of R. H. Tawney, *Religion and the Rise of Capitalism* (New York: New American Library, 1963), 99–102.

24. Part of the responsibility, in a complex issue like poverty, reaches, in some way, every person. But this responsibility is shared unequally—that which can be attributed to the poor is decidedly false or at least exaggerated in the interpretation to which we refer.

25. In effect, the Bible speaks very little of poverty. It refers, more often, to the poor. The biblical vocabulary is diverse; it does not allow for a conceptual definition of who is a poor person. Rather, like a photograph, it provides a description. This is the view of one of the pioneers of biblical study of the subject,

Albert Gelin, in his foundational work *Les pauvres et Yahvé* (Paris: Cerf, 1953), 19. See also Elsa Tamez, *La biblia de los oprimidos* (San Jose de Costa Rica: DEI, 1979).

26. With the expression *nonperson* we are designating the interlocutor of theologies of liberation, in contrast to the nonbeliever, the interlocutor of modern theologies.

27. For this reason, keeping in mind that the "economic, social, cultural and racial coordinates" are crucial to understanding poverty, we spoke of the poor as "peoples, races, and social classes" (Gutiérrez, *Theology of Liberation,* 226, 251; see also 255) and of the "exploited popular classes, oppressed cultures, and races experiencing discrimination" ("Praxis de liberación y fé cristiana," in Gustavo Gutiérrez, *La fuerza histórica de los pobres* [Lima: CEP, 1979], 65; see also 64, 90, 107, 111, 114, 125).

28. See the worthwhile historical studies on poverty done by Michel Mollat and colleagues, including the now-classic work *Études sur la histoire de la pauvreté (Moyen Age–XVIe Siécle),* 2 vols. (Paris: Publications de la Sorbonne, 1974), and for a later work, Alberto Monticone, ed., *La storia dei poveri: Pauperismo e assistenza nell'etá moderna* (Rome: Stadium, 1985).

29. "The woman in these groups [the poor] is doubly exploited, marginalized, and oppressed." Gustavo Gutiérrez, *Teología desde el reverso de la historia* (Lima: CEP, 1977), 34 n. 36, and "The Historical Force of the Poor," in *Signos de lucha y esperanza* (Lima: CEP, 1978), 173. Puebla picks up on this perspective some time later; see what was said by the Peruvian delegation to Puebla. In a paragraph entitled, significantly, "Liberacion de la Mujer," after affirming that "Medellín did not take up" this problem, the text notes that despite a new awareness of women's rights, "radically changing [a woman's] conditions of life and her social functions," the church and society still have an important task, since in many situations woman "is still not considered a person." CELAM III (Puebla, Mexico, 1979), *Puebla Conference: Final Document. Visión Pastoral de America Latina: Equipo de Reflexión, Departamentos y Secciones de CELAM* (Bogotá: CELAM, 1979), *aporte* 20, nos. 317–27.

30. The United Nations Development Programme (UNDP) report of 1996 concludes, from an economic viewpoint, that "the world is increasingly polarized, and the distance that separates rich and poor is greater every day." UNDP, "Human Development Report 1996: Economic Growth and Human Development," 2, http://hdr.undp.org/reports/global/1996/en/ (accessed August 9, 2006). It is based on worrisome statistics. In the last thirty years the proportion of global GDP held by the poorest 20 percent of the global population went from 2.3 percent (already a low number) to 1.4 percent. By contrast, the proportion of global GDP held by the richest 20 percent grew from 70 percent to 85 percent. The 1999 report observes that the "greatest fortunes of the world possess more than the total GNP of the group of less advanced countries, or 600 million citizens." UNDP, "Human Development Report 1999: Globalization with a Human Face," 3, http://hdr.undp.org/reports/global/1999/en/ (accessed August 9, 2006).

31. We are alluding, to be sure, to real poverty, which is at times called material poverty. For the moment, what we know as spiritual poverty or spiritual childhood, which occupies a central place in the biblical message, does not come into our consideration. It will be considered later.

32. This leads Peter-Hans Kolvenbach, superior general of the Jesuits, to say, "God has always been a God of the poor because the poor are the visible proof of a failure in the work of creation" and "The motive [for Jesus's prioritizing attention to the poor] is that, in the name of his Creator Father, the existence of the poor is declared scandalous, the failure of God's plan." Peter-Hans Kolvenbach, "El grido del poverii e il Vangelo," *La Civilittá Cattolica* 4 (1993): 117.

33. Johann Baptist Metz has recalled forcefully the importance of memory for the victims of history, in that it ties them, in a final way, to the passion of Jesus. Their victimhood is a painful component of the daily life of the poor, in which we also find projects, hopes, and joys.

34. The true difference is, rather, between theologies recognizing explicitly their social context and theologies thinking they are free from any historical context in which they exist.

35. Vatican II interrogated itself about the relation between the temporal realm and the growth of the reign of God. After a period of debate, it took a middle position without confronting the problem head on (see Paul VI, *Gaudium et spes,* December 7, 1965, no. 39, www.vatican.va/archive/hist_councils/ii_vatican_council/documents/vat-ii_cons_19651207_gaudium-et-spes_en.html (accessed August 9, 2006). See a discussion of this in Gutiérrez, *Theology of Liberation,* 216–21. Paul VI was more affirmative in *Evangelii nuntiandi* (1974): "How can we proclaim the new commandment [of love] without promoting justice and peace, the true human progress?" (no. 30, www.vatican.va/holy_father/paul_vi/apost_exhortations/documents/hf_p-vi_exh_19751208_evangelii-nuntiandi_en.html [accessed August 9, 2006]).

36. At the inaugural discourse of Puebla (1979), the pope had already spoken of an intrinsic link between the two commitments. CELAM III, *Puebla Conference.*

37. Marie-Dominique Chenu, *École de théologie: Le Saulchoir* (Tournai: Kain-lez-Tournai, 1937), 75.

38. Ibid.

39. This phrase was taken up as the title of an important book by Elisabeth Schussler-Fiorenza, *In Memory of Her: A Feminist Theological Reconstruction of Christian Origins* (New York: Crossroad, 1983).

Part Two

POVERTY, POETRY,

AND SCRIPTURE

Chapter 2

POVERTY, THE POOR, AND THE OPTION FOR THE POOR

A Biblical Perspective

ELSA TAMEZ

One of the contributions of liberation theology to biblical theology is to make clear how profoundly theological and biblical are terms such as *the poor, liberation,* and *option for the poor.* Gustavo Gutiérrez is the theologian to which we owe this fundamental contribution, which has become central and essential to all serious theological reflection in Latin America.

For centuries, theology and biblical interpretation in Latin America imported from Europe and the United States a concentration on such biblical themes as creation, salvation, faith, covenant, grace, sin, and resurrection. Meanwhile, it hardly occurred to anyone that the poor, oppression, social justice, and liberation were themes of theological importance; they were considered to be contingent and trivial, to be addressed by pastoral theology and not by systematic theology or biblical scholarship. Nevertheless, the experience of God in the concrete history of a continent "oppressed and believing,"[1] full of suffering and conflicts, changed that attitude.

41

Someone has said that if all the texts in the Bible that speak of the poor were cut out, very few pages would be left. I believe if theologians strained the Bible with a sieve to remove all historical material and keep only what they held to be "purely" spiritual and theological, the result would be a limited and insipid text, inapplicable to the real struggles of human life. The major portion of the Bible would be lost in the process.

Traditionally, theologians spoke of God's love for everyone, including the poor, but they mentioned the poor only as one group among others, sometimes just as an afterthought. They did not consider God's attitude toward the poor as something fundamental and essential to biblical theology. With liberation theology, however, biblical studies took a new direction. The new theology constituted an "epistemological rupture" in the sense that it drew less on preexisting theological concepts than on the reality of the Latin American context of oppression, poverty, and violence and the practice that this reality demanded. As Gustavo Gutiérrez always insists, theology comes out of our encounter with God in history because contemplation and the experience of God are part of the beginning stage of the theological task: "Our method is our spirituality."[2]

With the advent of liberation theology, then, the Bible became a fascinating book, influencing biblical studies worldwide. Popular readings of the Bible are now more encouraged and further explored, with great strength and richness.[3] Today there are many works in Spanish on the biblical and theological significance of the poor and the option for the poor.[4] They have appeared in other languages as well because the centrality of these issues to Christianity is considered a universal biblical principle, applicable not only to Latin America and the Third World but also to other churches and theologies.

This chapter addresses four topics: (1) poverty and the poor in the Bible, (2) the option for the poor, (3) the rights of the poor as rights of God, and (4) the challenges of the term *option for the poor*. I am going to concentrate here on economic poverty, which is the type that appears most often in the Bible, rather than discussing what is spoken of today as poverty of the spirit and evangelical poverty. The latter two are important, but the urgency of today's economic poverty, or rather destitution (in Guatemala and Nicaragua the children are literally dying of hunger) compels me to speak primarily about it. Further, the Bible speaks primarily of economic poverty. Therefore, I will concentrate on this dimension, and later I will present some challenges to the term *option for the poor* from a feminist perspective.

POVERTY AND THE POOR IN THE BIBLE

In 1979, I wrote a little book entitled *The Bible of the Oppressed*.[5] I am indebted to Thomas Hanks, my professor of Old Testament studies at that time, who spoke of oppression in biblical theology. Poverty, as a product of historical oppression, is a theme in biblical theology just as is covenant, creation, salvation, or grace. What is at stake is not only the relationship of God to the context of God's creatures but the life and death of God's creatures and all of creation.

Most of the research on poverty and the poor in the Bible makes it clear that the theme of poverty is intrinsically connected to the context of oppression. That is, the immense majority of biblical texts that refer to poverty specify who is poor, the causes of poverty, the mechanisms of oppression at national, international, and personal levels, and the struggles and unjust suffering of the poor. Poverty and oppression happen within the history, where God's revelation is made known. In Latin America there are numerous biblical studies based especially on Exodus, the prophetic books, Psalms, Ecclesiastes, the Gospels, some of Paul's letters, James, and Revelation. Almost all of these studies argue that the authors as well as the original audiences of these biblical writings saw the poor as people who had been impoverished: victims of oppression, whether caused by the governors of nations or empires, judges, priests, the wealthy who thought only about accumulating riches, or false prophets. In addition, Gustavo Gutiérrez's study on Job argues that Job represents all those who suffer unjustly and that his story invalidates models of a contractual relationship with God, in which God rewards those who obey him and punishes those who do not, insisting instead on a relationship that is mediated through grace.[6]

It is really surprising that for so many centuries it was believed that the Bible presented poverty as something that was determined by God and should be accepted. Poverty and the poor were spiritualized; poverty was not seen as an institutional sin. This is because the reading of the Bible reflected what the dominant society thought about poverty and the poor. Indeed, one still hears that the poor are poor because they do not care, lack initiative, and are lazy.

All this changed when the Bible began to be read in the light of the Latin American context. Since so many Latin American countries were involved in struggles for liberation, the Bible was read in the light of the praxis of liberation, and it was found that the biblical text contained "a subversive memory." The term *subversive memory* primarily calls to mind the Bible's account of the Hebrews' struggle for liberation from exploitation in Egypt, the prophets' denunciations of injustice, and the resistance to the Roman Empire expressed in Revelation. But *subversive memory* can also refer to the Bible's numerous mentions of the poor and poverty, and above all to its expression of God's option for the poor.

Today's poverty is tremendously subversive. As Honduran Cardinal Oscar Rodriguez Maradiaga said: "We have hit rock bottom, and worse, nobody wants to confront the greatest subversion of all time, the subversion of poverty, which is very different from the ideological struggle that cost the lives of thousands of persons in the 1960s and 1970s."[7]

The World Bank and the International Monetary Fund (IMF) know this, and consequently they are worried today about poverty. The subversive power of poverty lies in the increasing growth of unequal distribution of wealth, which is a taboo subject for the system's economists because it touches the structure of the economic order. For that reason they prefer to speak about aid from rich countries to solve the problem of world poverty.

THE OPTION FOR THE POOR IN THE BIBLE

The historical and concrete reading of poverty and oppression in the Bible began in Latin America in the 1960s. Since that time many Latin American theologians and others have always understood God's special love for the poor. In reading the Bible from the perspective of the poor, we see more clearly God's preference for them: the option for the poor is not one of a multitude of virtues, in which case it could be optional, but a biblical principle. Jon Sobrino speaks of the principle of mercy in the same sense and affirms its presence throughout the Bible.[8] Indeed, the two principles are interrelated. The option for the poor should be seen as an aspect of God's mercy, since it is God's merciful love that moves God to opt for the most needy of history. Mercy is shown not only to those who suffer economic poverty, injustice, and oppression but also to those who suffer the violence of racism, sexism, war, and many other discriminations. If we see the option for the poor as an expression of the principle of mercy, we can broaden the category of economic oppression to include other marginalizations. But it is even more important to see the two principles as complementary. They reinforce each other, balancing our humanity and effectiveness, our compassion and action, our emotion and reason. If we separate mercy from the option for the poor, we risk losing our effectiveness. Without the option for the poor, mercy is poorly understood. Without mercy, the option for the poor is purely rational and exterior to the Christian and human commitment. This is the reason that the option for the poor is an evangelical imperative more than a sociological imperative. If in fact it is a historical requirement of our responsibility as human beings living together, for Christians it is in addition a conviction of faith.

In the Bible we find the option for the poor not only in what we Christians call the Old Testament—in Exodus, the prophetic books, Psalms, Job, and the Wisdom and apocalyptic literature—but also in the central message of the Gospel of Jesus Christ: his whole life, passion, and resurrection. From the birth of the Messiah we can see God's option for the poor. In Luke 2:12 the angel says to the shepherds of Bethlehem: "This will be a sign for you: you will find a child wrapped in bands of cloth and lying in a manger."

The manger was a place where the animals were fed. The story tells us that they did not find lodging in the inn (*katalumati,* a humble place where travelers could spend the night, not *pandoxein,* a hotel) or in a room in a peasant farmer's house. They found it only in a stable, a place where poor peasant farmers put their animals. It is said that the houses of peasant farmers were generally one room. The people slept on one side and the animals on the other. In the center was the manger, the place where the animals fed.[9] It was there where Mary placed her child, whom Luke named Savior, Messiah, and Lord. This sign of the manger is repeated three times (Luke 2:7, 12, 16). For Luke this Savior is poor, and the angels see the manger as a sign, which gives great joy to the shepherds, who are also poor. This event, which for the consumer society is pure folklore, is truly an evangelical sign that indicates where God is found. Later, Paul theologizes this event in Philippians 2:4–7, when he exhorts the community to have the same mind as Christ and continues, "who, though he was in the form of God, did not regard equality with God as something to be exploited, but emptied himself, taking the form of a slave, being born in human likeness."

Let us read, then, in Jesus's social condition, an option of God to show God's historical face of solidarity with the poor. But not only that, the very practice of Jesus is clearly in their favor. We know that in Luke's Gospel Jesus initiated his ministry in Nazareth by reading himself the words of the prophet Isaiah that affirmed a new Jubilee: "The Spirit of the Lord is upon me, because he has anointed me to bring good news to the poor. He has sent me to proclaim release to the captives and recovery of sight to the blind, to let the oppressed go free, to proclaim the year of the Lord's favor" (Luke 4:18–19). Other Gospels also show this dedication of Jesus to all persons who are marginalized by society, including many women, the sick, the poor, and the defenseless, especially widows and children.

The proclamation of the reign of God, as a just society for all men and women, is directly related to the option for the poor, for it is good news for those who long for new life. The resurrection of Jesus Christ, God's vindicating act, also shows God's option for the crucified, who becomes the representative of the world's crucified. We say that the option of God for the poor is preferential in the sense that God loves all of God's creatures but has a preferential or special love for the poor precisely because of their disadvantaged position in an unequal and discriminating society. This is the reason we speak of the preferential option for the poor. This is valid if, in this understanding, no one is excluded from God's love. Nevertheless, closely analyzing this phrase, we can affirm better theologically that the option for the poor is not a question of preference. If it were preferential, that would mean the exclusion of others, such as the wealthy and oppressors. The foundation of the option for the poor is the intention to end structural sin that produces dehumanization for the poor as well as those responsible for the poverty. In other words, we can affirm that precisely because the love of God is universal, God opts for the poor so that there may no longer be excluded persons in society.

This understanding can be observed in Paul's rereading of the theme of election in Romans 9–11. In these texts, election is moved by mercy so that there is no longer exclusion, so that all peoples can receive the promises that God gave to Abraham and be God's people. God rejects exclusion and elects through mercy precisely because God elects the excluded, defenseless, and ignorant, to avoid all exclusion. If God elected Israel as God's people, it was because they were small and oppressed by other empires. God elects to include and liberate (Deut. 7:7, 8).[10]

Of course, the option for the poor is not only God's option or an option of Jesus Christ. It is also the option of Christians, all Christians, rich and poor, men and women. Jesus was a leader of a movement in the peasant region of Galilee, and he constantly taught with his life and words so that these peasants would follow him. He gave lessons about his option for the poor to the masses who listened to him and the Pharisees and scribes with whom he argued and discussed. In the Bible we find that the option for the poor is the option of the Triune God, the option that demands a presence within us as God's creatures. It is the option of the Triune God because it emulates the God of the Exodus and the prophets, and Jesus of Nazareth, the Son, and it is manifested in believers through the Holy Spirit.[11] If the Spirit of God and of Christ resurrected has been poured out in our hearts, as Paul says, then we act in harmony with the option of God and Jesus Christ, guided and strengthened by the Holy Spirit, which is, ultimately, the historical and concrete presence of God and Jesus the Messiah. The Spirit (of Christ and God) is *Emmanuel,* "God with Us,"[12] who, not being a phantom, acts through men and women disciples. In other words, the option for the poor, whether from God or Jesus the Messiah, becomes visible in history through those men and women who have received the Spirit. The body is the temple of the Holy Spirit, affirms the apostle Paul in 1 Corinthians 6:19. If the Spirit lives in our bodies, this means that our legs and arms, eyes and mouth are in charge of making visible the principle of the option for the poor.

The Rights of the Poor and the Rights of God

To speak of the "rights of God" could sound ridiculous. God is sovereign transcendence, and it does not fit to speak of God's rights and duties. It sounds disrespectful. Nevertheless, the Bible, which offers us criteria about the location of God and God's manner of being, shows us familiar, accessible, and loving images such as mother, father, helper, and friend. It also offers images of authority that defend the disadvantaged, such as a just judge faced with widows and orphans who ask for justice (Luke 18:1–8). The rights of the poor, as rights of God, also provide an image in human language to express the importance of the fear of God when some want to violate and crush God's little ones. The reflection below, marked by this language, is inspired by some biblical passages, as we will see.

Christian theology, in its essence, is marked by the faith in a crucified being who was resurrected by God. This being, named Jesus of Nazareth, toward the end of his ministry was arrested, tortured, and finally crucified by the military and legal forces of the Roman Empire. The beautiful, liturgical phrase that Christ died for our sins unfortunately often makes invisible this situation of conflict and takes it onto an abstract plane that is ahistorical and private. But the Gospels are very clear when narrating the life of Jesus of Nazareth. We Christians see in Jesus crucified, God crucified, an event considered ridiculous for Greek philosophical thought of that time and scandalous for the Jews (see 1 Cor 1:17–31).[13]

Leonardo Boff saw in the passion of Jesus God's maximum solidarity with humankind.[14] Historically this solidarity is represented in this Galilean peasant. To believe that God has also been crucified, we see that in the rights of the poor, persecuted, and crucified Jesus, God's rights are being trampled upon. Jesus was crucified unjustly, and, even worse, he was crucified legally, hiding the crime against an innocent. In this scene, Jesus is the representative of both sides: he is the representative of humanity in relation to the poor, marginalized, excluded, and persecuted, and in relation to God. Jesus unites the rights of excluded human beings and divine rights. For God, the crucified represents the disfigured face of all human beings whose rights have not been respected, the prayer that cries out unendingly to God because of the violation of the rights of the poor, women, indigenous peoples, blacks, the elderly, and children. For humankind, Jesus is God's representative, who reminds us that the rights of God have also been trampled upon because Jesus and all humans are creatures of God, created in God's image and likeness. This also reminds us that the end of the human being unjustly crucified is not condemnation to death but resurrection. In biblical theology we say that God, like the Roman Empire, also gave judgment, and God's verdict was resurrection for the crucified. That is the faith and hope for those who suffer oppression, exclusion, and all violation of human rights.

This Christian theological affirmation, in which we see the rights of God in the rights of the poor, excluded, and persecuted, is not just a new reading of the passion of our Lord Jesus Christ. In the Hebrew Bible we find affirmations that call for commitment in which the rights of God are touched when the rights of humans, especially the poor, are touched. In the first Creation story it is affirmed that God created woman and man in God's image and likeness. This implies that human beings have not only human rights but divine rights, which are the rights of their Creator. In the book of Proverbs we find clearly and repeatedly: "Those who oppress the poor insult their Maker, but those who are kind to the needy honor their Maker" (14:31). "Those who mock the poor insult their Maker; those who are glad at calamity will not go unpunished" (17:5). "Whoever is kind to the poor lends to the Lord, and will be repaid in full" (19:17). In these texts related to the poor and disadvantaged, we see that what is done to the neighbor is done to God.

And again, when in the New Testament we read that the body is the temple of the Holy Spirit (1 Cor. 6:19), this affirmation has very important implications. It invites us not only to take care of our own bodies because in them the Holy Spirit dwells but to see other men and women with respect because God also dwells in them. The knowledge that human beings are the temples of the Spirit creates a barrier for those who want to kill, rape, or destroy them. To abuse others is tantamount to attacking God.

All this leads us to affirm that today, in the atmosphere of war that surrounds us, God is being killed each time bombs are dropped over the innocent populations in Colombia, Afghanistan, Palestine, and so many other parts of the world. All the Christians of the world should be against the war in Iraq, where thousands of innocents are dying. If we understood and believed that the flame of God lives in all human beings, and even in nature, maybe we would stop some of our mortal aggressions done many times in defense of the good. The times are past in which persons were killed to defend God. We are beginning to understand little by little that in defending the poor and excluded ones we act like God and in favor of God. We are ultimately interconnected, and the rights of some are intertwined with the rights of others.

Not only in war but in daily life as well, God's rights are being violated in each woman who is beaten, in each child who is abused, and in many others who starve to death because of a world economic system that is wreaking havoc on the most vulnerable. We discriminate not only against our own kind but against God in racist and xenophobic attitudes and actions against our black, indigenous, immigrant, and homosexual neighbors. The rights of God and neighbor are being violated in the destruction of the environment because we all form part of the totality.

CHALLENGES TO THE TERM *OPTION FOR THE POOR*

I want to present two distinct concerns or challenges here: one concerns the lack of inclusiveness in the term *option for the poor,* and the other concerns the co-optation of the principle "the option for the poor" by the economic hegemony. The option for the poor, seen as an economic issue, is clearly a principle that has an irrefutable biblical foundation. This principle, in spite of possibly being subversive, fits perfectly within Christian orthodoxy. It has also been uncomfortable for the rich since the end of the first century in the first Christian communities, and it continues to be so today. The fathers of the church, such as Tertullian, Clement, Origen, and Cyprian, show a certain ambivalence with respect to wealth. On the one hand, they follow the Judeo-Christian prophetic tradition and have no problem in affirming that the love of money is the root of all evil (1 Tim. 6:10). On the other hand, because of the need for donations from the wealthy members of the Christian community, they find themselves obligated to give the offerings of the wealthy a redemptive meaning.[15] This ambivalence in official church history has been present for many centuries. Nevertheless, it has been unable to erase the essential principle of the option for the poor. This principle has come to light in distinct moments of history. Today the theology of liberation recovers it as its fundamental nucleus.

This does not mean that this terminology automatically includes all those marginalized and discriminated against within history. Women, indigenous peoples, blacks, homosexuals, and other discriminated persons and peoples have not necessarily felt included in a principle that is concentrated in the economic realm. Feminist liberation theologians have spoken of women as doubly or triply oppressed because of their class, gender, and skin color. In the option for the poor we feel included by our class as poor women but not necessarily by our gender. In the Bible the option for the poor sometimes does not include women. 1 Timothy strongly criticizes the wealthy and those who want to get richer (6:7–10), but he tells the women to listen to instruction in silence, not to teach but to be submissive (2:11–15), and to get married and have children (5:11–14) and says that in this way they can be saved (2:15). Let us say that we are in agreement theologically or evangelically that the option for the poor can have the sense of including those who have been excluded because of gender (such as women and homosexuals), ethnicity, skin color, and physical condition. But we have to recognize that in the Bible the option for the poor at the economic level is the most privileged. Because the Bible is a patriarchal and homophobic book, there is no explicit option for oppressed women or homosexuals as such.

The discussion about the inclusivity of the term *poor* is not new. Aiwan Wawa, a Panamanian Cuna theologian, has stated that it should be called the option for the impoverished "others." This would include the otherness of the indigenous culture, marginalized by its ethnicity and by its economic impoverishment. During the time of the dictators, when the blood of many martyrs flowed in our continent, we spoke of the option for the victims, with no need for theological debate. We women speak of "the option for the poor and excluded" men and women, and in this expression we find inclusion for all the marginalized, especially the economically excluded.

Thus, although the majority of liberation theologians insist that other discriminations enter the category "poor," in practice it is not like that. Those of us who suffer other marginalizations feel only partly included. Domestic violence, the beatings and assassination of women caused by rich and poor men, happen because the victims are women, whatever their social condition. So a Latin American feminist liberation theologian has two options. One is to include in her theology of liberation the struggle of women and to amplify the formula to the option for the poor and excluded men and women. The other is to pursue two theologies: a feminist Latin American theology that addresses the oppression and liberation of women and a Latin American liberation theology with the option for the poor because the challenge of the poor is a challenge for all the inhabitants of Latin America: men, women, indigenous, and blacks. The problem is that if the principle is not amplified into a formula that includes all those who are oppressed and discriminated against, we will have so many theologies of liberation that we run the risk of diluting the option for the poor, which is the fundamental and urgent challenge today in our impoverished continent and the rest of the world because of globalization. That is, because feminist theology, indigenous theology, and Latin American black theology are not able to leave to one side the option for the poor, the theology of liberation should include in its basic principle the option for all those oppressed and discriminated against. Just to affirm that in the option for the poor all are included is not sufficient.

The other challenge is the attempt by some to appropriate the principle "the option for the poor." Franz Hinkelammert has alerted us to this in his article "The Theology of Liberation in the Social and Economic Context of Latin America: Economy and Theology or the Irrationality of the Rationalized."[16] The challenge arises particularly because of the discourse of Camdessus, ex-general secretary of the International Monetary Fund (IMF), when speaking to the National Congress of Christian Business Executives of France in Lille in 1992. In this discourse Camdessus takes up the option for the poor from liberation theology and uses its terminology. For example, when he compares the power of the reign of God with that of the reign of this world, he asserts that the latter is founded on power, scarcity, the exaltation of rulers, border crossings, the spectacular, and the immediate, while the former affirms service, sharing, the exaltation of the excluded and weak, and strong relationships. And he continues: "My judge and my king is my brother who is hungry, thirsty, a foreigner, naked, sick, or a prisoner." Later he cites Luke 4:16–21, the mission of Jesus to proclaim good news to the poor and liberation to the captives.

For Camdessus, this ministry of Jesus expressed in Luke 4:16–21 is the task of the IMF. According to Hinkelammert, the empire represented in the IMF wants to appropriate the theology of liberation for itself. We know that the consequences of the structural adjustments demanded by the IMF have meant more hunger, unemployment, and death for the poor. One is absolutely astounded upon hearing discourses like this, knowing the havoc caused in the globalized economy by the so-called "free" market (see the case of Argentina, for example). If even the empire speaks of the option for the poor, we have a huge challenge before us. Here it can be seen very clearly that theological discourses, as liberating as they may present themselves, are insufficient if not founded upon and accompanied by social and economic analysis. Hinkelammert shows that a theology critical of the law and institutions would prevent the option for the poor from being be co-opted by the dominant ideology. This seems to me to be very important.

The revelation of God in the Bible occurs in contexts of poverty and oppression at different levels: international, national, and personal. In all of these we find a God who favors the poor, the weak and marginalized, whether that God is the Creator and Liberator from slavery in Egypt or the figure of Jesus of Nazareth. By continuation, the option for the poor becomes visible through Jesus's men and women disciples today. God's option for the poor includes not only God's solidarity and accompaniment in tribulations and struggles but God's identification to the degree that the rights of the poor are considered as God's rights. That is, the option for the poor is not just a theme but an evangelical principle and rule for all theological praxis and reflection.

Finally, the terminology of the principle "the option for the poor" is challenged today by other discriminations and humiliations that go beyond the economic. The expression "option for the excluded" or "option for the poor and excluded" would explicitly give room for other oppressions, discriminations, and humiliations. At the same time, the discourse of liberation theology about the poor and the option for the poor faces the challenge to make clear a discourse that cannot be manipulated and inverted as has been done by the ex–general secretary of the IMF. This is also a challenge for theologians of the First World, who focus more on the discourse than on the underlying realities and therefore easily turn it upside down.

NOTES

1. This well-known expression is from Gustavo Gutiérrez, *We Drink from Our Own Wells: The Spiritual Journey of a People* (Maryknoll, NY: Orbis Books, 1984), 28. It had a major impact on the Association of Third World Theologians (EATWOT) in the assembly celebrated in Sao Paulo, Brazil, in 1980.

2. Gustavo Gutiérrez, "Reflections from a Latin American Perspective: Finding Our Way to Talk about God," in *Irruption of the Third World, Challenge to Theology: Papers from the Fifth International Conference of the Ecumenical Association of Third World Theologians, August 17–29, 1981, New Delhi, India,* ed. Virginia Fabella and Sergio Torres (Maryknoll, NY: Orbis Books, 1983), 225.

3. In September 2002, the Assembly of the Network of Latin American Biblical Scholars (REBILAC) was held. Workshops on popular readings of the Bible are taking place in all of Latin America, and the magazine *Revista Bíblica Latinoamericana (RIBLA)* is contributing to the biblical movement with studies that combine academic work with pastoral work.

4. This includes not only books but theological dictionaries, innumerable articles, and conferences. One only has to search "option for the poor" on the Internet to become aware of this.

5. This book was translated into English as well as other languages. Elsa Tamez, *The Bible of the Oppressed* (Maryknoll, NY: Orbis Books, 1982).

6. Gustavo Gutiérrez, *Hablar de Dios desde el sufrimiento del inocente* (Lima: Centro de Estudios y Publicaciones, 1986), 32.

7. Quoted in Thelma Mejía, "La pobreza es subversiva," *La Nacion,* October 6, 2002, sec. 22A, www.nacion.com/ln_ee/2002/octubre/06/mundo4.html (accessed August 10, 2006).

8. Jon Sobrino, *El principio misericordia* (San Salvador: UCA, 1993), 31–45, translated as *The Principle of Mercy* (Maryknoll, NY: Orbis Books, 1994).

9. Herman Hendrickx, *The Third Gospel for the Third World,* vol. 1, *Preface and Infancy Narrative (Luke 1:1–2:52)* (Collegeville, MN: Liturgical Press, 1996), 183 ff.

10. Elsa Tamez, "La elección como garantía de la inclusión (Romanos 9–11)," *Revista Bíblica Latinoamericana [RIBLA]* 12 (1992): 153–66.

11. Jon Sobrino, "Opcion por los pobres y seguimiento de Jesús," in *La opción por los pobres,* ed. José Maria Vigil (Sal Terrae: Santander, 1991).

12. Gordon D. Fee, *Paul, the Spirit, and the People of God* (Peabody, MA: Hendrickson, 1996), 996.

13. Jürgen Moltmann, *The Crucified God: The Cross of Christ as the Foundation and Criticism of Christian Theology,* trans. R. A. Wilson and John Bowden (New York: Harper and Row, 1974).

14. Leonardo Boff, *Theologia desde el cautiverio* (Bogota: Indo-American Press Service, 1975), 151.

15. L. W. Countryman, *The Rich Christian in the Church of the Early Empire* (New York: Edwin Mellow Press, 1980), 131–213.

16. Franz Hinkelammert, "La teología de la liberación en el contexto economico y social de America Latina: Economía y teología o la irracionalidad de lo racionalizado," in *Por una sociedad donde quepan todos,* ed. Jose Duque (San José: DEI, 1996), 53–85.

Chapter 3

TOWARD THE CREATION OF TRANSFORMATIONAL SPIRITUALITIES

Re-engaging Israel's Early Poetic Tradition in Light of the Church's Preferential Option for the Poor

HUGH R. PAGE JR.

In his essay entitled "Reading Darkness, Reading Scriptures," New Testament scholar Vincent Wimbush asks those of us in the academic community to consider the implications of making African American experience the starting point for all hermeneutical engagements of Scripture.[1] He believes that this foregrounding of Black Diasporan life in the United States will accomplish several ends. First, it will facilitate the development of an agenda for biblical studies that is uniquely American. Second, it will enable African American life and culture to be of primary, rather than secondary, concern to the discipline. Readers will begin to understand how the experiences of *marronage* (flight), settlement, and identity construction influence

African American readings of Scripture.[2] Third, it will allow them to see the impact of what Wimbush calls "the individual and collective experience of trauma" on the formation of the canon. He notes that for African Americans the Bible is a "script/manifesto that defines and embraces darkness."[3] *Darkness* for him does not carry the usual range of meaning. He says: "I do not mean to play the usual rhetorical-symbolization games that set up endless but predictable polarities and dualities. I mean here simply that African Americans' engagement of the Bible points to the Bible as that which both reflects and draws unto itself and engages and problematizes a certain complex order of existence associated with marginality, liminality, exile, pain, and trauma."[4]

This essay asks a question related to the agenda set out by Wimbush: What would happen if the concerns of the poor and dispossessed were placed at the center, rather than the periphery, of the Bible scholar's research agenda? It also poses three additional queries. First, what do we learn about attitudes toward poverty from Israel's earliest literature? Second, how might such literature be read, interpreted, and appropriated from the standpoint of those whose status places them on social, political, religious, economic, and other margins rather than in the mainstream? Finally, how might such texts be employed in light of Catholic social teaching that asserts a preferential option for the poor?

My approach for examining and discussing the aforementioned issues will be descriptive, analytical, evocative, poetic, and theologically focused.[5] My hope is to look at these issues in a manner that promotes the use of the Bible's very earliest poems as building blocks for fashioning spiritualities that not only promote concern for the poor but encourage solidarity and action in concert with all who live outside the many interlocking social networks that make up our global community.[6]

My points of departure will be two signature papal encyclicals that establish parameters for theological reflection on poverty and wealth within the Roman Catholic social tradition and indeed within Catholic tradition as a whole: *Rerum novarum* and *Centesimus annus,* both of which I will consider from my standpoint as Bible scholar, theologian, and cleric. My goal in reading them will be to arrive at some principles for reading, interpreting, and appropriating Israel's early poems for speculative and constructive purposes.

Our encounter with the Bible in ecclesial, academic, and other settings is never singular. The interpretive act is radically contingent. Like "those who give their innermost selves over to ponder the law of the Highest," mentioned by the old sage Sirach, we must study carefully the repository of wisdom bequeathed to us by the ancients as found in Scripture (Sir. 39:1). The nature of this encounter is to a certain extent circular, given that our consciousness as people of faith has already been shaped in part by a tradition that has the First and Second Testaments as its foundations. However, it can also be seen as a pilgrimage along an eschatological spiral that takes us from familiar ground to new sites of sacred encounter, a journey that is simultaneously familiar and foreign. Such exploration of early Hebrew poetry promises to inform our thinking about what is necessary to build a more just and sustainable world and to provide us with new insights about our common life.

REFLECTIONS ON *RERUM NOVARUM*

I am struck by several features of the encyclical *Rerum novarum*,[7] all of which have implications for subsequent engagements with the Bible: (1) the sense of urgency it conveys with regard to addressing the needs of the poor; (2) its use of Scripture to construct a theological anthropology from which to critique dehumanizing ideologies and practices; (3) its subtly articulated suggestion that human labor is, in some measure, an artistic endeavor; (4) its assertion that the family, or "society of the household," enjoys an antiquity and status superior to that of any state; (5) its notion that private ownership is consistent with the natural order; (6) its articulation of the responsibilities that poor people and workers bear to the rich and employers; (7) its teleological vision in which social classes are reconciled through "neighborliness and friendship"; (8) its focus on the human person as steward of wealth and "servant of Divine Providence"; (9) its assertion that God's favor resides in special measure with the "unfortunate"; (10) its assertion that it is the responsibility of states to serve all constituents, and its focus on the unique opportunity afforded prosperous states so to do; (11) its claim that it is the duty of all humans not to subject themselves to conditions contrary to their nature and thereby impede their ability to serve God; (12) its theology of leisure rooted in the Sabbath; (13) its declaration that humans require freedom to act as individual agents and to form coalitions with others for mutual benefit; and (14) its contention that the law of charity must govern all human interaction.

Reflections on *Centesimus Annus*

In addition to establishing an important precedent for rereading encyclicals and, by implication, other texts within the Judeo-Christian tradition in light of new circumstances "to discover anew the richness of the fundamental principles" with which one might address the plight of the poor, *Centesimus annus* makes some assertions that have a bearing on the way one reads early Hebrew poetry and other biblical texts. These include (1) that no solution to social problems can be assured without recourse to the tenets of the Christian Gospel; (2) that new forms of poverty have emerged in the world community that require attention; (3) that the option for the poor is essentially "primacy in the exercise of Christian charity"; (4) that the sum total of human life consists of more than a web of social relationships; (5) that since 1945 both capitalist and postcolonial realities have to be factored into our understanding of the social forces shaping the world; (6) that the church's social teachings, as well as its theological anthropology, are the raw materials to be used in fashioning "an authentic theology of integral human liberation"; (7) that a new challenge to be faced in the global community is that of religious fundamentalism; (8) that knowledge, technical proficiency, and entrepreneurial ability are new possessions that many in the so-called First and Third Worlds lack; (9) that the problem of those who "live in situations in which the struggle for a bare minimum is uppermost" must also be part of the church's social agenda; (10) that lifestyles in which consumer choices motivated by "the quest for truth, beauty, goodness and communion with others for the sake of common growth" must be generated; (11) that a model of capitalism that has among its distinguishing features "free human creativity in the economic sector" within well-defined juridical, ethical, and religious boundaries is to be preferred over others; (12) that instead of economic models the church's contribution to the effort to address economic and other inequities is its social teaching; (13) that it is a fundamental Christian duty to support the value of freedom; (14) that the definition of the poor needs to be expanded so as to embrace economic and other forms of disenfranchisement and so as to include individuals, groups, and nations; (15) that war is to be eschewed in favor of peace and the creation of fully participatory national and global economies; and (16) that the church's social teaching should be treated not as mere theory but as "a basis and a motivation for action."

Other themes could be noted, but these are the ones that impressed me as most noteworthy and relevant in shaping an agenda for rereading early Hebrew poetry in a manner that makes the corpus accessible for theological reflection on contemporary poverty and ways to deal with it. Before proceeding, one interesting datum is worth noting. While both encyclicals touch upon issues that are treated in Israel's early poems, they neither quote them directly nor allude to them in explanatory notes. While there is no way of knowing, with any degree of certainty, the cause for this omission, one suspects it may be the result of misconceptions about the tone, original meaning, and canonical function of these texts, which are issues that a critical rereading in light of themes within the encyclicals themselves can help to clarify.

Some Principles for Re-engaging Sacred Scripture

What principles of engagement, therefore, can one derive from the aforementioned texts?[8] The first is that it is normative and acceptable to think in terms of the special needs and concerns of the poor as a starting point for theologically oriented biblical exegesis. The second is that interpretation of the Bible within the church should not be seen exclusively as an intellectual exercise in service to a privileged group of elites. It is, instead, an essential Christian discipline open to everyone. One might even go so far as to suggest that it is one source from which our solidarity with the poor derives its focus and vitality. The third is that, in reading Scripture, theological, anthropological, eschatological, and teleological concerns of both the text and our current life settings must be central.[9] Fourth, humans, as collaborators and co-creators with God, are engaged in tasks that bear their imprint as artists. Human life is, to use the language of Paul in his letter to the Ephesians (2:10), artistically wrought; it is a divinely inspired "poem" (Greek *poiema*), whose power and significance are seen in endeavors that uplift and liberate the human condition. As such, efforts to comprehend the many mysteries of human life need to resonate evocatively with the women and men who experience them on a daily basis.[10] The fifth principle is that at least some part of our encounter with Scripture ought to be geared toward the end of both revisiting and discovering texts that can assist us in formulating ecclesial policies and creating spiritualities that neither exploit the weak, nor demonize those outside the mainstream, nor exacerbate poverty on the national and international levels. The sixth principle is that reading strategies that democratize access to Scripture and envision it as a many-voiced icon of the communities that shaped and continue to utilize it should be employed.[11] The seventh, and final, principle is that Scripture needs to be accessed in ways that promote serious reflection on issues such as work, leisure, poverty, wealth, wages, and taxation in a manner that supports dialogue and peacemaking.

EARLY HEBREW POETRY: AN OVERVIEW OF A DISCRETE CORPUS

With these principles in mind, let us look at the twenty texts that represent what many scholars consider to be Israel's earliest poetic tradition. Early Hebrew poetry has been the subject of considerable interest for some time. For example, in the post-Enlightenment quest for answers to the vexing problem of biblical origins, scholars noted early on that certain biblical poems, particularly those located in the Pentateuch, held the key to understanding the faith of our forebears.[12] In the past sixty years, most of the pioneering work done on the corpus of early Hebrew poetry can be traced to William F. Albright and two of his most prominent students, Frank Moore Cross and David Noel Freedman.[13] The mantle has been taken up by several of their intellectual offspring.[14] Moreover, passion for this research trajectory, though not on par with that expressed for other areas in biblical studies, continues.[15] Nonetheless, questions continue to be raised about whether the poems are truly archaic or merely archaizing, and consensus is lacking on the appropriateness of the philological and prosodic criteria used by followers of Albright to sequence-date the poems.[16] Doubt has also been raised about their reliability as witnesses to Israel's early history, culture, and theology.[17] Like other subdisciplines within the larger universe of biblical research, the study of early Hebrew poetry has suffered to a great extent from postmodern resistance to totalizing discourse and skepticism about metanarration, as well as from postcolonial critiques of the use of the Bible and other ancient Near Eastern artifacts in the Western construction of the Orient as exotic and other.[18]

These things being said, and in spite of difficulties in dating supposedly ancient Hebrew poems and other biblical texts, I think that there is sufficient evidence to posit an early date for Exodus 15; Psalm 29; Judges 5; Numbers 23–24; Genesis 49; Deuteronomy 32–33; 1 Samuel 2; 2 Samuel

1:22 (same as Psalm 18), and 23; and Psalms 68, 72, and 78. There is also merit in treating them as a discrete corpus for the purposes of critical analysis and theological reflection.[19] Their placement within the canon suggests that they play a special role that includes reinforcing key themes, providing dissonant perspectives on difficult problems, and reminding the communities of faith that read and use them of the evocative, transformative, and liberative power of the poetic. There is little doubt that many of the poems contain a kernel of historical memory, impressionistically presented according to the norms governing the praxis of ancient Syro-Palestinian bards. However, their value to audiences from the thirteenth century BCE onward would certainly have extended well beyond their capacity to report historical events. My sense is that they were intended to be, and were perceived as, multifaceted and value-laden pieces offering cosmological, anthropological, theological, and teleological sketches that could be used in a variety of ways. Chief among these were what Wimbush calls *marronage*,[20] creative boundary transgression, community formation, identity construction, delineation of strategies to address social problems bred in crisis, and articulation of liberating lifeways. Moreover, the poems accomplish this, in many instances, by being multilayered—that is, through what might be termed a dominant and an oblique voice. The dominant voice carries the burden of narration and serves to engage the audience directly. The oblique voice operates just below the surface—between the lines, as it were. It takes the listener or reader on a tangent that leads ultimately to a maxim, observation, or realization necessary for survival in trying times. Table 3.1 illustrates how this works within the corpus. My arrangement of the poems follows that of Freedman.[21]

Freedman also proposes a three-part periodization for the poems. Exodus 15, Psalm 29, and Judges 5 belong to the period of Militant Mosaic Yahwism, twelfth century BCE. Genesis 49, Numbers 23–24, and Deuteronomy 33 belong to the period of the Patriarchal Revival, eleventh century BCE. Finally, 1 Samuel 2, 2 Samuel 1, 2 Samuel 23, 2 Samuel 22 (which is the same as Psalm 18), Deuteronomy 32, Psalm 78, Psalm 68, and Psalm 72 all belong to the period of Monarchic Syncretism, tenth century or later.[22] This breakdown is particularly useful in providing a framework for the theological themes found in the poems. It is also useful when one considers that a concern with the poor, as an identifiable group, and with poverty as an issue is found only in the third period, that of Monarchic Syncretism.

Table 3.1. Dominant and Oblique Voices in Ancient Hebrew Poems

Text	Key Theme—Dominant Voice	Key Theme—Oblique Voice
Exodus 15	God as victorious warrior and liberator	Deity as sole source of freedom
Psalm 29	God as cosmic and earthly monarch	Divine rule as ideal model for human governance
Judges 5	Charismatic leadership and tribal allegiance enable victory over adversaries	Community survival via creativity and transgressive strategies
Numbers 23–24 (7 small poems)	God as protector against incursions by adversaries	Benefit of peaceful encounters with neighbors awareness of ideology and other dynamics in community formation
Genesis 49	Theological justification for tribal primacy	Ancestral tradition as historical link and resource for reconceptualizing group identity
Deut. 33	Blessing of Israel as extended kin group; uplift of distinguishing tribal virtues	Divine approval of unity and and diversity in the formation of social aggregates
1 Samuel 2	Incomparability of God	God's commitment to faithful as well as the poor
2 Samuel 1	Celebration of warrior ideal	Folly of war and its inexorable toll
2 Samuel 23	God's blessing on a king	The vivifying effect of just governance
2 Samuel 22 (=Psalm 18)	God's special relationship with the House of David	Deity as source of power for effective leadership
Deuteronomy 32	God's special relationship with Israel	Uniqueness of Yahwistic faith claims and their effectiveness in social bonding
Psalm 78	High points and key themes in Israel's sacred saga	Knowledge of and fidelity to tradition as gateway to continued growth
Psalm 68	God's control of the universe and superiority	Central place of the poor in the larger cosmic scheme
Psalm 72	Correlation of monarchic competence, divine patronage, and fecundity	Interrelationship of divine governance, just rule, and prosperity

DIVINE PATRONAGE, MONARCHIC RULE, AND THE POOR

In Exodus 15, Psalm 29, and Judges 5, one finds a utopian vision in which God functions as divine patron, warrior, benefactor, and monarch. Divine rule clearly occupies a place of prominence, as does the loose political affiliation of extended kin groupings. Numbers 23–24, Genesis 49, and Deuteronomy 33 focus attention on social formation, intergroup dynamics, and the role of ancestral traditions in identity construction. One detects in these poems an emerging strong group orientation, to use the descriptive taxonomy of the anthropologist Mary Douglas, in which collectives such as family or clan are the loci of human interaction.[23] Items belonging to the Hebrew lexicon of social marginalization—that is, words associated with poverty, the poor, the needy, the lonely, prisoners, widows, and orphans, many of which are ubiquitous in the prophetic writings and Psalter—are lacking. This absence is not surprising if their vision is in fact an idealized one in which the sustenance of God and the supportive social web consisting of family and community have effectively eliminated all forms of disenfranchisement.

It is in four of the remaining eight poems, all hailing from the period of Monarchic Syncretism, that one finds specific mention of the poor. These are 1 Samuel 2 (the Prayer of Hannah), 2 Samuel 22 (i.e., Psalm 18), Psalm 68, and Psalm 72. Each of these texts offers a unique perspective on either God's special concern with the poor or the responsibilities that kings have toward them.

The Prayer of Hannah makes some remarkable assertions about the God of Israel's power, overarching social agenda, and intentions for the poor.

> Yahweh is a God of knowledge,
> And deeds are assessed by him.
>
> Warriors' bows are broken.
> Those who stumble about put on strength.
> Those who are sated must hire themselves out,
> While the hungry are full beyond measure.
> The barren woman has born seven children,
> While the one with many sons languishes.
>
> Yahweh causes death and life,
> He can bring one down to Sheol or raise one from it.

He humbles and honors,
Dispossesses and makes rich.

He will lift up the poor from the ground,
Raise the destitute from ash heaps,
In order to seat them among princes,
Indeed, to let them inherit an honorable throne.
For the earth's pedestals belong to Yahweh,
And he sets the world upon them.

(1 Sam. 2:3–8)

The text begins with a fundamental assertion about one of God's distinguishing traits and shifts into an initial eschatological vision in which war has ceased and the social order has been inverted. It then moves ahead with a description of God's ineffable power and concludes with the extraordinary assertion that the one who literally sets the earth solidly in its place not only has concern for the poor but plans to shake things up a bit by granting social status to those who have little.

2 Samuel 22, the text of which is found, with some slight modifications, in Psalm 18, juxtaposes God's disposition toward the arrogant with those who have been humiliated:

He will rescue people who have been humbled,
And take note of the proud to lay them low.

(2 Sam. 22:28)

Psalm 68 contains an even more extraordinary portrait of God as one who stands in solidarity with those outside the social mainstream.

God, in his holy place, is
Parent of orphans, legal champion of widows.
God gives those who are alone a home.
God leads prisoners to prosperity,
But those who are rebellious live in desolation.

(Ps. 68:5–6)

Later, the psalm goes on to suggest that when God led Israel into the wilderness as triumphant Divine Warrior, no doubt a reference to the Exodus event, the natural world blossomed and provision was made for the poor:

The earth shook and the heavens opened,
Before God, the One from Sinai,
The very God of Israel.

O God, you poured out showers of rain.
You fortified your inheritance when it was weary.
Your community made a home within it.
From your goodness, you provided for the poor, O God.
(Ps. 68:8–10)

Psalm 72 configures the responsibilities of kings toward the poor in a manner fully congruent with the attitude of Israel's God toward them. It is said that he "will adjudicate disputes among the people righteously and judge the poor in a just manner" (72:2). In verse 4 we find reference to the king's patronage of both the poor and their children. The most moving description of monarchic duties is found in verses 12–14:

Indeed, he will come to the aid of the poor
And the afflicted that have no support.
He will take pity on the needy and the destitute.
He will save the lives of those who have nothing.

He will redeem them from oppression and violence,
For their blood is precious in his sight.
(Ps. 72:12–14)

These evocative statements about God's concern for the poor and baroque descriptions of the duties rulers have toward them are consistent with religious and political tropes found elsewhere in the ancient Near East. Within this larger milieu, care for the human family is part of the divine job description. Moreover, kings are supposed to rule justly, adjudicate equitably, and take care of those who exist on the social margins. However, these statements take on a slightly different tone in an early Israelite context. There, the administrative Deity of the universe, the chief executive officer of the cosmos, is concerned with, committed to, and hears the prayers of the poor. Royal protection of the poor is not simply intended to be part of state propaganda, at least not from the point of view of the bards who preserved Israel's epic traditions or the prophets who inherited and transformed them. For these creative geniuses, care for the poor was part of God's immutable agreement with Israel and the entirety of the human family.[24]

CREATING TRANSFORMATIONAL SPIRITUALITIES

While it may well be possible to take issue with the appropriateness of Wimbush's claim that the Bible, in its entirety, was generated by people living in what he terms "emergency mode," it would be extremely difficult to argue with the appropriateness of this claim for the early Hebrew poems.[25] The poems function rather like the lyrics of blues songs. They entertain, instruct, challenge, subvert, and elicit both contemplation and catharsis. They scandalize with their specificity, cajole, and disturb. They signify the sources of life's difficulties, name them, and help to exorcise them. In so doing, they embrace life and hope. As Stephen Reid reminds us in his comparison of the biblical lament genre and the blues, two characteristics of both are "tenacity" and a reminder to "take time with our heartache."[26] Similarly, early Hebrew poems make us slow down, take stock, and reassess. They transmute the strong feelings that arise in response to life's ambiguities and unresolved injustices. Their performance, whether spoken, sung, or passively absorbed through reading, creates a moment of spiritual convergence in which we become one with those whose experiences are described. What Albert Murray says in his study of the blues is equally true of early Hebrew poetry:

> Also always absolutely inseparable from all such predicaments and requirements is the most fundamental of all existential imperatives: affirmation, which is to say, reaffirmation and continuity in the face of adversity. Indeed, what with the blues (whether known by that or any other name) always somewhere either in the foreground or the background, reaffirmation is precisely the contingency upon which the very survival of man as human being, however normally unsatisfied and abnormally wretched, is predicated.[27]

Moreover, these poems jar us from complacency and compel us to create spiritualities of transformation in response to dehumanizing conditions and problems such as poverty. Entering into dialogue with them is not for the fainthearted. They challenge us to envision a world in which the reality of poverty is as absent as are descriptions of it in Israel's very earliest strata of poetry. They ask that we maintain our historical memory, expand our theological horizons, and reassert our commitment to life-giving traditions, even as we create new and maximally inclusive matrices for social interaction, ecumenical engagement, interfaith dialogue, and mutual support. Finally, they compel us to work with government officials and other leaders to make certain that the written and unwritten social charters out of which the fabric of our social life is woven are honored. We need not fear that an active engagement with early Hebrew poetry will somehow take us far from the tenets of the Christian Gospel, for its essential trajectory and elegant truths are found there. In fact, if one looks at the implied spiritual praxis of the Magnificat (Luke 1:46–55) and the Beatitudes (Matt. 5:3–12; Luke 6:20–23), one will find many points of agreement with the countercultural lifestyle subtly articulated by Israel's first poets.[28]

In sum, our earliest Jewish forebears speak eloquently to us through the corpus of ancient Hebrew poetry. They encourage and empower us to make the construction of a just and sustainable world—"a world," to quote one of the closing lines of the film *The Matrix*, "without borders or boundaries, a world where anything is possible"—part and parcel of everything that we think, every endeavor that we undertake, and every dream that we dream.

NOTES

1. Vincent L. Wimbush, "Reading Darkness, Reading Scriptures," in *African Americans and the Bible: Sacred Tests and Social Textures,* ed. Vincent L. Wimbush (New York: Continuum, 2000). Those of us who study any aspect of African American biblical interpretation owe a great debt to Wimbush, who has articulated a bold agenda for Bible scholarship. He is also responsible for introducing the term *engagement* to describe the relationship between African Americans and the Bible.

2. Ibid., 23.

3. Ibid., 16.

4. Ibid., 17.

5. H. L. Goodall Jr., *Writing the New Ethnography* (Walnut Creek, CA: AltaMira Press, 2000); Stacy Holman Jones, *Kaleidoscope Notes: Writing Women's Music and Organizational Culture* (Walnut Creek, CA: AltaMira Press, 1998); G. E. Marcus, "What Comes (Just) after 'Post'? The Case of Ethnography," in *The Handbook of*

Qualitative Research, ed. Norman K. Denzin and Yvonna S. Lincoln (Thousand Oaks, CA: Sage Publications, 1994); Norman Denzin, *Interpretive Ethnography: Ethnographic Practices for the Twenty-First Century* (Thousand Oaks, CA: Sage Publications, 1997). My interest in finding ways to stand in solidarity with those outside the social mainstream has taken on added urgency as a result of working with several of my colleagues at Notre Dame (Lionel Jensen, George Lopez, Richard Pierce, Donald Pope-Davis, and Lynn Todman) in the past several years on a variety of special initiatives aimed at building linkages between the university and its surrounding community. In writing this essay, I have followed the lead of anthropologists such as Goodall, *Writing the New Ethnography,* and Jones, *Kaleidoscope Notes,* both of whom have suggested the adoption of new parameters for writing in the social sciences and have created a series of reflections on this topic that are descriptive, analytical, and poetic. In so doing, I hope that the essay's tone is resonant with the spirit of the ancient corpus of poetry that it engages. Perhaps it will encourage Bible scholars now and in the future to produce what some have called *messy texts.* Such works, according to Denzin—reprising Marcus's definition in "What Comes"— "are many sided, intertextual, always open ended, and resistant to theoretical holism, but always committed to cultural criticism" (*Interpretive Ethnography,* 224). Writing of this kind promises to enable theological reading and interpretation of early Hebrew poetry that keep its vitality and transformational power alive for faith communities today and in the future.

6. Alister McGrath, *Christian Spirituality: An Introduction* (Oxford: Blackwell, 1999), 2. McGrath's definition of spirituality as "the quest for a fulfilled and authentic religious life, involving the bringing together of the ideas distinctive of that religion and the whole experience of living on the basis of and within the scope of that religion," expresses most clearly my understanding of the term. The spiritualities of which I speak need not be limited to adherents of Christianity. The Bible has had (and continues to exercise) an enormous impact on Western institutions, public discourse, and literature. Even those who consider themselves outside the Judeo-Christian religious continuum may discover in its pages—and those of other sacred writings in our global religious environment—insights and intuitions with which to create compassionate and empathetic approaches to life.

7. David J. O'Brien and Thomas A. Shannon, eds., *Catholic Social Thought: The Documentary Heritage* (Maryknoll, NY: Orbis Books, 1992), 14–39, 439–88. For a full text of this encyclical, as well as the encyclical *Centesimus annus,* discussed below, the anthology of O'Brien and Shannon can be consulted. For the purposes of this chapter, use was made of the official online versions of both encyclicals, available at www.osjspm.org/cst/rn.htm and www.osjspm.org/cst/ca.htm respectively.

8. Donald Dorr, *Option for the Poor: A Hundred Years of Vatican Social Teaching,* rev. ed. (Maryknoll, NY: Orbis Books, 2002), 2–3. See Dorr's classic treatment of these and other encyclicals. Special attention should be paid to his summary of the three components basic to the idea of the option for the poor and description of what it denotes:

> An option for the poor is a commitment by individual Christians and the Christian community at every level to engage actively in a struggle to overcome the social injustices which mar our world. To be genuine it must come from a real experience of solidarity with the victims of our society. This means that one aspect of an option for the poor has to do with sharing in some degree in the lives, sorrows, joys, hopes, and fears of those who are on the margins of society.

My goal is to offer a somewhat different perspective on the encyclicals that might initiate a larger discussion on the part of theologians and others about their implications for biblical interpretation.

    9. Sheila G. Davaney, *Pragmatic Historicism: A Theology for the Twenty-First Century* (Albany: State University of New York Press, 2000), x, xi, 60, 154–55, 180, 187–88. This principle is consistent with the aims of what Davaney calls pragmatic historicism, an approach to theological inquiry that places it—in her words—"at the intersection of traditions" and embraces a broad spectrum of academic and other interlocutors in the social sciences.

    10. T. V. F. Brogan, "Poet," in *The New Princeton Encyclopedia of Poetry and Poetics,* ed. T. V. F. Brogan and A. Preminger (Princeton: Princeton University Press, 1993), 920–24. The emphasis on human life as poem accentuates the role of God as divine artist and concomitantly draws attention to the special place that poets occupy in the ancient and modern theological spectrum. Those whose works are found in the Bible can be understood as "makers" of oral and written traditions that create and sustain communities of faith. Moreover, they create—through the power of words—a sacramental space where the eschatological conjunction of past, present, and future can take place. See Brogan, "Poet," on the poet's roles as individual, seer, maker, and social actor.

    11. Susan E. Gillingham, *One Bible, Many Voices: Different Approaches to Biblical Studies* (Grand Rapids, MI: Eerdmans, 1998), 3–4; Harold Bloom, *The Anxiety of Influence: A Theory of Poetry* (New York: Oxford University Press, 1993), xi–xlvii, xix. I have long found it beneficial to think of the Bible metaphorically (both the Old/First and New/Second Testaments) as a single text that contains a *choir of descanting theological voices.* The truths expressed in its *theological libretto* are wide ranging, and its *teleological score* is characterized by both harmony and dissonance. I am not the only scholar to have taken this interpretive trajectory. Gillingham has noted in her well-articulated, thorough, and balanced introduction to biblical studies that "the Bible is a pluralistic text, made up of many parts with many divergent views about God and his relations with the world" (3). She also argues, quite convincingly, that the Bible's polyphony makes its constituent books "well-suited for a multifaceted method of study, whereby the diversity evident in the making of the Bible is matched by a diversity of methods in the reading of it" (4). What Bloom says about both the "influence process" and the literary nature of the critical enterprise is also pertinent. Of particular note is his statement that "authentic, high literature relies

upon troping, a turning away not only from the literal but from prior tropes. Like criticism, which is either part of literature or nothing at all, great writing is always at work strongly (or weakly) misreading previous writing. Any stance that anyone takes up towards a metaphorical work will itself be metaphorical" (xix).

The Bible is high literature. Many of the books and individual passages contained in it were, no doubt, esteemed as such by those responsible for the selection and editing of its final form. In this light, interpretive strategies that are theologically driven and artistic are necessary for the text to remain a life-giving and liberating entity within those communities that honor its authority and sacred character. Furthermore, they enable the Bible's unity and diversity to serve as a textual icon for what those who read it can become—a living choir whose *singularity* of purpose is expressed in the *descant* that their thoughts, actions, and dreams express.

12. Robert Lowth, *Lectures on the Sacred Poetry of the Hebrews,* Anglistica et Americana 43 (Hildesheim, NY: George Olms, 1969), 94. See, for example, Lowth's comments on Gen. 9:25–27; 27:27–29, 39, 40 in his well-known lectures on Hebrew poetry.

13. William F. Albright, *From the Stone Age to Christianity* (Garden City, NY: Doubleday, 1957); William F. Albright, *Yahweh and the Gods of Canaan* (Garden City, NY: Anchor Books, 1969); Frank Moore Cross, *Canaanite Myth and Hebrew Epic: Essays in the History of the Religion of Israel* (Cambridge, MA: Harvard University Press, 1973), *From Epic to Canon* (Baltimore: Johns Hopkins University Press, 1998), and *Leaves from an Epigrapher's Notebook: Collected Papers in Hebrew and West Semitic Palaeography and Epigraphy,* Harvard Semitic Studies 51 (Winona Lake, IN: Eisenbrauns, 2003); Frank Moore Cross and David Noel Freedman, *Early Hebrew Orthography,* American Oriental Series 36 (New Haven, CT: American Oriental Society, 1952), and *Studies in Ancient Yahwistic Poetry,* Biblical Resource Series (Grand Rapids, MI: William B. Eerdmans, 1997). The catalog of books and articles produced by Albright, Cross, and Freedman is too extensive to cite here. Some key works can be noted. Albright's two major treatises—on the religion of Canaan and Israel *(Yahweh)* and the development of monotheism *(From the Stone Age)* respectively— provide access to the gestalt of his life's work. Cross's magnum opus is his critically acclaimed monograph, written some thirty years ago, on the epic traditions of early Israel *(Canaanite Myth).* To this can now be added both his most recent work on the history, literature, and religion of Israel and a (lightly edited) collection of his most influential articles. Cross and Freedman's most famous joint venture consists of their coauthored dissertation completed under Albright's direction at Johns Hopkins University and subsequently published under their names in two volumes *(Early Hebrew Orthography).*

14. Noteworthy contributions have been made by David A. Robertson, *Linguistic Evidence in Dating Early Hebrew Poetry,* SBL Dissertation Series 3 (Missoula, MT: Scholars Press, 1972); Stephen A. Geller, *Parallelism in Early Biblical Poetry,* Harvard Semitic Monographs (Missoula, MT: Scholars Press, 1979); M. O'Connor, *Hebrew Verse Structure* (Winona Lake, IN: Eisenbrauns, 1980); Theodore Hiebert, *God*

of My Victory: The Ancient Hymn in Habakkuk 3, Harvard Semitic Monographs 38 (Atlanta: Scholars Press, 1986).

15. Johannes C. de Moor and Wilfred G. E. Watson, *Verse in Ancient Near Eastern Prose,* Alter Orient und Altes Testament 42 (Kevelaer: Butzon und Bercker, 1993); Steven Weitzman, *Song and Story in Biblical Narrative: The History of a Literary Convention in Ancient Israel* (Bloomington: Indiana University Press, 1997). The collection of essays on prose-embedded verse in the ancient Near East edited by Johannes C. de Moor and Wilfred G. E. Watson and the recent monograph of Weitzman—whose evocation of choral imagery in describing the function of Exod. 15 resonates with my metaphorical conception of how the Bible functions as a whole—can be cited as evidence of continuing scholarly interest in the texts that fall within the corpus of early Hebrew poems. Though these works focus attention by and large on the literary, structural, and canonical dimensions of poetic compositions surrounded by prose (in biblical and other texts) rather than strictly historical-critical issues (e.g., authorship, date, *Sitz im Leben*), these works do further our understanding of the reception history of the texts in question. In fact, they suggest that the key to understanding the formation of the Pentateuch and the Deuteronomistic history may well be found in a closer examination of narrative-embedded poems in these large literary aggregates.

16. Joseph Blenkinsopp, *The Pentateuch: An Introduction to the First Five Books of the Bible,* Anchor Bible Reference Library (New York: Doubleday, 1992), 19, 159. See, for example, the balanced critique offered by Blenkinsopp. He notes the strength of Albright and Cross's hypothesis regarding the existence of a poetic *Vorlage* as the basis of the Pentateuchal narrative and the inherent limitations of the prosodic criteria employed by Albright, Cross, and Freedman to date purportedly early poems such as Exod. 15.

17. Keith Whitelam, *The Invention of Ancient Israel* (New York: Routledge, 1996), 8–9, 71–121; William G. Dever, *Who Were the Early Israelites and Where Did They Come From?* (Grand Rapids, MI: Eerdmans, 2003), 227–41. For example, Keith Whitelam, who builds on the work of Philip Davies, T. L. Thompson, Robert Coote, and N. P. Lemche—believes that biblical scholars have fabricated various conceptions of ancient Israel to forward academic, political, and other aims, many of which have had less than salutary long-term effects on our global community. Dever seeks a via media that allows archeologists and biblical scholars to reach détente by carefully delimiting the communicative parameters of the primary materials available to them, noting the strengths and weaknesses of the methods employed in their interpretation, and searching for points of convergence where separate paths of data may ultimately meet.

18. See, for example, Edward W. Said, *Orientalism* (New York: Vintage Books, 1979); A. K. M. Adam, *What Is Postmodern Biblical Criticism?* Guides to Biblical Scholarship, New Testament Series (Minneapolis: Fortress Press, 1995); and Fernando Segovia, *Decolonizing Biblical Studies: A View from the Margins* (Maryknoll, NY: Orbis Books, 2000).

19. Too often, the drive for academic supremacy and the positing of suppos-edly novel approaches to long-standing hermeneutical problems is used as an ex-cuse to dismiss the groundbreaking advances made by senior colleagues. Today, solid work conducted a decade or more ago is often consigned to obscurity before it can be read, absorbed, expanded, and further developed by a new generation of scholars. This is, to my mind, a lamentable breach of charity. The work begun long ago by Albright, Cross, and Freedman on early Hebrew poetry deserves to be carried forward. Failure to do so would represent poor stewardship of their life-long effort to delimit this corpus using philological and literary criteria.

20. Wimbush, "Reading Darkness," 23–25, 31 n. 12. Wimbush uses this term to encompass responses of "deformation" and "flight" that are part of the black ex-perience in America; he appears to be referencing the processes of voluntary com-munal disengagement and escape that enabled African Americans to pursue free-dom from enslavement and to work toward social and political independence. The term *marronage* is based on the English word *maroon,* the name given to African American slaves who escaped captivity and established separate lives independent of plantation communities.

21. David Noel Freedman, "Divine Names and Titles in Hebrew Poetry," in *Pottery, Poetry, and Prophecy: Studies in Early Hebrew Poetry,* ed. David Noel Freedman (Winona Lake, IN: Eisenbrauns, 1980), 77–79.

22. Ibid., 78–79, 118.

23. Mary Douglas, "Introduction to Group/Grid Analysis," in *Essays in the So-ciology of Perception,* ed. Mary Douglas (London: Routledge and Kegan Paul, 1982).

24. Norbert F. Lohfink, *Option for the Poor: The Basic Principles of Liberation The-ology in the Light of the Bible* (Berkeley, CA: BIBAL Press, 1995), 30, 32–33, 41. This is in keeping with what Lohfink has asserted in his incisive assessment of the bib-lical foundations for the concept of the option for the poor. He rightly calls atten-tion to the radical nature of the exodus tradition in light of ancient Near Eastern discourse about concern for the poor and disenfranchised. He is also on point when he affirms that there is something unique in the biblical portrait of a God who *re-moves* those who suffer from both tyrannical systems that dehumanize and insti-tutions responsible for systemic forms of oppression. The early Hebrew poetic cor-pus appears to put forward the idea that God sanctions the formation of alternative communities in which values antithetic to those of any dominant (and oppres-sive) ethos become the normative basis for daily life.

25. Wimbush, "Reading Darkness," 21.

26. Stephen Breck Reid, *Listening In: A Multicultural Reading of the Psalms* (Nashville: Abingdon Press, 1997), 8–9.

27. Albert Murray, *Stomping the Blues,* 25th anniversary ed. (New York: Da Capo Press, 2000), 6.

28. Don Cupitt, *Mysticism after Modernity* (Oxford: Blackwell, 1998), 3. What such an engagement may well do is lead us to think further about the ways that early Hebrew poems *destabilize,* by their very presence in the canon, dominant po-

litical ideologies and theological themes encoded in other biblical texts. For example, is it possible that one of their purposes is to remind communities of faith—past, present, and future—that God's grace is available to all and cannot be impeded by any human structures, particularly those designed to oppress? Along these lines, what Cupitt has said about the deconstructive agenda of Christian mystics may well apply to certain ancient Hebrew poets: "[T]he writers commonly called 'mystics' were usually (though not quite always) persons of low ecclesiastical rank, from the inferior clergy, the religious, and the laity. They included relatively large numbers of townspeople, of women, and of poets. In their devotional writings they are conspicuously silent about the great salvation-machine and all its concerns. Recalling the older charismatic and more democratic tradition, they try to write their way and ours to a condition of personal religious happiness" (3). If Cupitt is correct, then Bible scholars, historians, theologians, and others should look at these poems for clues about the possible social location of their authors and consider the implications of those findings for contemporary spiritual formation.

Part Three

POVERTY, PATRISTICS,

AND MARTYRDOM

Chapter 4

THE CAPPADOCIAN FATHERS
AND THE OPTION
FOR THE POOR

BRIAN E. DALEY

Few of us, probably, associate the fathers of the church with the phrase *the option for the poor.* Sowed in the conscience of the world and the church by the Latin American bishops at Medellín in 1968, and again at Puebla in 1979, as well as by Gustavo Gutiérrez in his seminal book *A Theology of Liberation,* this phrase seems to focus on the obligations of Christians to the least of our brethren in this modern world with its growing and apparently unbridgeable gaps between the rich and the poor, North and South, the power of technologically based affluence and the hopelessness of want and exclusion. It is perhaps all the more striking, then, that Pope John Paul II, in his 1987 encyclical *Sollicitudo rei socialis,* insists that "the option or love of preference for the poor . . . is an option or a special form of primacy in the exercise of Christian charity to which the whole tradition of the Church bears witness."[1] What I would like to offer in this brief chapter is a glimpse of just one significant, if curiously unstudied, moment in the growth of that tradition: the reflections of the three fourth-century Greek bishops commonly known as the Cappadocian fathers—Basil of Caesarea, his brother Gregory of Nyssa, and their friend Gregory of Nazianzus— on the anthropological and moral issues raised by wealth and poverty and on the central Christian obligation, in their view crucial to our salvation, of actively and practically loving the poor.[2]

Most people familiar with the development of Christian theology will think, first, of the crucial role these three Cappadocians played in shaping the language and concepts by which we speak of the mystery of God as a Trinity of hypostases or "persons," who form and act as a single, utterly inconceivable reality. Doubtless, too, their share in the early stages of ancient controversy over the personal unity of Christ, as God and a human being, will come to mind, as well as their highly developed theology of the human person, their view of human salvation as an endlessly growing share in the life of God, and Gregory of Nyssa's first sketches of a Christian theology of mystical prayer, most notably in his homilies on the Song of Songs. Yet beyond all these seemingly rarefied issues, the three theologians shared an urgent concern to draw the attention of their contemporaries to the plight of the poor, the diseased, the marginalized, the "insignificant," to use Gustavo Gutiérrez's term, precisely as a challenge to faith in the transforming work of an incarnate, self-communicating God. As Christian humanists, pioneers in the first self-conscious attempts by Christians to use and reshape the intellectual and linguistic techniques of classical Hellenism in the service of the Christian Gospel, they saw it as part of their philosophy to turn the gaze of their hearers, imaginatively and dramatically, toward the homeless beggars in their town squares—the new Lazarus crouching at their gates—and to remind more affluent Christians of the fundamental obligation that lies on all of us to share what we control of the world's goods with something approaching an even hand. At the heart of their appeal lay their theological principles: the central identity of the human person as bearing the image of God, the promise of human growth toward the full restoration of that image in the person of Christ, and the moral imperative, the vision of human virtue, that flows from this understanding of our nature and destiny.

As is true of many Christian prophets and reformers, these three writers came from what we would call the upper middle class of their own society and were thoroughly immersed as young men in the traditional educational rituals of their culture. Basil of Caesarea was born around AD 330, the eldest son in a large and well-connected Christian family in the

Roman province of Cappadocia in central Asia Minor. During his formative years as a student of rhetoric and philosophy in Athens in the mid-350s, Basil shared both a house and a growing interest in Christian theology with a fellow Cappadocian, Gregory of Nazianzus, the son of a small-town bishop. Nazianzus was perhaps a year or two older than Basil and was an intense and highly verbal young man who seemed always to live on the edge between the heights of intellectual and literary acclaim and the depths of self-pity. On their return to their rugged homeland, Basil invited Gregory to spend several months with him on his family's rural estate, leading the life of simple, contemplative retirement so favored as an ideal by ancient pagans and Christians alike, a Christian, ascetical version of Cicero's "dignified leisure" that they used, in part, to study the works of Origen.

At Christmas in 361, Gregory was virtually forced by his father to be ordained as a presbyter so that he could take a more active role in the pastoral leadership of his father's little church of Nazianzus. His friend Basil, a much more public person by temperament, also decided to be ordained for the service of Eusebius, the bishop of Caesarea, the provincial capital. Basil's younger brother Gregory, later bishop of Nyssa, a married man who had also received an extensive early education in science, philosophy, and letters, seems to have been ordained a presbyter as well, sometime in the late 360s.[3]

On Bishop Eusebius's death in 370, Basil drew on all his family and personal connections to have himself elected Eusebius's successor and, as metropolitan bishop of Cappadocia, exercised outstanding leadership, over the next nine years until his death, in promoting both a new form of active, ecclesially committed monasticism and the theological tradition of the Council of Nicaea, which asserted the full participation of the Son and the Holy Spirit in the substance and activity of the transcendent God. As part of his campaign to secure the churches of Cappadocia in the hands of like-minded leaders, he persuaded both his friend Gregory and his younger brother Gregory to become bishops as well, although neither of them seems to have shared Basil's taste or talent for pastoral leadership. They did share his passion for rhetorically sophisticated preaching, however, and his sense of the form of life, the *politeia,* to which faith in the Gospel invites us: a form that all three, along with other late-fourth-century Christian intellectuals, referred to as "philosophy," the true quest of wisdom for which pagan philosophy since Socrates had served merely as prologue.

It was as part of this ministry of Christian rhetoric that all three Cappadocians composed sermons on love of and service to the poor.[4] In the spring and summer of 369, during a crippling drought that left central Anatolia dangerously short of water and food, Basil, still a presbyter and patron of pastorally active ascetics, delivered three powerful homilies aimed at stirring the wealthier members of the Caesarean congregation to share their surplus food with the starving, not simply as a gesture of kindness, but as a straightforward human and Christian obligation. The first of these (number 6 of Basil's homilies) begins with Jesus's portrait of the "rich fool" in Luke 12:16–21. Subtitled "On Greed," it argues that all the earth's produce is given to us by God for our common use and that individuals are simply stewards of a common supply. Drawing on a theme already sounded by the Stoics, Basil insists that the vice of greed, in a world intended by its creator for common occupation and use, is to hoard more than one actually needs of the world's goods while others remain in want:

> Who, then, is greedy? The one who does not remain content with self-sufficiency. Who is the one who deprives others? The one who hoards what belongs to everyone. Are *you* not greedy? Are *you* not one who deprives others? You have received these things for stewardship and have turned them into your own property! . . . The bread that you hold on to belongs to the hungry; the cloak you keep locked in your storeroom belongs to the naked. . . . You do an injury to as many people as you might have helped with all these things![5]

Basil's seventh homily, subtitled "Against the Wealthy," has its scriptural base in Matthew 19:16–23, the story of Jesus's conversation with the rich young man. It is, for the most part, a reflection on the psychology and the destructive effect of pursuing wealth: the addictive power of affluence, its spiral of mounting, self-induced need, and its effect of leading the wealthy to seek other forms of domination over others:[6]

> Nothing can withstand the force of wealth. Everything bows to its tyranny, everything trembles before its lordship; each of those who has suffered unjustly is more concerned not to experience some new evil than to bring the perpetrator to justice for what has happened before. He drives away your yokes of oxen, he plows and seeds your field, he harvests what does not belong to him. And if you speak out

in resistance, you are beaten; if you complain, you are held for damages and led away to prison.[7]

The reason people are significantly richer than their neighbors, Basil insists, is ultimately that they choose not to be aware of the needs of their neighbors. "Surely the more you abound in wealth," he remarks a little simplistically, "the more you are lacking in love!"[8] In light of the famine, those who have a surplus are simply obliged, in Basil's view, to begin sharing it immediately with those in dire need.

Basil's Homily 8, "A Homily Delivered in a Time of Famine and Drought," draws on the Old Testament prophets to interpret Cappadocia's present crisis. Basil is willing to read the times as a sign of God's anger and judgment, a "visitation" of the Lord intended to call his congregation to conversion. They are deprived of God's usual blessings on the land, notably rain, "because we receive but do not share, we praise his generosity but deprive the needy of this very thing in ourselves."[9] Human reason and even the behavior of the irrational cattle urge us to share the world's produce with each other. Greek philosophical sects, as well as the early community depicted in Acts, shared a table: "Let us imitate that first band of Christians, when all things were held in common—when life and soul and harmony and the table all were shared, when fraternity was undivided, and unfeigned love formed many bodies into one."[10]

More practically, Basil suggests that the affluent members of his congregation appoint one ascetical, disinterested overseer, such as himself, to supervise the distribution of their surplus for the benefit of the poor.[11] Apparently his preaching had its desired effect. Gregory of Nazianzus, in his panegyric delivered a year or two after Basil's death in 379, tells us that Basil opened and personally worked in a refuge and soup kitchen in Caesarea during that famine year[12] and that after he became bishop Basil raised the money to build an elaborate hospice for the homeless, the sick, and travelers just outside the ancient city, which formed the nucleus of Caesarea's later expansion.[13] Even ancient rhetoric could be effective in fundraising!

Basil's brother Gregory has also left us two powerful homilies on much the same theme, apparently preached as part of a Lenten cycle and possibly dating from the time when Basil, then bishop, was promoting his hospice project in the early 370s.[14] The first homily, subtitled "On Beneficence," connects the community's efforts at self-restraint during Lent with a heightened concern for the destitute in their city, especially the homeless and the refugee. Appealing to his congregation to be generous in direct aid to the poor, Gregory alludes to the judgment scene in Matthew 25, assuring his hearers that in that final reckoning the poor whom we have helped will be our advocates before God, for "they bear the face *(prosopon)* of Christ"; just as we are all the stewards of creation, they are "the stewards of our hope, the doorkeepers of the kingdom."[15] Gregory's second homily, "On Loving the Poor," is grounded again in the text of Matthew 25. Here, however, the particular focus is an appeal for generosity and hospitality toward lepers, who apparently have appeared in Caesarea, a crowd of destitute pariahs shunned by family and friends and living in the open air. Gregory dramatizes their presence with all the skills of a trained rhetorician, just as he dramatized the exquisite luxuries of the wealthy in his first homily: their deformities, their almost clownish attempts to attract the attention of passersby, become in his hands a macabre and moving piece of theater. The purpose of the drama, clearly, is to contrast the present state of these unfortunates with what Gregory keeps insisting is "our common nature" as human beings: to be one "born in the image of God, entrusted with the governance of the earth and the rule over all creatures, here so alienated by sickness that one hesitates to recognize him,"[16] but God's image all the same. Recalling the brevity of the present life and our common hope for eschatological transformation, Gregory argues that the best way to begin healing our own spiritual wounds is to care for their bodily ones.[17]

Probably shortly after Gregory of Nyssa delivered these homilies, Gregory of Nazianzus also composed his own homily "On Loving the Poor," a long and immensely powerful sermon that has come down in his corpus as Oration 14.[18] Gregory Nazianzen actually incorporates into his homily a number of passages directly borrowed from his namesake's second sermon, a practice commonly accepted in antiquity as a flattering gesture of agreement, and develops an equally powerful portrait of homeless lepers roaming the squares of a Cappadocian provincial city. For Gregory Nazianzen as for Gregory Nyssen, *philanthropia,* the active love of our fellow men and women that is most tellingly expressed in love of the poor, is the highest of all the human virtues, "since nothing else is more proper than this to God,"[19] who will save us "by the grace and philanthropy of our Lord Jesus Christ."[20] After himself satirizing the self-indulgence of the rich and underscoring the frailty and shortness of all human life, Gregory evokes the contrast between the exalted vocation of all human beings and the demeaning barriers we erect between ourselves:

> Recognize from where it is that you have being, breath, the power of thought, and greatest of all, the power to know God and to hope for the Kingdom of Heaven, for equality with the angels, for the vision of glory . . . , for the chance to become a child of God, a fellow-heir with Christ, even (I make bold to say) to become yourself divine. From where do all these gifts come, and from whom? . . . Who endowed you with all the gifts by which the human person stands out over all other creatures? Is it not he who now, before all else and rather than all else, demands from you kindness toward other human beings *(to philanthropon)?* Are we not ashamed, then, if receiving so much from him, either in fact or in hope, we do not give back this one thing to God: to show love toward others *(to philanthropon)?* . . . God is not ashamed to be called our Father, though he is our God and Lord; shall we, then, deny our own human family?[21]

These appeals by the three Cappadocian bishops for an active concern for the poor and marginalized as a central element of a Christian's way of life did not come from thin air. Like John Chrysostom's better-known sermons on Lazarus and the Rich Man, preached in nearby Antioch less than two decades later, they draw on a long, if not always so powerfully articulated, tradition of Jewish and Christian recognition that the poor among us are the objects of God's special concern and must therefore be our concern as well. Ancient Greek and Roman society, it is often pointed out, showed little concern for the poor as a group particularly deserving of care; the great public benefactions expected of wealthy citizens and aspiring politicians were understood more as an occasion for them to display their wealth and achievements than as remedies of injustice or exercises of compassion.[22] Ancient Israel, by contrast, recognized that the God who created all peoples and who called Abraham's children into a special covenant is the God who "raises the poor from the dust and lifts the needy from the ash heap" (Ps. 113:7). So it was a central concern of Israel's God to forbid members of his people to oppress the socially and economically disadvantaged: the stranger, the widow, the orphan, the dependent poor (Exod. 22:21–25; cf. Lev. 19:13): "If there is among you a poor man, one of your brethren," Deuteronomy urges, "in any of your towns within your land which the Lord your God gives you, you shall not harden your heart or shut your hand against your poor brother, but you shall open your hand to him."[23] The disciples of Jesus remembered him as one whose prophetic vocation was, in Isaiah's phrase, to "preach good news to the poor" (Luke 4:18, quoting Isa. 61:1; cf. Luke 7:22, Matt 11:5) and who proclaimed that God's kingdom was open especially to them (Matt. 5:3; Luke 6:20). Recognizing Jesus as the one who "emptied himself" of his divine status and took on the "form of a slave" (Phil. 2:7), Paul could write: "You know the grace of our Lord Jesus Christ, that though he was rich, yet for your sake he became poor, so that by his poverty you might become rich" (2 Cor. 8:9). In the context of this biblical tradition, and this view of Christ as the Son of God who had taken human poverty on himself, early Christian theology and practice saw the poor as occupying a distinctive place within the community and as requiring particular attention. In the words of the second-century moral treatise the *Shepherd of Hermas,* the rich and the poor each have their proper "work" to do: "The poor person works with prayer, in which he is rich, which he received from the Lord . . . , and the rich person likewise, without hesitating, shares with the poor the wealth which he received from the Lord. And this work is great and acceptable with God."[24] By the mid–fourth century the Christian community had won a reputation for their practice of *philanthropia,* especially toward the poor and marginalized, so much so that the Emperor Julian, in his efforts to revive Hellenic religion as a cultural force, strongly criticized human greed as the root cause of poverty and urged a generosity and hospitality among Hellenes that would be at least as vital as that of "the impious Galileans"![25]

What was new in the sermons of the three Cappadocians on loving the poor was their ability to give new depth and theological grounding to this ancient Jewish and Christian instinct by contextualizing it within a clear vision of God as judge and savior, within a Christology, a Christian anthropology, and a Christian eschatology that were thoughtfully anchored both in the Scriptures and in a long philosophical tradition. For all three of them, as indeed for Julian, the goods of the world that supply our needs are the gifts of a beneficent creator, intended for the support of all creatures.[26] If we are to perfect our humanity by imitating God, we must strive first of all to imitate his *philanthropia.*[27] This is the supreme human virtue, Gregory Nazianzen insists, because it most closely reflects God's own mercy,[28] yet at the same time this love of humanity is, like all the virtues, perfectly natural to us because our nature is made in God's image.[29] It is greed, and the violence and domination to which greed leads us, that are in fact contrary to nature and therefore destructive and vicious; greed makes a person into "a brutal tyrant, an intractable barbarian, a craving beast . . . far more ferocious than the entire animal kingdom,"[30] insists Gregory of Nyssa. All three of these writers, in fact, draw on the ancient utopian topos that the original state of humanity is one of equality among persons, an equality of status that is meant to lead to equality in possessions. Gregory Nazianzen writes:

> [God] has spread out unsettled land for all on earth, and springs and rivers and forests . . . , not putting them under the power of force or the limits of law or the divisions of geographical boundaries, but setting them forth richly as common possessions for all, and not in any way diminished because of this. What is of like rank in nature he honors with an equality of gifts, and so shows how rich his own generosity is. But human beings, in contrast, bury their gold and their soft, unneeded clothing in the ground, . . . all tokens of violence and discord and primeval oppression, and then raise their eyebrows in incomprehension. . . . [They forget] that the things we call poverty and riches, freedom and slavery, and all other such things, are only later acquisitions of the human race, and like a kind of common disease that accompanies sin and is a symptom of it. "From the beginning," however, as the Lord says, "it was not so" (Matt. 19:8).[31]

Since they were theologians, preachers, and pastors, the Cappadocians' version of this argument for philanthropy based on our original human state is centered on the New Testament conviction that this humanity has been definitively renewed in Jesus, the "new Adam," the divine person with a human face in whom our own human transformation has begun. And it is Christ, as our eschatological judge, who remains, in their view, both the norm and the object of all our philanthropy. So Gregory Nazianzen closes his oration with an appeal that really summarizes the rationale of all three writers for an option or preferential love of the poor:

> If you believe me at all, then, servants and brothers and sisters and fellow heirs of Christ, let us take care of Christ while there is still

time; let us minister to Christ's needs, let us give Christ nourishment, let us clothe Christ, let us gather Christ in, let us show Christ
honor—not just at our tables, as some do, nor just with ointment,
like Mary, nor just with a tomb, like Joseph of Arimathea. . . . But
since the Lord of all things "desires mercy and not sacrifice" (Hos.
6:6; cf. Matt. 9:13), and since "a compassionate heart is worth more
than tens of thousands of fat rams" (Dan. 3:40 LXX), let us give
this gift to him through the needy, who today are cast down on the
ground, so that when we all are released from this place, they may
receive us into the eternal tabernacle, in Christ himself.[32]

For Christians then and now, Gregory reminds us, the option for the poor
is nothing less than the choice to follow Christ, to offer him our service,
and to love him through his Body.

NOTES

1. John Paul II, "Sollicitudo rei socialis," www.vatican.va/phome_en.htm
(accessed May 24, 2006), no. 42.

2. I have already treated the thought of the three Cappadocian fathers on
poverty and wealth, and the nature of their appeal to more affluent Christians to
care for the sick and the poor of their day, in a longer article: Brian E. Daley, "Building a New City: The Cappadocian Fathers and the Rhetoric of Philanthropy," *Journal of Early Christian Studies* 7 (1999): 431–61.

3. For an argument in support of this conjectural early dating of Gregory of
Nyssa's ordination, see ibid., 450.

4. For a recent analysis of these homilies in the context of late antique pagan,
Jewish, and Christian attitudes to the poor, see Susan R. Holman, *The Hungry Are
Dying: Beggars and Bishops in Roman Cappadocia* (New York: Oxford University Press,
2001). In an appendix to her book, Holman offers new translations, from which I
quote in this chapter, of Basil's Homily 8, "In Time of Famine and Drought," and of
Gregory of Nyssa's two homilies entitled "On the Love of the Poor." Translations in
this chapter of passages from Basil's other writings are my own. I have translated
Gregory of Nazianzus's Oration 14, "On the Love of the Poor" and hope to include
it in a forthcoming volume of translations from Gregory's works. None of these
homilies were available in English before the appearance of Holman's book.

5. Basil, Hom. 6.7 (J.-P. Migne, ed., PG 31.276C8–77A8). For Stoic parallels,
see Cicero, *De officiis* 1.7.21–22, who argues that private property is not part of
the original or "natural" state of humanity; and Seneca, Ep. 90 (to Lucilius), 18 and

36–43, who sees avarice as both the foundation of private property and the root cause of poverty (38).

6. Basil, Hom. 7.4–5.

7. Basil, Hom. 7.5 (PG 31.293C10–96A3).

8. Basil, Hom. 7.1 (PG 31.281B8–9).

9. Basil, Hom. 8.3 (PG 31.309A11–14).

10. Basil, Hom. 8.8 (PG 31.325A2–B4).

11. Basil, Hom. 8.4 (PG 31.313D).

12. Gregory of Nazianzus, Or. 43.35–36.

13. On the *Basileias,* see Gregory of Nazianzus, Or. 43.63; Sozomen, *Historia ecclesiastica* 6.34; Firmus of Caesarea, Ep. 43.

14. For dating, see Daley, "Building a New City," 449–50.

15. Gregory of Nyssa, Or. 1 *(De pauperibus amandis)* (A. van Heck, ed., in *Gregorii Nysseni De pauperibus amandis orationes duo* [Leiden: Brill, 1964], 460; trans. Susan Holman, *Hungry Are Dying,* 195).

16. Gregory of Nyssa, Or. 2 *(De pauperibus amandis)* (A. Van Heck, ed., in *Gregorii Nysseni De pauperibus amandis orationes duo* [Leiden: Brill, 1964], 480, 477; trans. Holman, *Hungry Are Dying,* 203, 201).

17. Gregory of Nyssa, Or. 2 (Van Heck 485; trans. Holman 200–210).

18. For the argument for dating this homily in the early 370s, see again Daley, "Building a New City," 454–55.

19. Gregory of Nazianzus, Or. 14.5 (J.-P. Migne, ed., PG 38.863C1).

20. Gregory of Nyssa, Or. 1 (Van Heck 469; trans. Holman 199).

21. Gregory of Nazianzus, Or. 14.23 (PG 38.888A–C).

22. For a good recent discussion of modern scholarship on the place of the poor in ancient Greek and Roman society, see Holman, *Hungry Are Dying,* 3–42. See also Evelyne Patlagean, *Pauvreté économique et pauvreté sociale à Byzance, 4e–7e siècles* (Moutons: École des Hautes Études en Sciences Sociales, 1977).

23. Deut. 15:7–8. On the obligation for farmers to leave some of the fruit of their harvest at the edges of their fields for the poor and wandering people to gather, see Lev. 19:9–10.

24. *Shepherd of Hermas,* Similitude 3 (51.5–7) (Graydon F. Snyder, trans., in *The Apostolic Fathers* [Camden, NJ: Thomas Nelson, 1968], 6:97–98).

25. See Julian's fragmentary *Letter to a Priest* 289A–93A, 305CD, in *The Works of the Emperor Julian II,* ed. and trans. Wilmer Cave Wright (Cambridge, MA; Harvard University Press, 1913) 298–308, 336–38.

26. So Basil, Hom. 6.2; Gregory of Nyssa, Hom. 1 (Van Heck 465); Gregory of Nazianzus, Or. 14.23.

27. Gregory of Nazianzus, Or. 14.5; Gregory of Nyssa, Or. 1 (Van Heck 469; trans. Holman 199).

28. Gregory of Nazianzus, Or. 14.5.

29. Gregory of Nazianzus, Or. 14.26–27; for a classic presentation of this view, see also Gregory of Nyssa, *On the Making of the Human Person* 5, 16.

30. Gregory of Nyssa, Hom. 1 (Van Heck 465; trans. Holman 197). In a curious contrast to Gregory's suggestion that greed makes us bestial, Basil argues that it is simply a human failing: animals share pasture and water, but only humans hoard. See Basil, Hom. 8.8.

31. Gregory of Nazianzus, Hom. 14.25 (J.-P. Migne, ed., PG 38.889C–892A). For this idea of unnatural human greed as the source of differences in wealth, see Irenaeus, *Adversus haereses* 4.30.1; Basil, Hom. 6.2–3 and Hom. 8.8; Gregory of Nyssa, Hom. 1 (Van Heck 465); and Julian, *Letter to a Priest* 290A–91A. For the Stoic background of this notion of an original equality, see above, n. 5.

32. Gregory of Nazianzus, Or. 14.40.

Chapter 5

THE LATIN AMERICAN MARTYRS

Summons and Grace for the Church

JON SOBRINO

In the final third of the last century, there were many martyrs in Latin America: peasants, workers, students, lawyers, doctors, teachers, intellectuals, journalists, catechists, priests, religious, bishops, and archbishops who remind us of Jesus crucified. Along with these martyrs, groups consisting mainly of the poor were assassinated in great massacres. They died defenseless and remain anonymous. They remind us of the suffering servant of Yahweh. Thus it is quite appropriate to speak about a martyrial church.

In that martyrial church there also appeared a generation of bishops of extraordinary evangelical caliber, a religious life (symbolized by the Confederation of Latin American Religious [CLAR]), and numerous renewed priestly groups. In that church there originated a theology—that of liberation—that centered faith, hope, and love on the poor. Finally, in this church there emerged base ecclesial communities, communities of the poor, of lay women and men who brought the people of God to maturity.

This martyrial church is, we believe, the finest fruit of the Gospel in many centuries. However, in this chapter we will not present this church;

rather, taking it as a starting point and considering the contemporary church, we will analyze how the martyrs of the last thirty years can configure it today. More concretely, we will consider how, for the church today, these martyrs become a summons and grace, both of which are central components in the "call to holiness" with which John Paul II challenged us in his *Ecclesia in America*.

THE NECESSITY OF A SUMMONS FOR THE CONTEMPORARY CHURCH

First thesis: A summons to the church is necessary and healthy. The martyrs are the ones who can summon with greater vigor because they constitute a powerful historical mediation of the God that summons the church. That summons should take into account today the ecclesial regression that has occurred since Medellín. This first thesis precedes the body of the chapter, but understanding it is fundamental to comprehending the necessity of the church being summoned and the capacity that the martyrs have to do this.

The State of the Church

The present-day martyrs directly summon historical reality—economic, political, military, and ideological structures and their agents. The fundamental summons consists in asking these structures to account for what they have done, what they do, and what they will do before the crucified peoples. Nevertheless, this questioning goes ignored, and normally, in these instances, those who are summoned not only do not feel summoned but defame the martyrs if they can. In any case, they are enthusiastic to bury the martyrs for good, as has happened and, in some form, continues to happen in El Salvador. The worst consequence of this is that society is impoverished; it is deprived of the humanizing potential of the martyrs.

The fundamental summons of the martyrs is directed to the world of sin; however, it is also directed toward the church. That this summons is both possible and necessary is well known. The church has recognized itself as *semper reformanda* (always reforming itself), as in the patristic writers. If we move from these words to reality, we may ask if the church as a whole is better or worse today than formerly. Compared to the church of fifty years ago, the changes and advances are clear. But if the contemporary church is compared to the church that emerged in Vatican II and Medellín, one cannot deny that there has been a regression and that we find ourselves in this regression currently.

Good things are being sustained by the church, at times with great merit and despite many obstacles, and some new ones are even emerging, but the signs of regression are unmistakable and mark the church's current direction. When talking about a summons, we will not concentrate on the limitations and sins that have always affected the church, recurring scandals in history still going on today, but rather on the decrease and loss of good things that were real but are now dying the death of a thousand qualifications. Using biblical words, one could formulate the summons to the church in this manner: "Where is your first love? Where is the audacity of Medellín? Where is the willingness to risk everything to save the poor of this world?" These are some of the questions by which the summons may be expressed as an examination of conscience.

In terms of the church *ad intra* (as it looks into itself), there is a decrease in intraecclesial fraternity and an excessive emphasis on the church's hierarchical, controlling dimension, manifested in a fear of the popular base, the laity, and especially women. The church does less to foster the maturity of the people of God, tolerating and even encouraging spiritualized movements that remove themselves from God's creation and become esoteric and above all, infantilizing. There is a decrease in catholicity and collegiality. A church that favored ecclesial localism, so as to be universal in a Catholic manner, not uniformist, and that promoted a generation of local bishops in Latin America comparable only to the prophetic bishops from the time of colonization, once again becomes exaggeratedly centralized and uniformist, lacking the honesty it takes to recognize the need for those types of prophetic bishops and lacking the courage to promote them—in fact, in many instances doing the opposite. As for collegiality, the new type of bishop does not offer much in terms of the universal church.

Regarding the church's mission, there is a decrease in the option for the poor, in the option for all that includes popular awareness, praxis, conflict, and prophecy. Despite many documents and words, many of them good, we have passed from a church of the poor, one oriented utopically toward their defense and prophetically toward the denunciation of their oppressors, to a church that, in compensation, desires to return to normality, to a harmony with the powers of this world, who co-opt the church even when the church critiques them.

Last, regarding the church's Christian foundation, there is a decrease in creaturely humility, so that, even when in dialogue with the world, the church struggles to maintain its leading role as if it were above all creation. There is a decrease in a theological creaturely consciousness, in which one allows God to be God before those developments that appear as signs of the times: laity, women, new theologies, inculturation. There is a decrease in following Jesus of Nazareth, evangelist and prophet, as if the Spirit could usher in a Christianity that had no need of Jesus.

This characterization is simplistic. After all, there continues to be commitment, solidarity, accompaniment, and even martyrdom; we need only to recall Bishop Juan Gerardi. There are illuminating social encyclicals and, above all, the daily activities of communities. However, if we look at things in their totality, their emphases and tendencies, what is encouraged and what is resisted, above all at the highest levels of leadership, along with what there is in the way of opposition to commitment and solidarity, what has been said so far appears objectively true. The "ecclesial winter" is real. The words below of José Comblin are strong but lucid, and necessary if we are to change the church. He says, comparing today's church with that of Medellín,

> Today, the dominant impression is that the church, for the most part, in the shepherds and the sheep, is returning to the past. It maintains the same language, but the practice is different. It returns to the sacristies and the parish houses. It no longer hears the voice of the poor majority, but listens rather to its traditional public, those that attend the cult. The church is once again concerned with itself. It seeks to reclaim positions of power: cultural, political, and even economic. Once again it cultivates only religious sentiment, emotions. Of course, it does not lack clients because the neoliberal model has increased the anxiety, desperation, insecurity, and ignorance of the people.[1]

The Capacity of the Martyrs to Summon

Thus the church needs conversion and change, but if it is left to its own inertia and its administrative and canonical mechanisms, conversion and change will be difficult. There is a serious need for a summons of the church, but the church experiences great difficulty in allowing itself to be called to account. Moreover, the church can attempt to justify itself by saying that surely it need not give an account to anyone except God, so that only God may summon the church. The church may ask for God's pardon, but it does not appear to be sincerely open to the summonses that human beings can make. There are always exceptions, but the idea that the church enjoys a special status that protects it from a summons is dangerous and impoverishing. The question, then, is whether and how this summons can take place.

We begin with the most fundamental idea, with the God in whom the church believes and who can therefore summon the church. Now, this God is not just any god, distant in transcendence, but the God who became human reality in Jesus Christ. Thus the problem of God's summons of the church translates into the summons that Jesus Christ makes to the church. No one can deny this possibility, although the story of the Grand Inquisitor ("Lord, do not return")[2] makes manifest the fear that we feel at the thought of Christ coming to us. But the problem does not simply end there. For the glorified Christ can summon the church existentially and with vigor only through historical realities.

The presence of Christ in historical realities is traditionally accepted by the church, although its different denominations maintain this with varying nuances. Christ continues to be present in the Eucharist, in the preaching of the Word, in the community, and in the pastors. This is well known; however, according to the Gospel and the *orthodoxia* of the Latin American Church, Jesus Christ is most present, and present also as summons, "in the poor" (Matt. 25:31–46). Medellín recalls this, adding, "Their cries rise to the heavens."[3] Puebla proclaims that Christ "with particular tenderness . . . chose to identify Himself with those who are poorest and weakest" (Matt. 25:40).[4] From the poor, then, Jesus Christ can summon the church, and the church remains vulnerable to that summons.

Let us go one step further. The reality of the poor reaches its maximum expression in the martyrs, those who have suffered the ultimate impoverishment. Seen from the perspective of Latin America's recent reality, martyrs are those who have lived like Jesus and who have been assassinated for the same causes Jesus was (Oscar Romero), as well as those who have been massacred in massive, cruel, unjust, and indefensible ways because their deaths are necessary to maintain injustice (the massacres of El Mozote, Guatemala, Haiti, Rwanda, and so on).

Taken together, these martyrs are the ones who summon the church, or, put another way, if they do not have the capacity to summon the church, then it is doubtful that anything, or anyone, can. Quantitatively, they are so numerous that they are impossible to ignore. Qualitatively, both the horror and the love that they express are such that they can shock and encourage. Furthermore, they make it impossible to use the excuse that "only God can summon the church" because they are the presence of Christ among us today. They are the suffering servants of Yahweh who bear the sin of the world and of the church. They are the crucified Christ. Their blood is precisely that which explains the spilling of Christ's blood. As Irenaeus says, "If the blood of the righteous were not to be inquired after, the Lord would certainly not have had blood [in his composition]. . . . 'All righteous blood shall be required which is shed upon the earth, from the blood of righteous.' . . . He thus points out the recapitulation that should take place in his own person of the effusion of blood from the beginning, of all the righteous men and of the prophets, and that by means of Himself there should be a requisition of their blood . . . saving in his own person at the end."[5]

Obviously, not only the martyrs can summon the church. A peasant woman can do it, a contemplative monk, a woman working in a sweatshop, or a laborer. However, the primordial summons has its origins in the presence of blood spilled unjustly: "What have you done? I hear the blood of your brother crying to me from the soil"(Gen. 4:10). Naturally, the concrete content of the summons to the church depends on who is summoning it. Thus the martyrs have a specific summons at this time, which is fundamentally a time of regression. They are able to shake the church as only love and blood can, and they demonstrate the road that must be followed to return to the church of the poor, of which they are its chosen representatives. "We need someone to be a prophet for us too and call us to conversion and not let us set up religion as something untouchable," said Archbishop Romero.[6] Next we shall concretize the fundamental contents of the summons and of the offer of grace that the martyrs make according to the Christological schema of incarnation, mission, cross, and resurrection.

INCARNATION: OVERCOMING UNREALITY

Second thesis: Through Medellín, the Latin American Church has been incarnated, has been made "real." Yet today that is a grave and fundamental problem because a church that is not real cannot comply with the exigency of incarnation or participate in its dynamism. It falls into Docetism, losing its identity and relevance. The martyrs summon the church and animate it to be a "real church."

The church should be willing to be summoned as to whether it is a Christian Church, the Church of Jesus, the sacrament of salvation. However, we should begin with something more basic that, for lack of a better term, we will formulate in the following manner: whether the church is real. In this lies the first summons of the martyrs.

The Most Flagrant Reality: Unjust Poverty

We will not linger on this point, but we must mention it, at least minimally, because although they do not constitute all of reality, poverty and injustice, as well as failures of the species and of the human family, are at the root of any summons of the church. Daily experience and annual reports of the United Nations demonstrate that unjust poverty is the most stinging problem in our world.

From the Latin American continent to the entire planet, the majority of human beings are poor men and women, mostly women. To say it qualitatively, the poor of this world are those stooped under the weight of existence—those whose most important task and major difficulty is simply surviving. They are the silenced who do not have dignity or even any voice, the impotent who do not have the power to exercise their rights, those who are rejected because they cannot achieve the dictated requisites of the imposed culture, the insignificant who count for nothing. The poor are defined as those who do not exist, and they arrive at this situation because they have had everything taken from them. In the time of Jesus, the poor were the miserable, the sick, women, tax collectors, and sinners. In the present, one must add to these the excluded, immigrants and members of certain races and cultures, all of whom experience worse injustices if they are also poor women.

To say it quantitatively, two statistics are sufficient: 1.5 billion human beings have to live on less than one dollar a day, and according to the United Nations the ratio between rich and poor, which was 1:30 in 1969 and 1:60 in 1991, grew to 1:74 by 1999. This does not represent the totality of reality. After all, in the middle of this aberrant situation there exist goodness, commitment, hope, and even joy. However, it does represent the worst part of reality. The philosopher Ignacio Ellacuría apprehended reality as, above all, inhuman poverty, the cruel and unjust death of the poor majority. He did this to the point that he even critiqued Heidegger: "Maybe instead of asking why there is being rather than nothingness, he should have been asking why there is nothingness—no being, no reality, no truth, etc.—instead of being."[7] As a theologian, Ellacuría searched for the sign of the time and concluded, "This sign is always those people crucified in history."[8]

This same vision of reality is the precious inheritance of the Latin American Church. Medellín began with these words: "The misery that besets large masses of human beings . . . as a collective fact, expresses itself as injustice which cries to the heavens."[9] For Puebla, "The situation of inhuman poverty in which millions of Latin Americans live is the most devastating and humiliating kind of scourge."[10] With or without globalization, with old or new paradigms, this reality not only has not diminished but keeps increasing as we begin the twenty-first century.

Thus from this reality comes the question of whether we live in this world and are therefore real or not. From here emerges the summons to incarnation: the only way to regain dignity and overcome the shame of living in an artificial world. This means not only living physically in this world but allowing the world's reality to configure us. In other words, if Sumpul and El Mozote, Zaire and Rwanda do not configure our knowing, our acting, our hoping, and our celebrating, if they do not move our intelligence and our hearts, we are not in reality in any way. Not only are we not human, ethical, or Christian, but, more radically, we are not real. We have fabricated an alternative historical, cultural, and religious world in which to take refuge and defend ourselves from true reality. In Kant's thought, we remain immersed in the slumber of unreality.

Unreality as Ecclesial Docetism

To illustrate the previous notion, it might be helpful to remember that from the beginnings of Christianity unreality was a very serious problem under the heresy of Docetism. From the beginning, Docetism, the negation of Christ's humanity, was a very grave, if not the most significant, problem for the church. It was the most difficult to overcome, evidenced by the fact that it took much longer for the church to define the true humanity of Christ, at Chalcedon in 451, even though it was evident in the New Testament, than his true divinity, defined at Nicea in 325, which was not as evident.

Docetism is also an ecclesial problem. This may sound strange because one would think that the church would have the contrary problem
of being too human, even sinful. Yet things are not this way. The church is
in the world, but it has the recurring tendency and temptation to create
for itself its own ambit of doctrinal, pastoral, liturgical, and canonical reality that distances it from and defends it against the world. The tendency
and temptation are to exist in a world of so many poor without letting
that reality affect the church's faith, mission, theology, internal organization, or dimension of the people of God—as evidenced in the church's way
of naming bishops, its understanding of its priestly ministry as exclusively
masculine, and other such issues. The poor tend to be taken into account
as receptors of social ministry and some ethical practices, but essentially, at
the level of identity and true ecclesial power, the church does not give the
sense of being real because it is not a church of the poor.

This is a most serious problem, not just for the church's relevance in
a world of poverty, but also for its identity. The prologue of the Gospel of
John expresses the "will to reality" of God, a will that consists not solely
of becoming flesh but of becoming flesh that is vulnerable. In the language
of later Christology, the reality that the Son assumes is not simply *humanitas* (humanity) but *sarx* (the weakness of flesh). Moreover, as is demonstrated in the Christological controversies of the first centuries, with an
insistence only on Christ's *humanitas* (what we call factuality) one cannot overcome Docetism. To overcome Docetism truly, the Son must become *sarx*.

Thus *humanitas* without *sarx,* factuality without reality (of the world
of the poor) continue to be serious ecclesial problems. Homilies, documents, and messages that do not make the reality of poverty central, even
though they might mention it, and do not discuss the injustice and corrup-
tion in which poverty originates or the covering up that accompanies it,
produce a sense of unreality because they express no commitment to enter
into the conflict, to work against injustice and suffer the consequences.
They are what José Comblin calls "words, words, words."[11] The same sense
of unreality is produced in seminaries where formation means protecting
seminarians from reality and in spiritualities, ministries, and movements
that understand human existence as transcendent from history, with infantilizing consequences.

Often important ecclesial events, like a visit by the pope, are organized
in such a way that they too produce a sense of unreality. During the pope's
visit to El Salvador in 1996, the majority of the people present were poor,

but the only part of their reality that appeared was their religious enthusiasm, more or less deliberately stirred up. What did not appear was their poverty, their fears, their disenchantment, their vulnerability, or their true faith and hope; their reality did not appear. In terms of the visit's organization, the poor functioned more as a backdrop than as the reality that defines a country, while at center stage were minorities that do not represent reality: government officials and politicians, the powerful and wealthy, and the church in proximity to them. The pope's visit did not help reality to blossom, nor, judging from its consequences, did it have much influence on it.

The consequences of what we have called Docetism, or unreality, are many. The option for the poor does not occupy a definitive place but lives in equilibrium with another option that, when it comes down to it, appears to be much more primary and more real: the option of harmony with the established powers. The church stands, not radically in being or action with the poor, but with other things. These may be necessary, and even good, but they do not go to the essence of its existence. Preserving the institutional organization, stopping sects, maintaining the number of faithful, and maintaining an alienating religiosity and fidelity—even to obsession—to the magisterium all carry much more weight than the reality of the poor.

This unreality, more than possible theological exaggerations, puts the deepest identity of the faith in peril. To put it in technical terms, not living reality as it is makes it very difficult to gain the perspective and the hermeneutic necessary to understand what is fundamental to the faith: the incarnation of the Word in the weakness of reality and the salvific dynamism of that type of incarnation. Unreality leads instead to the contrary, the dis-incarnation of poverty and incarnation of power, and the search for the salvific, not in the weakness of the flesh (in *carne*), but in power.

The Summons and Grace of the Martyrs: To Be a "Real Church"

While what has been said above is variously applicable according to the situation, time, and place, overall the danger of unreality cannot be ignored. The way we are going, it would seem that the official church and numerous groups and movements have embraced a vision that does not require them to be active and present in reality. In this situation, the martyrs summon, as Antón Montesinos did five centuries ago: "Are you all sunk in the deepest sleep?"[12] How can you take no part in, or relativize, the suffering of the majority? Where are the homilies and pastoral letters of the 1970s and 1980s that put the real truth into words and analyzed its causes? Where is the confrontation and denunciation of this world of sin, not just social doctrine and dialogue? Above all, where is the move toward the poor, taking part in their impotence and destiny, putting into service all that one is and has?

The martyrs summon, and they do so with credibility. One cannot ignore them without falling into hypocrisy because they were, above all, "real," whether they were passive and anonymous martyrs who lived the reality of poverty, insignificance, and powerlessness directly and immediately or active martyrs directed toward serving the passive and anonymous ones, putting their voices at the service of those with no voice and their power at the service of those with no power. For this reason, the martyrs can summon the church concerning its reality and unreality. Moreover, their martyrdom adds radicality.

The martyr Archbishop Romero offers, more clearly than any words, an example. Romero built a real church. Though this church had its limitations, mistakes, and even sins, it was real, Salvadoran. As his oft-quoted words say, "I rejoice in the fact that our church is persecuted, precisely for its preferential option for the poor, and for trying to incarnate itself in the interest of the poor."[13] Even more clearly, he states, "How sad it would be, in a country where such horrible murders are being committed, if there were no priests among the victims! They are the testimony of a church incarnated in the problems of its people."[14]

But Romero's church was also real because it incarnated itself in the positive reality of the people. Before its suffering and resistance, it said to Christians, "If someday they take away the radio stations from us, if they close down the newspaper, if they don't let us speak, if they kill all the priests and the bishops too, and you are left a people without priests, each one of you must become God's microphone, each one of you must become a messenger, a prophet."[15]

In the midst of the generosity and commitment of the people, Romero felt proud of the church and took joy in it: "You are a church that is so alive! A church so full of the Spirit!"[16] These words are not mere piety, or even about commitment: rather, they offer the knowledge of whether a church is real or not. The church of Oscar Romero was real; conversely, a church that is not poor in times of poverty, that is not persecuted in times of persecution, that is not assassinated in times of assassination, that does not commit itself in times of commitment and does not generate commitment in times of indifference, that does not have hope in times of hope and does not encourage hope in times of disillusion, is not a real church. "Overcome unreality" seems to be the principal summons to the church by the martyrs. Yet the martyrs are a grace as well because their example and their memory inspires the task.

MISSION: SALVATION OF REALITY

Third thesis: The Latin American Church has sought the salvation of an entire crucified people. Currently, it concentrates more on an interior and individual salvation. The martyrs summon and encourage it once again to overturn history and save the crucified people.

Martyrs and the Salvation of a People

The martyrs whom we have called active produced concrete signs of salvation and, like Jesus, were interested in the salvation of persons. But they also lived for the historical and structural salvation of the people. We emphasize this because today structural salvation has become something suspicious and is being forgotten, even theoretically.

However, the martyrs did not think this way. From one martyr to another, Ignacio Ellacuría defined Archbishop Romero not simply as a good man and holy priest but as one "sent by God to save his people."[17] This salvation has an essentially historical, popular, and structural dimension. In the words of Archbishop Romero himself, to save means to speak the truth in the name of all the people: "These homilies try to be these people's voice."[18] Salvation means giving hope to an entire country: "Upon these ruins will shine the glory of the Lord."[19] In Ignacio Ellacuría's words, to save means to "overturn history," not just mend it; it means to promote justice and announce a utopia, a civilization of love that must be a civilization of poverty to be real. It is to announce to the people that "God, the Savior, God the liberator can be seen."[20] Salvation and history, salvation and people were correlative realities for the martyrs.

Pathos, Martyrdom, and Liberation

Such pronouncements are important because they express essential and cumulative dimensions of the mission of the church. They are words of inspiration and pathos, which today tend to be forgotten. The church no longer speaks, as it once would, about transforming structures, saving a people, creating a historical utopia, establishing the reign of God. The tendency now is to concentrate on and encourage individual salvation—familiar to the extreme, good and necessary—more than that of a people, interior salvation more than historical. Salvific acts tend to be more charitable than liberating: they may aid the weak, but they do not confront their oppressors. This tendency is understandable, given the immense difficulties, the immediate and concrete needs, the disenchantment and state of orphanhood of the poor. However, it is dangerous, for what is disappearing from the mission of the church is what the magisterium, in language seldom cited but nonetheless important, has usually termed integral liberation, the fullness of salvation, and so also a historical salvation of a whole people.

This is not to say that the martyrs who sought salvation of a people were ignoring, or even making secondary, the personal salvation that comes specifically in the personal encounter with God. "I wish, dear brothers and sisters, that as a result of today's preaching each of us would come to know God," said Archbishop Romero.[21] "To be human one must be 'more than human,'" Ignacio Ellacuría would recall, citing St. Augustine.[22] It is, therefore, a self-serving deception to affirm that those who sought the liberation of the people were, in principle, reductionists.

Though perhaps in a different way, reductionism is, rather, the problem of the church today, and a serious one. In this individualistic and interior reductionism, the relevance and identity of the church, in a world of poor peoples who urgently need salvation, hang in the balance. A church that is not oriented to the salvation of those people becomes a closed sect, the modern reduction of Essenes, or else it becomes a massive institution, removed from reality and alienated from the people, intent on a sociocultural Christianity, although now more gentle and inane.

This is not the place to go into detail about how an ecclesial mission would overcome the lack of popular and structural salvific pathos. It is sufficient to mention the need to maintain what was central from Medellín onward: the struggle against injustice and for a just and humane society, which Ellacuría termed the "civilization of poverty," and, together with others, to propose paths of resolution, however modest they may be. Today we can add new tasks to this, or at least new dimensions to the continuing task: the struggle against falsehood, the liberation of the truth, and the unmasking of the giant cover-up in our world. Also imperative is the encouragement of an adequate "ecology of the Spirit," that is, the necessary purification of the air that the human spirit must inhale in the present (pseudo-) culture, to take part in the battle that today wages around snatching away the hope of the poor.

We cannot analyze each of these tasks. However, for this as for any other description of the work of the church it is important to emphasize two essential elements that are being forgotten. One is the pathos of historical praxis in the church's mission, adding, though it may not be popular today, the agonistic or struggling dimension of Christian life. The other element is the all-encompassing horizon of praxis: in the language of the Gospel the reign of God, in present-day language the salvation of a people. We must remember that this all-encompassing liberation includes the life of the poor in all its fullness: the ability to be a home (*oikos,* which is also the root of "economy"), the ability to be a fraternal family, the ability to express oneself in culture and art, the ability to speak and be heard, and the ability to be a people of God so that the poor are not fearful of God but feel welcomed by God.

The Summons and the Grace of the Martyrs: Saving a People

Why should we turn to the martyrs to summon the church to its praxis of historical salvation? Can we not find inspirational biblical and magisterial texts for this purpose? The answer is that these martyrs provide a particularly forceful summons because, at this time, there is a direct relationship between martyrs and the salvation of a whole people. This novelty, which has wide-ranging implications for the church and for peoples, has rarely, if ever, occurred in history.

On the one hand, the passive and anonymous martyrs, the great majority, the crucified peoples, are, in their very tragic reality, an absolute demand that the church work, not for just any salvation, but for the salvation of a people. On the other hand, the active martyrs summon this praxis because through and in this praxis their lives were robbed of them. It is simplistic to ask oneself, in the form of an option, whether they gave their lives for Christian reasons or political ones, for their faith in God or for their commitment to the people. They gave their lives, as Jesus did, out of love for a people, to save a people, so that that people can one day be the people of God in the reign of God.

One might object that this language is better suited to the past and that the current situation requires realism when we speak of integral liberation, the salvation of a people. This is true in part. Fundamentally, however, whatever the actual worldly or ecclesial sensibility, the summons to the church should persist: whether in its mission the church does or does not slide along the slope of the private and the ahistorical, that which is devoid of social impact; whether the church does or does not satisfy itself with doing good but not liberating deeds or with alleviating problems without working to eradicate their roots; or whether it has or has not succumbed to a postmodernity without utopia, or to a neoliberalism that is contrary to utopia, that will tolerate religion as long as it does not question reality and will even support it as soon as religion can be manipulated in its favor, although the poor might not be aware of this.

Here the martyrs reappear. They summon the church to examine whether it has allowed itself to be moved to the utmost, without reservation, without withholding anything for itself, by the crucified peoples of our present world, at the beginning of the twenty-first century. The martyrs certainly summon the church on whether it is faithful to the inheritance of Jesus and to the inheritance that the martyrs themselves have left us in abundance: to live and do everything one can to save a people.

What is more, they do not just summon; they also illuminate and inspire us at a crucial moment, crucial because we must be clear that it is not the church that creates the mission but the mission that creates the church. It is not an already constituted church that decides what ought to be done. Rather, in the practice of doing and going about the work of salvation the church constitutes itself into a determined kind of church. Depending upon this action and work, upon the salvation that the church wishes to bring into the world, the character of the church will become evident. This is why it is necessary to postulate as adequately as possible what this mission consists of, a problem more primary than the question of its ministry, its liturgy, or its canons.

Today we hear a great deal about plans and methods of ministry, and for good reason. But we hear very little of mission, and it even seems that there is some fear of engaging this theme seriously. In the best of cases it is presupposed, simplistically, that the matter has already been settled at Vatican II and Medellín. But it is quite clear that this is not the case because we see mission defined, not from these paradigms, but rather independently of them and in some cases in opposition to them.

In this situation we must return to the martyrs and their mission. The martyrs have not given their lives merely for some good deeds or some small liberations but for something deeper and more inclusive: for the salvation of a people and, within it, of persons. This mission generated a certain type of church, one that included much from the Jesus movement. Because of this the martyrs question, and summon, the church regarding whether its mission in the present is oriented toward the salvation of a people, and whether, in that case, it is gestating a church that resembles Jesus. But they are also, yet again, both encouragement and grace for this task.

THE CROSS: SHOULDERING THE WEIGHT OF REALITY

Fourth thesis: The Latin American Church has shouldered the weight of reality, carrying out its mission in the presence of and in opposition to the antireign. Today it is wont to ignore structural conflict and the carrying of what is onerous in reality. Because of this, it loses reality, salvific capacity, and credibility. The martyrs summon the church and encourage it to shoulder once again the cross of reality.

Reality as the Antireign That Deals Death

To speak of shouldering the weight of reality is not masochism. It should rather be the most obvious task in a historical reality such as ours. The passive, anonymous martyrs demonstrate this clearly, and they demonstrate their defenselessness against this cruel weight that overcomes them. They are the *analogatum princeps* (principal analog) of what it means to shoulder the weight of reality.

But we wish to focus now on the active martyrs. For them, shouldering the weight of reality was not masochism, or a purely mystical and intentional desire to identify with the crucified Christ, as is often presented, but rather an attempt to identify in an honest way what was real. Properly understood, Jesus's command to "take up your cross and follow me" (Matt. 10:38; Mark 8:34; Luke 9:23) is tautological because to follow Jesus, to live like him and do what he did, leads to bearing what he bore, the cross. One thing we must be clear about when analyzing the summons of the martyrs to the church is what the cross signifies and whence comes the need to carry that cross.

The cross is not merely the suffering that comes from our limited human nature, although one must obviously have respect and compassion in the face of such suffering and try to eliminate or alleviate it. Such is the suffering expressed in anguish, illnesses, failures, disappointments, misunderstandings, the death of loved ones, the fear of death, all very painful things that at times can be even more painful, subjectively, than the cross of martyrdom. Though an expression of the limitation of human reality, it is still not formally "cross." We insist on this because the church has a long tradition of alleviating the kinds of suffering we have mentioned and of participating in them to alleviate the suffering of others, which is worthy but still does not mean the same thing as "carrying the cross."

The cross is, plainly, the death that ensues from defending the oppressed and struggling against the oppressor. Analogously, the cross means the type of suffering that this fundamental struggle generates: harassment, defamation, persecution, exile, incarceration, torture, and other such things. In other words, the cross indicates a relationship to injustice, such that in a world where there was no injustice there would be suffering, undoubtedly, but no cross. According to this, subjectively the cross comes from the willingness to incarnate oneself in the conflictive nature of history. Objectively, it presupposes a conflictive structure of reality, a vision that may or may not be shared by philosophy, sociology, and politics but that is clear in the Christian vision: it is the historico-theologal structure of reality, dialectic and conflicting.[23]

The Bible, with scarce knowledge of sociology, economics, and politics, continues to offer this great intuition about the structure of reality, which is difficult to find elsewhere and which, because it is so revealing, is ignored and covered up, even in many Christian theologies. In Johannine language, what is malignant is deadly, and reality is stricken with that specific deadly malady. It is no surprise, then, that human beings who are honest in dealing with reality and committed to its transformation are given death. The contrary would be abnormal because it would signify either that reality was no longer deadly or that in the church and in the world there were no more believers or persons dealing honestly with that reality.

The Temptation of the Church: To Avoid Conflict

Currently there is not much real confrontation in Latin America between the church and the world of sin, although there may be verbal debates.

The excessively simplistic justification for this is merely that things have changed. But the analysis of what has changed tends to be seriously inadequate, and there is, above all, a lack of logic, as if in a changed situation, which need not be different in fundamental things, the conflict between the God of Jesus and the idols had automatically disappeared. For the theorists of neoliberalism to praise the present situation is one thing, but for the church to fall into the trap of not immediately denouncing the fundamental conflict, and to not involve itself in that conflict, is grave. Evil is not simply evil; its essence is to generate conflict, to "act against." The church, then, should adopt a stance before an evil that is conflictive, even if this complicates things very much.

It is true that there are verbal confrontations between the Vatican, governments, and international organizations around the problem of the right to life. In other areas, however, such as the economy, human rights, and armaments, the ecclesial denunciation, though frequently ethical and accurate, is normally co-opted, such that there are conflictive texts but no real conflicts. The church today carries no important cross for having said such things. The situation was quite different in the time of Monsignor Romero, Dom Helder, Angelelli, Don Sergio, and Proaño, to mention only those bishops that have died. Their denunciations were not co-opted but combated.

Currently, in various countries and certainly in El Salvador, some episcopal appointments have been intended precisely to avoid conflict and to secure, after fifty years, good relations between civil and religious powers. There are worthy exceptions among the bishops, but the communiqués of the episcopal conference are meager in their denunciations when compared to the magnitude of the tragedy, and though they describe reality at times with a certain linguistic vigor, they fail to analyze the depth of its causes or to mention with any precision those who are responsible. The consequence is that they do not generate conflict. In my opinion, we cannot say that the church today is either the Socratic sting, or the revealing pen of Ellacuría, or the incorruptible word of Monsignor Romero.

As Christians, we need not be a-critical, nor need we deceive or be self-deceived. And in any case, we must maintain something of the Pauline *parrēsia* (confidence), bravery, or audacity and not fall into cowardice. There is no need to offer a watered-down, bland Christianity that could speak in the same way to victims and their executioners, let alone a Christianity that has more to say to the executioners than to the victims, more to Pinochet than to the disappeared, even if this is done in an elegant way and to avoid greater evils. We need not make of Christianity "cheap grace," which, as Bonhoeffer said, is the greatest danger to Christianity. Although the phrase should be properly understood and all the sacrificialist after-taste should be removed from it, it is important to keep in mind the intuition of the New Testament about the cost of our salvation so that we do not trivialize Christian existence: "You have been rescued not by something passing, gold or silver, but with precious blood" (1 Pet. 1:18 ff.).

Our church and our faith are based on a conflict, a cross, and, because of this, a resurrection. To forget this is the end of Christianity. "Times have changed," some say, with the hope of communicating to the believer, subliminally, that the cross and resurrection may be good things, necessary for liturgy, private devotion, and one's personal life, but that they say nothing ultimate or serious about the reality that the church should evangelize. This is not so. There are changes in the political arena, but it would be a grave error to equate this arena with the deeper reality. Changes in the political superstructure need not change the deep theologal or metaphysical structure of history, which effects the carrying forward of the confrontation. It is another thing to say that this confrontation, fortunately, need not take the bellicose and brutal form, in many countries, that it did some decades ago. But we should not think that conflict no longer exists in history and that the church should not become involved in it. In any case, the church should not play along with the system, acting as if now everything were substantially improved or at least on the right track.

The Summons: Without Bearing the Weight of Sin There Is No Salvation

Without bearing the weight of the world there is, of course, no incarnation, but without it, the church would also not bring salvation or be credible. This need not be a philosophical truth, but it is a Christian truth that without struggling against sin from within, shouldering its weight and its consequences, there is no redemption. Though in theory we might have much to get beyond, a spurious sacrificialism, and though in practice things may have changed, it is still true that "if a grain of wheat does not fall to the earth and die, it will not bear fruit, but if it dies it bears much fruit" (John 12:24). This is what the martyrs express without saying a word, by merely being it. Some, however, made it explicit.

In giving an honorary doctorate to President Oscar Arias, Ignacio El-lacuría, in the middle of a political discourse, in the presence of ambassadors and of ex-president Cristiani, cited, in Latin, the words *"Sine effusione sanguinis, nulla redemptio"* (Without the shedding of blood, there is no salvation) and added, "Salvation and liberation of peoples must endure many difficult sacrifices."[24] This must all be understood and historicized in situations that do not involve war. But the thesis remains: without a willingness to get involved in the conflict of reality, to shoulder its weight and to pay some price, the church will not bring salvation. Nor will it have credibility. When the United Nations' reports on the world situation speak of tragedy and inhumanity, it becomes impossible to have credibility if we lack the willingness, at least, to struggle against these realities and to suffer the consequences. And last, it is impossible to verify that the church is acting in a Christian way. If in no way the church fares as Jesus fared, it is unclear why that church should be understood and accepted as the Church of Jesus. Monsignor Romero said it quite clearly: "A church that suffers no persecution but enjoys the privileges and support of the things of the earth—beware!—is not the true church of Christ."[25]

The martyrs are those who summon the church to take up the cross, because they did. But they also demonstrate that this is the way a church can bring salvation to the poor majorities, have credibility, and be welcomed and loved by the poor as the Church of Jesus. With their example they encourage us to do this.

RESURRECTION: TO GET CARRIED AWAY WITH REALITY

Fifth thesis: Though obviously in an analogical sense, it can be said that the martyrs have appeared to the church. They continue to summon, encourage, and facilitate its ability to live now as a resurrected church in history, with freedom, joy, and hope.

In the previous theses we have historicized the incarnation, mission, and cross of the church through the martyrs, which can be done easily. By embarking now on the resurrection, we move in a different kind of reality, and analogy imposes itself on our analysis. Regarding the martyrs, we will construct two reflections on a resurrected church. The first is that the martyrs are a very special grace, analogous to the apparition of the Crucified-Resurrected One; something ultimate has been given us, and this reality shoulders our weight. The second is that, insofar as they are already resurrected as vanquishers of negativity and death, the martyrs invite us to live as a resurrected church in history.

Grace: Something Has Been Given Us

In the New Testament it is proclaimed that Jesus has been resurrected by the Father and that he has appeared to his disciples, women, and men. Our point now is to emphasize two things. The first is that Jesus allows himself to be seen *(opthe):* that is, both the apparition of Jesus and the Jesus that appears are a gift and grace; what is allowed to be seen is good, and the one who allows himself to be seen is grace. The second is that the fact that the resurrected Jesus allows himself to be seen does not eliminate the fact that he also allowed himself to be seen during his life. Although the New Testament does not use this language, it has to do with what we might call the historical *opthe:* the Jesus who went about doing good allowed himself to be seen. The apparition of the Resurrected One was the greater grace, to put it that way, but from that point the disciples understood that the life of Jesus was grace: "In him the goodness of God has appeared." Said in the simplest way possible, in the total "appearance" of Jesus, historical and eschatological, something good has been given us: we have been introduced to reality's dynamism of goodness, and this shoulders our weight.

This is crucial as we analyze the importance of the martyrs for the church. Analogically, we can say that throughout history there have been apparitions; here the *opthe* occurs again. Monsignor Romero said very simply: "If they kill me, I will be resurrected in the Salvadoran people."[26] And this is how many experience it, in the case of Monsignor and of other martyrs. But, as in Jesus's case, this resurrection of the martyrs irrupts together with their historical life. This was also grace; it allowed itself to be seen in the word of truth of Monsignor, his praxis of justice, his fortitude amid persecution, and his unconditional love of the poor until the end. From an existential and experiential point of view, the death of the martyrs helps the church to open its eyes to their goodness. And this goodness, when understood, seems to overflow and flood us; it invites us and helps us also to be good ourselves. It is the primordial grace of reality, which shoulders our weight and so graces us.

The fundamental thing we would like to emphasize in this last excursus is the summons to the church to allow itself to be graced by the martyrs and to live as a resurrected church in history. We will return to this latter point, but now we will focus on the moment of allowing oneself to be graced, allowing oneself to be carried. This allowing of oneself always has against it, as a danger, hubris, the arrogance of humanity. Therefore, even if we digress a bit, we should reflect on two aspects of this danger. To illustrate them, let us briefly analyze what can happen in the processes of canonization, which we mention because it is a very real issue for us right now, as Romero's process is already under way.

The Martyrs as Grace for the Church.   First, we must maintain that the martyrs are grace for the church, a primary mediation of the Crucified-Resurrected One. Therefore the processes of canonization should express the grace that the martyrs are for the church. This does not mean that the process should not be regulated (canonized), but the process should not obfuscate the grace, nor should it give the impression, if we can use this language, that it is the church that is gracing, or doing a favor for Romero. Rather, it is he who graces, who does a favor for the local and the universal church. In this sense, more fundamental than the analysis given to whether Romero possessed virtues, orthodoxy, and ecclesiastical obedience, is the analysis of whether Romero—his life, his work, his martyrdom—has been recognized and accepted by the people of God as grace, something that, in his case, has quite clearly happened. Grace does not live off the process of canonization, but vice versa.[27]

Maintaining the Totality of the Martyrs.   Second, we must maintain the totality of grace that is expressed in the martyrs. That is, we should maintain their final moment, the formally martyrial moment, together with their life and praxis, keeping in mind, furthermore, that very frequently, in the case of the Latin American martyrs, their martyrdom is the culmination of an entire life. Here we have a dialectic: the life explains the martyrdom and the martyrdom expresses the life. We insist on this because it is an important current problem. It is clear that the powers of this world would like to bury the martyrs, even if they do it elegantly. But it is also true that some ecclesial powers intend to domesticate them, precisely because of what we have said in this chapter: they are the historical mediation of the summons of God.

Hopefully this will not occur in Romero's case, but it could happen that a Monsignor Romero who was not the "true" Monsignor Oscar Romero, a good, pious, zealous, priestly, but definitely watered-down Romero, might be canonized. It must be maintained that the "true" Monsignor Romero lived simultaneously for the justice of the poor and the glory of God and that he consequently struggled against injustice and against the gods of death. This was the whole Oscar Romero, the "true" Monsignor Romero. This, and no other, was the Romero that wound up a martyr.

If the official church canonizes a martyr, it cannot be said that it has forgotten him or her, but one might ask what aspect of the martyr the church wishes to keep alive and active in history. So that the mode of remembering a martyr does not spoil what truly occurred, it would help if the canonization took place close to the events, something that could truly happen in the case of Monsignor Oscar Romero. But it is equally important not only that the moment of the martyr's death be remembered but also that his or her life be valued and proposed as a model, the life that really made the martyr a witness to God, to truth, and to love and that led to his or her martyrdom.

The New Testament gives us a great lesson about this mode of proceeding. The resurrected Christ, although he was already in eschatological reality, allowed himself to be seen with the wounds of crucifixion, as the one who offered pardon and peace, and prepared a table to be shared: all things that were typical of Jesus of Nazareth while he was alive. This is how present-day martyrs should be remembered and modeled. What is more, the New Testament makes us vigilant against the danger of using a manipulated image of the Resurrected One. It was to defend against this danger that the Gospels were written, and, crucially, what is narrated in the Gospels is the life of the Christ that was Jesus. That life, consummated forever, was what the evangelists proposed as good news and as a life to be carried forward. Analogously, this should also occur in the remembrance of the martyrs.

To Live as Resurrected Ones in History

We have said that in the resurrection something appears to us, something is given us: the fullness of life. But the resurrection also carries the essential dimension of triumph and victory over negativity. What aspects of that triumph and victory can be expressed today in the life of the church, such that we may live now as resurrected people under the conditions of history? In my opinion what can happen is a historical reverberation of the resurrection, as expressed in freedom, joy, and hope. To this the martyrs invite us.[28]

Freedom as the Triumph over Egocentrism.   Freedom reflects the triumph of the Resurrected One not because it alienates us from our material reality but because it introduces us into historical reality so that we may love, without anything in that reality serving as an obstacle to that love. In a Christian sense, the free person is the one who loves and, in the end, only loves, without allowing any other perspective to derail him or her from love. Speaking in paradoxical language, freedom is attaching oneself to history in order to save it, but in such a way that nothing in history ties one down or enslaves one to prevent one from loving.

In history there are different kinds of love. In a world of poor and of victims, many—or some—can sincerely affirm that they have dedicated their lives to the poor and the victims and that they sincerely love the poor. But normally that love comes with ties to other loves, including legitimate ones: to the party, the popular and revolutionary organization, the religious congregation, the ecclesial institution, which always mitigates, conditions, or distorts the exercise of the first love for the poor (to say nothing of ties to ambitions for wealth and power). Thus it can be said that, although the love is real, it is not total love because the ties persist, understandable and legitimate as some of them are in themselves. But some people, like Monsignor Romero, loved the poor and loved nothing above them, without ulterior motives, without allowing other loves, however legitimate, to derail him from that fundamental love, and without allowing the risks he ran for that love to make him more prudent.

In that type of love, liberty makes itself present, to a greater or lesser extent, depending on the case, but in a real way in the martyrs. Christian freedom is, in the ultimate sense, freedom to love. It is Jesus's own freedom when he affirms, "No one takes my life, I give it" (John 10:18). It is Paul's freedom that "is enslaved to all, to win all" (1 Cor. 9:19). This freedom has nothing to do with stepping out of history. But neither does it have anything to do directly with the right to one's own freedom, although this right is legitimate and its exercise is necessary and pressing within the church. The freedom that expresses the triumph of the Resurrected One consists in not being tied to history in history's enslaving aspects (fear, paralyzing prudence); it consists in the maximum freedom of love to serve, not allowing anything to put limits on, or be an obstacle to, that love. The martyrs, especially the great majority of them for whom death came as the culmination of persecution, summon us and encourage us to freedom.

Joy as Triumph over Sadness.   The other dimension of the triumph of the resurrection is joy, and joy is possible only when there is something to celebrate. To live with joy means having the capacity to celebrate life; the question is whether such celebration exists. Once again, this can sound extremely paradoxical in situations of extreme suffering like that of the crucified peoples, but it happens. "The opposite of joy is sadness, not suffering," Gustavo Gutiérrez says he overheard in a base community.

That life can be celebrated and that joy is possible are fundamental to living as resurrected people. It is the joy of communities that, despite various hardships, get together to sing and recite poetry, to demonstrate that they are happy because they are together, to study the Bible, and to celebrate the Eucharist. To be honest with their own lives, they feel that they must also celebrate. It is the joy of Monsignor Romero, who was accosted by all sides and by all the powers that be but who rejoiced in visiting the communities and who even exclaimed—apparently with rhetorical flourish but with great truth—"With this community it is not difficult to be a good pastor." It cost him his life, but the people gave him a joy that no one could take away from him. In that joy he made the triumph of the Resurrection historically present. The martyrs summon us to that joy in the church and they encourage us toward it.

Hope against Resignation.   If anything expresses the Resurrection it is the triumph of hope. "You killed him, but the Lord raised him up," says Peter (Acts 2:23–24). God does justice not to a cadaver but to a victim. This is how the desire that the oppressor not triumph against the victim becomes reality.

Hope is, and continues to be, against hope, perhaps more so each day. But a church with hope is a church that is already living a resurrected existence. The martyrs, insofar as they express the darkness of assassination, can be the greatest test for hope but also its biggest source because they also express the brilliance of a death on behalf of love. In fact, this is how the church began, when hope did not die with the death of Jesus but rather a fuller hope emerged, although always a crucified hope. This can also occur today, and therefore I conclude with some words on hope by Ignacio Ellacuría from a short time before his martyrdom:

> All this martyrial blood, shed in El Salvador and in all of Latin America, far from moving people to dejection and despair, infuses a new spirit of struggle and a new hope in our people. In this sense, if we are not a "new world" or a "new continent" we are, clearly and in a verifiable way—and not precisely on account of the foreigners—a continent of hope, which is an extremely interesting symptom of a future society in the face of other continents which have no hope, only fear.[29]

Freedom, joy, and hope are realities that triumph over the negativity of history. They could easily be considered forms of historical resurrection. The martyrs inspire us toward this. And a free, joyful, and hopeful church lives already as a resurrected church.

The Latin American Church has been a persecuted and martyrial church. Its martyrs, objectively, are similar to Jesus because they followed Jesus until the end and were given death for being defenders of the oppressed, as Jesus was, and thus witnesses to the God of life. They are martyrs for the reign of God and for humanity.

Today, at the start of a new millennium, the Church of Jesus continues to need, in different situations, the spirit and the pathos of its martyrs. In this lies its identity and also its relevance. If we look at our world, filled with human wreckage and victims of an unequal system, only a church that picks up on the legacy of the martyrs will have credibility among the poor and those in solidarity with them. If we look at God, at faith in God, which is often difficult in our day, only a martyrial church can pronounce God's name with credibility. The Second Vatican Council has already advised us that "believers can thus have more than a little to do with the rise of atheism . . . to the extent that they conceal rather than reveal the true face of God."[30] And Scripture condemns with stronger words: "Because of you the name of God is blasphemed among the nations" (Rom. 2:24).

The martyrs, then, have not used the name of God in vain; rather, with their lives and their deaths, they have demonstrated the true face of God. In the martyrs' churches the name of God is not blasphemed but blessed, or at least respected. Therefore I close with these words of gratitude for the Latin American martyrs: "Because of you the name of God is blessed among the poor."

Notes

1. José Comblin, "Medellín ayer, hoy y mañana," *Revista Latinoamericana de Teología* 46 (1999): 79.

2. See Fyodor Dostoevsky, *The Brothers Karamazov* (Farrar, Straus and Giroux, 2002), bk. 5, ch. 5.

3. Conferencia General del Episcopado Latinoamericano (CELAM) II (Medellín, Colombia, 1968), "Peace," no. 14, and "Justice," no. 1, in *Liberation Theology: A Documentary History,* ed. and trans. Alfred T. Hennelly (Maryknoll, NY: Orbis Books, 1990), 109 and 97, respectively.

4. Conferencia General del Episcopado Latinoamericano (CELAM) III (Puebla, Mexico, 1979), *Puebla Conference: Final Document,* no. 196, in *Puebla and Beyond: Documentation and Commentary,* ed. John Eagleson and Philip Scharper, trans. John Drury (Maryknoll, NY: Orbis Books, 1979), 148.

5. Irenaeus, *Adv. har.* 5.1.1.7 ff., in "Ante-Nicene Fathers," vol. 1, Christian Classics Ethereal Library (CCEL), www.ccel.org/fathers2/ANF-01/anf01–63.htm #P9086_2625724 (accessed August 10, 2006).

6. Archbishop Oscar Romero, Homily, July 8, 1979, in *Oscar Romero: The Violence of Love,* comp. and trans. James R. Brockman (Maryknoll, NY: Orbis Books, 2004), 143.

7. Ignacio Ellacuría, "Función liberadora de la filosofía," *Estudios Centroamericanos* nos. 435–36 (1985): 50.

8. Ibid.

9. CELAM II, "Justice," no. 1, in Hennelly, *Liberation Theology,* 97.

10. CELAM III, *Puebla Conference: Final Document,* in Eagleson and Scharper, *Puebla and Beyond,* 128.

11. Comblin, "Medellín," 79.

12. Antón Montesinos, *Three Dominican Pioneers in the New World: Antonio de Montesinos, Domingo de Betanzos, Gonzalo Lucer,* trans. Felix Jay (Lewiston, NY: Edwin Mellen Press, 2002), 18.

13. Archbishop Oscar Romero, Homily, September 15, 1979, in *Oscar Romero: Reflections on His Life and Writings,* ed. Marie Dennis, Renny Golden, and Scott Wright (Maryknoll, NY: Orbis Books, 2000), 86.

14. Archbishop Oscar Romero, Homily, June 24, 1979, in Dennis, Golden, and Wright, *Oscar Romero,* 86.

15. Romero, Homily, July 8, 1979, in Dennis, Golden, and Wright, *Oscar Romero,* 91.

16. Quoted in Jon Sobrino, *Monseñor Oscar A. Romero: Un obispo con su pueblo* (Santander: Sal Terrae, 1990), 54

17. Ignacio Ellacuría, "Monseñor Romero, un enviado de Dios para salvar a su pueblo," *Revista Latinoamericana de Teología* 19 (1990): 5–10.

18. Archbishop Oscar Romero, Homily, July 29, 1979, in *The Church Is All of You: Thoughts of Archbishop Oscar Romero,* ed. James R. Brockman (Minneapolis: Winston Press, 1984), 92.

19. Archbishop Oscar Romero, Homily, January 7, 1979, in Jon Sobrino, *Oscar Romero: Profeta y mártir de la liberación. Testimonios de Mons. Germánchmitz y Mons. Jesús Calderón* (Lima: Centro de Estudios y Publicaciones, 1982), 50.

20. Ignacio Ellacuría, "Utopia y profetismo," *Revista Latinoamericana de Teología* 17 (1989): 184.

21. Archbishop Oscar Romero, Homily, February 10, 1980, in *Archbishop Romero: Martyr and Prophet for the New Millenium,* ed. Rev. Robert Pelton (Scranton, PA: University of Scranton Press, 2006), 8.

22. Ellacuría, "Monseñor Romero," 9.

23. In history there are rival gods in conflict: the God of life and the idols of death (the absolutizing of economic, military, cultural, and religious power). Correspondingly, there are mediations, forms of society, at war: the reign of God, of justice and fraternity, on one side and, currently, societies configured according to neoliberal capitalism on the other. Last, there are mediators at war: all those who, knowingly or not, have continued the cause of Jesus and, on the other side, financial systems, securities corporations, multinationals, et cetera. According to all of this, "the cross" is that which necessarily intervenes on behalf of a mediator that struggles against an unjust mediation.

24. Ignacio Ellacuría, "Words on the Occasion of the Honorary Doctorate in Political Science to Dr. Oscar Arias, President of Costa Rica," mimeo, San Salvador, September 1989, p. 6.

25. Archbishop Oscar Romero, Homily, March 11, 1979, in Brockman, *Church Is All of You,* 66.

26. Archbishop Oscar Romero, Homily, March 19, 1980, in Dennis, Golden, and Wright, *Oscar Romero,* 21.

27. Let us say that, if what the canonizers have before them is definitely grace, it would be good if they were stricken with it and were to demonstrate this in their mode of proceeding. Also, they should minimize, as much as humanly possible, sin and hubris.

28. For a more detailed treatment, see Jon Sobrino, *Christ the Liberator: A View from the Victims,* trans. Paul Burns (Maryknoll, NY: Orbis Books, 2001), chs. 3 and 5. From there we draw much of what appears in subsequent paragraphs.

29. Ignacio Ellacuría, "Quinto centenario: ¿Descubrimiento o encubrimiento?" *Revista Latinoamericana de Teología* 21 (1990): 281.

30. Paul VI, "Gaudium et spes," www.vatican.va/archive/hist_councils/ii_vatican_council/documents/vat-ii_cons_19651207_gaudium-et-spes_en.html, no. 19 (accessed May 25, 2006).

Part Four

POVERTY, POLITICS, AND
APOCALYPTIC MYSTICISM

Chapter 6

THE CHRISTIAN OPTION
FOR THE POOR

DAVID TRACY

Some years ago I wrote a small book entitled *Plurality and Ambiguity*. One reviewer of that book, the philosopher Richard Bernstein, stated that the entire book was a reflection on a single sentence of Walter Benjamin: "Every great work of civilization is at the same time a work of barbarism."[1] That seemed to me entirely accurate.

This essay is also only a reflection on the theology of another prophetic-mystical thinker of our period, Gustavo Gutiérrez. The central theological problem of our day is not the problem of the nonbeliever but the problem of those thought to be nonpersons by the reigning elites.[2] That strikes me as exactly right. This does not mean, for Gutiérrez or for me, that the theological problem of the nonbeliever, including the nonbeliever in the believer, is now resolved. But it does mean that only when the issue of those others explicitly or implicitly thought of as nonpersons takes priority will even the problem of the nonbeliever receive new thought. This means that within Christian theology, as within the Christian churches, the option for the poor should be at the heart of every serious Christian theology today.

Just as Emmanuel Levinas has shown how philosophy today should begin not with the modern problem of the self but with the problem of the other, so too should Christian theology, in its distinct turn to the other, especially, but not solely, the oppressed, repressed, and marginal other, make the contemporary turn-to-the-other, as opposed to the modern turn-to-the-subject, the starting point, not conclusion, of all genuine Christian thought.[3]

This issue is, of course, too large and complex, both philosophically and theologically, to treat in a single chapter. I will instead treat two central aspects of it. First, I will address the basic paradigm that Gutiérrez and others have named the mystical-political dimension of all Christian theology and that I name the prophetic-mystical dimension. Second, I will show how a move into a rethinking of Christology in this paradigm, with the additional expansion of the prophetic to the apocalyptic Second Coming, for example in Metz and Ashley, strengthens and focuses the kind of Christology needed for a theological defense of the option for the poor.[4] First, however, I would like to offer a reflection on the basic paradigm itself.

THE MYSTICAL-PROPHETIC PARADIGM

Awareness, wide-awakeness, and right mindfulness of our participation in the whole and, for Christians, our participation in God is the basic character of a mystical form of theology. The term *mystical* is accurate enough in a general sense. But in a more exact sense the word is meant to refer not only to the intense awareness of the great mystics but also to practices of awareness and to reflective, even argumentative, modes of theological awareness, as well as contemplative or enlightened states of awareness that are usually understood as beyond meditation (which still needs language, concepts, and images, as in Ignatius Loyola's use of images in his *Spiritual Exercises*).[5]

The same kind of difficulty in naming occurs in our second choice for this more self-aware mode of the basic polarity of all religions, namely distance and participation. In the history of Western religions, the word *prophetic* first reminds most readers of the great prophetic traditions of ancient Israel and their continuation in Rabbinic Judaism, Christianity, and Islam.

Indeed, a peculiarity of *any* prophetic sense that makes it unlike mysticism, unlike contemplation, and unlike apocalypticism is the desire for

clear language to express, for the ordinary person in terms he or she can understand, the obligations of the individual, the responsibilities of the community, and the honor to be accorded those communal responsibilities
"under heaven" or "under God." Language and history are central here, and
a religious sense of participation through distancing oneself before some
primordial whole renders one responsible to the community, family, ancestors, the heavens, and God. For the ancient prophets of Israel, language
should be utterly clear so that the promise and threat are clearly understood by all. To be sure, for the prophetic consciousness, some transcendent distancing Other speaks through the prophet to the people and the
rulers. The prophet is aware of a great distance from that Other who demands to be heard whether the prophet wishes it or not (witness Lamen-
tations on being a prophet, or Jeremiah, or the fears of Isaiah). Yet the
prophet must speak—and must speak with sufficient clarity so that "all
who have ears to hear may hear."

Moreover, several, though not all, of the classical prophets, Amos and
Isaiah especially, could not be more clear in the demand for justice for the
destitute and the oppressed in an unjust society. Neither could the Jesus of
Luke's Gospel or implicitly of Mark's. Neither could Martin Luther King
Jr., Elizabeth Cady Stanton, or Gustavo Gutiérrez. Prophets must use the
power of language, a power at once distancing them from a primordial
sense of the whole and allowing them to speak to history and a people in
a particular historical situation in words that anyone can, in principle, understand. It is not difficult to understand Amos. Prophets are often impatient with mystics. They accuse them, often wrongly, of a lack of social
awareness. Prophets are usually also impatient with apocalyptic writers.
They accuse them, often rightly, of uttering a language so obscure and
obfuscating that it cannot be understood by all, indeed can lead to a ridiculous fundamentalism (let us calculate the days to the end time on the basis
of the symbolic numbers of the text; let us make Russia "the bear of the
North" that will hasten Armageddon; when should the thousand-year
reign of Christ begin?). Prophets, on the other hand, usually want clear, direct speech to empower their call from a transcendent God, and their demands are for action now. They do not speak their own words but instead
testify to the distant, disruptive, proclamatory Word of the Transcendent
Other, "Thus says the Lord." But prophets must use language, that most
necessary of distancing phenomena, clearly, cleanly, and well, so that the
people may hear and act, responding with ethical-political responsibility

to the summons of the God to whom the prophet witnesses. Prophets often denounce iconic images as idols or as pagan. Just as a mystical contemplative's main temptation is to withdraw from social action, so the prophet's main temptation is to see any icon, any image, any ritual or sense of participation as idolatry. These are the great temptations rather than necessities of the religious life for mystical and prophetic types.

The question recurs: Must the mystical and prophetic finally prove dialectical oppositions such that the twain can never meet? Or are the mystical and prophetic forms, like the religious sensibilities of participation and distance and the religious forms of manifestation and proclamation empowering them, finally polarities? That remains the most important question of any religion attempting to live authentically in a multireligious world with both self-respect and a willing self-exposure to the other.

Every religion is grounded in some manifesting or proclamatory event. In the prophetic biblical traditions, this could not be clearer. We probably could not understand Judaism without the founding revelatory events of Sinai and Exodus. It would be impossible to understand Christianity without the revelatory event of Jesus as the Christ. It would be equally impossible to understand Islam without understanding that the central revelatory event is not a historical-religious event like Sinai and Exodus, or a religious-historical event and person like the unsubstitutable Jesus as the Christ, but a text, the Koran, given by God to the last of the prophets, Mohammed. Both Judaism and Christianity also need a text, the Bible, but that text, unlike the Koran, is understood not as the revelation but as the canonical witness to the revelatory event. In Islam alone among the three radically monotheistic religions, the revelatory event *is* the text: the Koran, to which the prophet Mohammed canonically witnesses. All three religions, in my judgment, are fundamentally proclamation-prophetic religions whose power of distancing moves religion from an earlier manifestation through nature and cosmos to proclamation in and through history.

The move, within Christianity, is from the disruptive, proclamatory, and prophetic Word, as in the prophet Jesus's own eschatological sayings, parables, and proverbs, to the manifesting, meditative Word of Logos in the Gospel of John. This trajectory to mystical participatory form had already begun, of course, in the classical Wisdom traditions of the Jewish Scriptures (now named, for Christians, their First or Old Testament). Greek reflective questions, it seems, *pace* all anti-Hellenizers, are already being posed in inner-Jewish, Christian, and Islamic terms. Sometimes these questions took a critical turn. The extraordinary achievement of Jewish, Christian, and Muslim readers was their insight that belief in a transcendent Creator-God need not destroy, though it might indeed disrupt and transform, the ancient conception, described in all the ancient Greek-inspired philosophies, of a participatory, manifesting synthesis of the human, cosmic, and divine realms and of the *plenum* implied in those philosophies.

There was no need to choose between the Jewish Creator-God and the ancient synthesis of those early Jewish, Christian, and Muslim hermeneutics upon which theologians insisted. Just think: when these strands came together in medieval critical thought, the manifested, wide-ranging, reflective inquiry of the Greeks returned in new forms. God's creative act did not have to be understood merely as the efficient causality of the Aristotelians. The transcendent Creator-God would be, in that case, the cause of, but completely transcendent to, not immanent in, the created human and cosmic realms. But what if the causality of creation is not purely efficient but also final and formal, or perhaps, more exactly, quasi-formal? Then the Creator-God of the Scriptures is not only the origin of all but, as origin, the sustainer of all and the final end, final cause, of all reality.

This remarkable Jewish-Christian-Muslim reflective achievement could comprehend philosophically, and thereby theologically, how the Creator-God of the Bible is both transcendent to all creation and, as such, immanent in all creation. These thinkers were aided by the peculiarly biblical readings they accorded to Plato's *Timaeus* and its creation account.[6] These readings saved the ancient manifesting participatory synthesis of the human, the cosmic, and the divine, and the plenum within it, for thought and life (e.g., the manifesting-proclamatory Christian sacraments). This challenge was as difficult for the medieval Jewish, Christian, and Islamic thinkers to resolve—and they did resolve it—as the crisis of the nonperson is today for all sensitive Jewish, Christian, and Islamic thinkers.

Religion as proclamatory Word posits itself by implying its other, the manifesting participatory Sophia, as feminist theologians have shown. In Christianity, a combining of the Logos of Wisdom traditions, the Gospel of John and its attendant Logos theologies, and recent Sophia theologies, as well as the classical retrievals of the ancient synthesis and the plenum, enriched the liturgical-sacramental lives of Christians and produced Greek-inspired creation theologies of the transcendent-immanent God. In Judaism, a similar mingling of traditions produced Maimonides' conception of the theological-sacramental power of the law and Rosenzweig's conception of the Jewish liturgical year. In Islam, a belief in the one and transcendent God, Allah, grounded the ancient synthesis in the philosophies and theologies of such thinkers as Ibn Siva and Ibn-Rushd. The ancient synthesis, and the participatory plenum pervading it, was not destroyed but disrupted, transformed, and reposited by the Jewish, Christian, and Muslim thinkers in the Middle Ages. The prophetic Word posits itself by implying its other: reflective-contemplative, mystical.

The prophetic *optum* for the poor proclaimed by Luke's Jesus and the apocalyptic disruptions of all elites, including the original disciples, proclaimed by Mark's Jesus posit themselves by implying the participatory mystical Wisdom of John's Logos. There is no choice, for Christians, between the love emphasis of John's Gospel, that "love-intoxicated Gospel" as Augustine called it, and the justice emphasis of Luke and Mark. In my judgment, by rendering explicit the option for the poor as central to their self-understanding, Christians have a great opportunity to rethink the issue at the heart of Christianity, namely the relationship between love and justice. Love is too insubstantial if its demand for equality does not include the demand for justice for all rendered unequal, the poor. There is no Christian justice if it is not grounded in the participatory love of God made manifest in Jesus the Christ. Neither justice nor love, and therefore neither the prophetic nor the mystical, can live without implying each other. It does little good to speak, as some Christian elites now do, of a "special love" for the poor. The only special love worth mentioning here is a demand for justice. One very good and sound way to ensure the demand for justice is to drop the language of special love and speak more plainly and clearly of an option for the poor. Only then, I have come to believe, will the ethical-political dialectic of love and justice, like the prophetic mystical polarity empowering it, find its proper Christian focus. This can be seen even more clearly in the return of apocalyptic, not only prophetic, language in Christian thought today.

APOCALYPTIC AND CHRISTOLOGY

Christian apocalyptic thought, with its dualisms, its sense of an end, and often its violence, can seem an unlikely contributor to a contemporary theological enterprise affirming the option for the poor. Better to speak, most theologians seem to think, of eschatology. Better to rely on prophetic, not apocalyptic, language as the disruptive language we need, since indeed we do need prophetic language. Indeed, that is the reasonable case most Christian theologians, even eschatologically oriented ones, tend to make. There are grounds for this modern Christian theological suspicion of apocalyptic as opposed to eschatological language. If apocalyptic language, which so fragments the continuity of history, does not also fragment itself through, for example, the deliteralization upon which Augustine insisted in *The City of God,* and upon which such theologians after Augustine as Rudolf Bultmann, Reinhold Niebuhr, and Karl Rahner also insisted, then all could be lost for Christians.[7] For all that Christians would then possess would be a diminished and incomplete form of apocalypticism that could protect them from experiencing the void revealed in the terror of history, as that history is experienced by marginalized and oppressed peoples. By literalizing when the end will occur and by violently dividing all reality into two opposing forces on behalf of a community's sense of injustice, such apocalypticism hardens into a finally fundamentalist self-righteousness.

Ernst Käsemann may indeed have exaggerated in detail, as many New Testament scholars would now say. But in principle his famous statement remains properly provocative: "Apocalyptic is the mother of all Christian theology."[8] It is impossible, as far as I can see, to understand the New Testament without apocalyptic, and I do not mean this only in the obvious sense of the important apocalyptic texts there: Thessalonians, Matthew 25, almost the whole of Mark, and especially the *fascinans et tremendum* power of Revelation.

The New Testament does not merely begin chronologically with Mark's strange apocalyptic Gospel. It ends, not in triumphalist closure, even after the Resurrection, but with the plaintive unsettling cry "Come Lord Jesus, come" (Rev. 22:20). The whole Christian Bible ends with that cry.

The New Testament cannot be adequately understood without that apocalyptic tone of "Come." One always needs, with the great historical critical exegetes of our time, to remember the historical settings and the social locations of these New Testament texts. The fall of Jerusalem as a tragedy, indeed an apocalyptic tragedy, was important not only for the Jews but for Jewish Christians and for all four Gospels, probably including Mark. The importance of the historical mission to the Gentiles and all the other major historical events that influence the texts we now read is embedded in the New Testament. But above all we need to have great sensitivity, which is often lacking, to the event that did not occur, the Second Coming of Jesus Christ, the Son of Man, and what that might mean for a reading of the New Testament itself.

For example, when theologians and the whole Christian Church employ the great symbols for Christology, they usually employ the three classical Christological symbols: Incarnation, Cross, and Resurrection. Because these reveal who Jesus Christ is, and thus for Christians reveal who God is and who we human beings might become, each of them has received hundreds of interpretations from the very beginning.

There are four Gospels—five if you add Paul, as you should. Without the symbol of Incarnation, for example, where is the Christian affirmation of Jesus Christ as God? Where is the affirmation of the disaster still attendant upon much Christian denigration of the body, and especially sexuality, all too clear a case of Christianity forgetting both body and creation? An incarnational perspective, as in Francis of Assisi and Clare, is crucial for any further Christian understanding of how we actually participate in nature and owe justice to our fellow creatures, not only human creatures. It was, I admit, Buddhists who gave me this insight on Francis, whom they considered the most radical religious figure in the entire West. Moreover, recent Christian feminist, womanist, and *mujerista* theologies have persuasively shown how Christianity seems to have trapped itself in Hellenistic categories of soul and body, male and female, mind and passion. Without changing these, Christianity could again lose its biblical Jewish antidualistic roots.

With the classic symbol of Incarnation, even the cross becomes differently understood, or, at least, further understood. For the cross of the Crucified One as viewed through the symbol of Incarnation can also be seen, as Eliade argued, as the cosmic tree of the ancients and of so many ancient religions. The tree, the cosmic tree in Hinduism and in so many indigenous religions, manifests the synthesis of the divine, the cosmic, and the human realms, for it reaches with its branches to the whole cosmos in the air and reaches with its roots to the power and joy of the earth itself.[9] With the Incarnation, belief in resurrection becomes genuinely not a belief in Greek immortality of the soul but, with Luke and Paul in their distinct ways, a resurrection of the body, reminding Christians over and over that the body is good. Redemption does not replace the goodness of creation, and Christians must be in communion with all the living and the dead.

Without the classic symbol of Cross, Christian life and thought is always in danger of sentimentalizing Christianity into a "have a nice day"
greeting card without suffering, without a sense of evil, and without re-
mainder. For the lifting up of the cross may well be, as John insists in his
incarnationally oriented Gospel and as von Balthasar's whole theology attempts to express, the manifestation of God's beauty and glory. Even in
John, who anti-Gnostically grounds the crucifixion in a history-like, realistic Passion narrative, Christology is cross centered. Cross, suffering, pain,
death, and disgrace attend the Johannine Jesus. Certainly with Paul and
his almost obsessive refusal to let go of the thought that even the Christian cannot finally think, God is disclosed not as the God of glory but as
the crucified God in Jesus Christ and him crucified.

Without the cross, I repeat, where would the great movements in theologies of liberation find a way to understand the conflict, the pain, and
the negativity in every historical struggle for justice? Without the cross,
could we Christians even begin to face the ruptures of our own history,
with our betrayals, through the centuries, of the option for the poor, as
well as the ruptures of all history of which we have knowledge, that void
exposed in the Shoah and every other instance of the useless, innocent,
unjust suffering of whole peoples, in what even Hegel called "the slaugh-
ter bench of history"?[10]

With the cross, one need not worry that Christianity will descend
to what Nietzsche feared it would always descend to: a reactive, weak,
finally somewhat embarrassing sentimental religion that cannot bear cross
and power. With the cross, Christianity should be able to face the reality
of force that, as Simone Weil insisted so well, affects every human life,
even eventually the life of the privileged, who will also die. For force, as
she argues, physical force, intellectual force, spiritual force, affects us all
through sickness, old age, disease, and death; it is the power that prolep-
tically draws us all further into what? The void, or God.[11] With the cross,
any Christian belief in resurrection will be shorn of all temptations to individual and historical triumphalism and all non-sense about the ease of
death. Like Paul, we face death as the final earthly power to which all of
us must one day yield.

The equally necessary symbol of Resurrection presents its own demands in relationship to Incarnation and Cross. Against any fatalism and all
dolorism (loving suffering for its own sake), in every struggle for justice or
for material life itself, as Marxists rightly insist, the Resurrection empowers the kind of hope that is believably real as a struggle against injustice.

Hope is neither optimistic nor pessimistic. Optimism and pessimism are largely matters of temperament and response to life's experiences. Resurrection hope does not know but endures; one continues the struggle in the hope of a share in the vindication in the life and death of this unsubstitutable Jesus Christ, the Risen One. Historical struggle must be materialist and thereby can overcome pessimism and optimism alike and live in the hope heard in the slave narratives of "Roll, Jordan, Roll" and the great spirituals and blues of African Americans, a people with a history whose horror seems never to end, and whose struggle for justice goes on and on and on with hope, with bursts of fury, rage, anger, laughter, and joy, and with life, and matter, and spirit.[12] With Resurrection, the incarnational trust in body, flesh, and creation is strengthened and moved past any temptation to nature romanticism into a struggle for the body and for earth—indeed, as Paul expresses it, for all creation groaning to be free—and, above all, with all humans unjustly treated. With Resurrection, Cross will never give in to the temptation to fatalism, to despair.

The necessity for each of these classic symbols, Incarnation, Cross, and Resurrection, for understanding Christ and thereby naming God by naming the Jesus narrated and confessed by Christians as the Christ has never been more clear. We need all three symbols and their tensions and their relationship to Jesus. The ever-changing need to relate these symbols to one another in ever-new combinations, in fidelity to the pluralism beginning in the New Testament itself and continuing throughout the entire history of Christianity and now in a global Christianity, shows once and for all how no theology and no naming of God through Christ Jesus can be built on only one of these symbols.

The cry of hope and love rebounds through Incarnation and Resurrection. And the cry of justice now as the option for the poor resounds through Cross and Second Coming. Only all four symbols, united, of course, to the lives of Jesus that they interpret, can bring Christian theology to the full-fledged option it needs now, the option for the poor.

With so intense a struggle to understand who Jesus Christ is for Christians, and thereby how to name God, and hope for what human beings might be, in the classical Christological symbols of Incarnation, Cross, and Resurrection, it may be strange to plead as I now do, even against my former self and against all I have formerly written on Christology (which was always on the three symbols), for serious attention to and incorporation of a fourth, too often neglected symbol: the apocalyptic symbol of the Second Coming of Christ. But the great symbol of an apocalyptic Second Coming of Christ is not, I have come to believe, a luxury item for Christian self-understanding or for the name of God. Apocalyptic is as what Jacques Derrida nicely calls "a certain tone in contemporary culture and thought."[13] It is a tone that must be heard, especially by Christians attempting to live a Christian life and think a fully Christian vision of history and time. The radical "not yet" of the apocalyptic power in the symbol of the Second Coming destabilizes all Christian thought, and that for the better. Once deliteralized and stolen back from the date-setting literalists, the Second Coming, I am convinced, is as powerful and as central a symbol for Christian self-understanding of Jesus Christ and for naming God as the other three. The New Testament as a whole, I repeat, unfolds between its two great destabilizing, fragmenting, and fragmented texts the extraordinary fragmentary text of the Gospel of Mark, as distinct from the continuous realistic narrative of the Gospel of Luke and of Acts, and at the end the even more fragmentary book of Revelation. Mark's brief account of the Resurrection, which he surely affirms, disallows any Christian triumphalism and ends, most scholars agree, with the women at the tomb fleeing in fear and terror (Mark 16:8). The book of Revelation, that last book of our Bible, that unsteady collection of fragments from ever-new genres, hymns, warnings, epistles, heavenly journeys, mediating angels, narratives, nonclosures, ruptures, and interruptions of history, seems held together, if at all as a text, at times only by what appears to be the obsession of the author or authors theologically to cry, "Not yet, not yet," and to have messianic times come into history, even after the incarnation, the cross, and the resurrection of this Jesus, the Christ.

To be sure, the end times have already happened in Jesus Christ. They have already begun. But they are "not yet." For Christians, the Bible does not end like a classical folktale with "and they all lived happily ever after." It ends rather with a cry, a plea, a prayer, a passion, and "Come Lord Jesus, come." Perhaps the unjust marginalization of those who join the so-called fundamentalist groups has forced them into their love of the book of Revelation, a love that shares the obsessive quality of parts of the book itself regarding the numbers to count, the symbols, the geography involved, and the countdowns for what Hal Lindsay, the most prominent fundamentalist spokesman of apocalypse, has named "the late great planet earth."

I cannot share any fundamentalist readings of the book of Revelation. But I have now come to see how foolish the rest of Christians have been to ignore that book and to ignore the apocalyptic Second Coming. Why do we ignore it when our name for the liturgical season of Advent is the only word left in English to my knowledge that speaks of that other notion of the future, of God's coming from the future to the present? How can Advent become just a preparation for the Incarnation and Christmas? What of all the readings of the Second Coming? What does one do with them?

The embarrassment, if that is what it is, of many theologians like Bultmann and Rahner regarding the apocalyptic has effectively handed over the great symbolic text of the book of Revelation and the apocalyptic power pulsating like a bloodstream throughout the New Testament to Christian fundamentalists, are all too certain about what this symbol must mean not only for the individual but for historical countdowns. The fact is, however, that the New Testament ends in nonclosure, with a prayer, a passionate cry of "come." It ends with a fragmented text that barely holds itself together save by the power of its demands for justice now shouted by a desperate people. It begins with a strange Gospel, the strangest of the four, Mark, which is apocalyptic through and through. It ends Christologically, having already affirmed the symbols of Incarnation, Cross, and Resurrection, with a fourth symbol that we too easily forget, the apocalyptic Second Coming of Christ, which destroys at its core any Christian temptation to triumphalism, whether it be theological toward the Jews, as in supercessionism, or political, as in Christianity become Christendom and empire, ignoring the option for the poor and extending only special love. Without the symbol of the Second Coming, without apocalyptic, Christianity can settle down into a religion that no longer has a profound sense of the "not yet" and of God's hiddenness in history, a religion without any sense of the need for action for justice in the option for the poor.

NOTES

This essay is offered as a tribute to my good friend Gustavo Gutiérrez.

1. Richard J. Bernstein, "Plurality and Ambiguity Review," *Journal of Religion* 69 (January 1989): 85–91.

2. Gustavo Gutiérrez, *On Job: God-Talk and the Suffering of the Innocent,* trans. Matthew J. O'Connell (Maryknoll, NY: Orbis Books, 1987).

3. Emmanuel Levinas, *Totality and Infinity: An Essay on Exteriority,* trans. Alphonso Lingis (Pittsburgh: Duquesne University Press, 1969).

4. Johann Baptist Metz, *Faith in History and Society: Toward a Practical Fundamental Theology,* trans. David Smith (New York: Seabury, 1980); J. Matthew Ashley, "Apocalypticism in Political and Liberation Theology: Toward an Historical Docta Ignorantia," *Horizons* 27 (Spring 2000): 22–43.

5. *Spiritual Exercises of St. Ignatius Loyola,* trans. Elizabeth Meier Tetlow (Lanham, MD: University Press of America, 1987).

6. *Plato's Timaeus,* trans. Francis M. Cornford (Indianapolis: Bobbs-Merrill Educational Publishing, 1959).

7. Augustine, *City of God,* trans. John Healey (London: J. M. Dent, 1945); Rudolf Bultmann, *Theology of the New Testament,* trans. Kendrich Grobel (New York: Scribner's Sons, 1951); Reinhold Niebuhr, *Nature and Destiny of Man* (New York: Scribner's Sons, 1943); Karl Rahner, *Foundations of Christian Faith: An Introduction to the Idea of Christianity,* trans. William V. Dych (New York: Seabury, 1978).

8. Ernst Käsemann, "The Beginnings of Christian Theology," *Journal for Theology and the Church* 6 (1969): 40.

9. Mircea Eliade, *The Sacred and the Profane,* trans. Willard R. Trask (New York: Harcourt Brace, 1959).

10. Georg Wilhelm Friedrich Hegel, *Lectures on the Philosophy of History,* rev. ed., trans. J. Sibree (New York: Wiley, 1944), 21.

11. Simone Weil, "The Love of God and Affliction," in *The Simone Weil Reader,* ed. George Panichas (Wakefield, RI: Moyer Bell, 1977), 439–68.

12. Eugene D. Genovese, *Roll, Jordan, Roll: The World the Slaves Made* (New York: Pantheon Books, 1974); James H. Cone, *The Spirituals and the Blues: An Interpretation* (Maryknoll, NY: Orbis Books, 1991).

13. Jacques Derrida, "On a Newly Arisen Apocalyptic Tone in Philosophy," in *Raising the Tone of Philosophy: Late Essays by Immanuel Kant, Transformative Critique by Jacques Derrida,* ed. Peter Fenves (Baltimore: Johns Hopkins University Press, 1993), 117–71.

Chapter 7

THE TURN TO APOCALYPTIC AND THE OPTION FOR THE POOR IN CHRISTIAN THEOLOGY

J. MATTHEW ASHLEY

The Basque theologian Gaspar Martinez has recently argued for a striking similarity in the work of three theologians who began their careers during or immediately following the Second Vatican Council.[1] Johann Baptist Metz, Gustavo Gutiérrez, and David Tracy, he asserts, all took as their task a deeper theological engagement with society and history, each according to his different context. For so doing, each of them drew the accusation of forgetting, diminishing, or domesticating the transcendence of God. Martinez shows that this accusation is unfounded. Indeed, what is remarkable is that in turning to history each of them was compelled to re-turn to God, and to a God who is not less transcendent, less "other," for having been found by passing through society and history, but who, precisely because of that passage, must be named by ever more radically apophatic strategies. For Metz, engaging post–World War II German society and history meant joining the struggle to save the Enlightenment from its own self-destructive dialectic. Running up against the theoretically unresolvable obstacle to that project—Auschwitz, the Shoah—Metz was compelled to re-turn to a God who is irritatingly eschatological, about whom one cannot build virtuoso speculative systems, but about and *to* whom one can and must speak an apocalyptic language best modeled by Job and by Mark's Jesus. For Gutiérrez, working in a continent riven by the suffering of the innocent, a suffering that resists, indeed annihilates, those who struggle to end it, this return to God is found in a deepening of the exodus paradigm so prominent in his early work by means of a reading of the book of Job. This reading locates the category under which to talk about the mystery of God as that of the utter gratuitousness of God's love, a love that defies human expectations of a quid pro quo love (even when the quo is action in history on behalf of justice) precisely as it calls forth the grateful response of fidelity to God's call for compassion and justice for the "nonperson."[2] David Tracy's early attempt to find a way for theology to press its claims in a pluralistic public square here in the United States has been complicated, irritated, and interrupted by his growing awareness that theology has to attend more fully to the critiques of that alleged publicness by the "masters of suspicion" both past and present and his realization that theology must retrieve forgotten or repressed ways of naming God as the wholly other so that faith and theology are not constrained in advance to enter that public square with nothing but more of the same. In sum, as Karl Rahner, who had such an impact on each of these men, insisted, Christian faith and therefore theology as well are ultimately grounded in a trusting, hopeful surrender to the mystery of God; but, as these theologians' work has shown, this surrender need not, indeed must not, happen without passing through history, even and especially a history in which, as Walter Benjamin so graphically put it, "every great work of civilization is at the same time a work of barbarism."[3]

As Martinez shows, then, the theological itineraries of these three thinkers strikingly exemplify Gustavo Gutiérrez's reminder that the best, most *theo*-centric theologies are the self-avowedly contextual ones. Two further homologies will serve as the foci of this essay. First, there is now a general agreement among these three important postconciliar theologians that the way to pass through history toward an authentic naming of God is to enter history in solidarity with the poor. Of course this has always been the case with Gutiérrez. If anything, what one finds in examining Gutiérrez on this point is both an intensification and a broadening of the category of poverty: from a definition that focused, but never exclusively, on economic destitution to a definition in terms of the marginalization, be it based on class, culture, gender, race, or what have you, that threatens to make persons "nonpersons," such that they die before their time. Poverty, as he simply puts it, means death.[4] Metz has moved steadily in this direction ever since he began his efforts to develop a new political theology in the 1960s. He has primarily been guided by the problem posed by suffering, particularly by suffering unjustly inflicted on the innocent. In recent years Metz has come increasingly to speak of one authority that we cannot allow to be dissolved either by modernity's critique of the authority given to tradition or by postmodernity's critique of the authority given to reason and the rational: "the authority of those who suffer,"[5] an authority not just for Christian theology or faith but for any humane culture and politics.[6]

Finally, David Tracy, always sympathetic to liberation theology, has given ever-greater priority over the past decade to responding to the questions posed by the existence of "the nonperson," not just as an alternative in competition with the Enlightenment, modern questions raised by the existence of the nonbeliever (both the overt atheist without and the potential atheist created *within* every believer by the modern scientific, cultural, political, and economic revolutions), but as the only adequate route by which the latter questions can be answered at all. As he says in chapter 6 of this volume,

> The central theological problem of our day is not the problem of the nonbeliever but the problem of those thought to be nonpersons by the reigning elites. . . . This does not mean, for Gutiérrez or for me, that the theological problem of the nonbeliever (including the nonbeliever in the believer) is now resolved. But it does mean that only when the issue of those others explicitly or implicitly thought of as nonpersons takes priority will even the problem of the nonbeliever receive new thought. This means that within Christian theology, as within the Christian churches, the option for the poor should be at the heart of every serious Christian theology today.

The final homology that we can observe between these three theologians is the turn to apocalyptic. Metz, of course, is most well known for advocating this turn. Beginning in the mid-1970s he began insisting on the importance of apocalypticism for Christianity's self-understanding, particularly in the face of what he saw as the enervating grip of "timeless time," time as an empty continuum in which nothing new can really happen but only an endless extrapolation of what has been.[7] He has described the attempt to do justice to Christianity's apocalyptic traditions as "the hem of my theological approach,"[8] and with the passing decades he has become, if anything, even more insistent on this point.[9]

Gutiérrez does not press the case for an apocalyptic eschatology with anything like Metz's vehemence, but like many liberation theologians he has made use of the conceptual resources of utopia, particularly as found in the work of Ernst Bloch, in whom it has clear and emphatic apocalyptic overtones.[10] Moreover, again like all liberation theologians, Gutiérrez rejects conceptualizing history and historical change in terms of a model of development, according to which the only rational way to think of future forms of society is to understand them as developing or evolving out of currently existing forms. The point of choosing the root metaphor of liberation is in part to insist on the need for interrupting the current development or evolution of historical processes, which is precisely the point that Metz has been pressing with his turn to apocalypticism.[11]

A much clearer instance of the presence of apocalyptic themes, and particularly of the apocalyptic schema of history, can be found in Jon Sobrino's recently completed two-volume Christology. Among the most striking instances are these: his linking of the traditions about Jesus's resurrection with their background in Second Temple Jewish apocalypticism,[12] his theological interpretation of history as a battle between the God of life and idols of death,[13] and his reflections on the apocalyptic motif of martyrdom.[14] As we shall see, Sobrino's Christology will repay further attention, insofar as it is the clearest present instantiation of Tracy's claim, in his chapter in this volume, that "a move into a rethinking of Christology in this paradigm [the mystical-political paradigm of political and liberation theology], with the additional expansion of the prophetic to the apocalyptic Second Coming, . . . strengthens and focuses the kind of Christology needed for a theological defense of the option for the poor."

This brings us, then, to Tracy and his remarkable opening to apocalyptic texts, a turn evident in his chapter in this volume entitled "The Christian Option for the Poor."[15] Here, as Tracy himself concedes, he is amending the position he took in his most sustained Christological reflection to date: *The Analogical Imagination.* In that text Tracy argues that, together with the genre of doctrine and early Catholicism, the genre of apocalypticism (he does not mention the symbol of the Second Coming) should be a "corrective" (important but not constitutive) for the reading of the kerygmatic and narrative witnesses to the event and person of Jesus Christ in the New Testament that is organized by the central Christian and Christological symbols of Incarnation, Cross, and Resurrection.[16] For Tracy the symbol of the Second Coming is itself co-constitutive with the other three for any adequate understanding of Jesus Christ, and thus of any naming of the God of Jesus.

To be sure, Tracy has always appreciated apocalypticism's importance. He showed more openness than many to the apocalyptic "turn" of his friend Johann Baptist Metz. But he has also always struck me as having even greater sympathy with Metz's teacher, Karl Rahner, who remarked of his student's virtual obsession with retrieving apocalyptic thinking: "You may be right, you may be right; but, how are you ever going to get this across to people?"[17] How indeed? How does one convey the meaning of apocalypticism in our scientifically informed, intellectual, and social worlds? How does one talk about a Second Coming, of a saving end to history, when, as Rudolf Bultmann famously remarked, "Everyone of sound judgment knows that history kept on going and will keep on going"?[18] The thesis I shall explore in what follows is that apocalyptic needs the option for the poor as much as the converse. On Tracy's terms, I will argue not only that the option for the poor in Christian theology needs a turn to apocalyptic to develop an adequate Christology, as Tracy clearly asserts, but that only by taking "the option for the poor in Christian theology" can the turn to apocalyptic be gotten across, both in a way that is adequate to the (to most moderns scandalous) depth of its provocative biblical exemplars and in a way that avoids its all-too-manifest aberrations. I conclude with some remarks about what this test case can tell us about the meaning of the option for the poor in Christian theology.

THE URGENCY AND SALVIFIC SCANDAL OF APOCALYPTICISM

The sound judgment that history kept on going and will keep on going seems unexceptionable in many contemporary university settings. For the majority of the world's people, however, it is a death sentence. For them, for history to keep on going as it does now means death before their time, as Gustavo Gutiérrez has so incisively put it. For many it means sudden, violent disruption and death, as it did for the victims of El Mozote in El

Salvador, the Shoah in Europe, or the Middle Passage between Africa and the Americas. For the rest, it means the slow physical or cultural death of oppression and poverty, directly inflicted or indifferently allowed, collateral damage to seemingly ineluctable processes of globalization. It is when one makes an option for these, and when one hears their anguished cry for life and for justice, that one feels the deep and deeply Christian power of the symbol of the Second Coming, proclaiming an imminent interruption to a history that so horribly "keeps on going."

If we accept a definition of theology as "giving an account of our hope" (1 Pet. 3:15), an *intellectus spei* (Jon Sobrino), or a hermeneutics of hope (Gustavo Gutiérrez), and if we dare not narrow the circle of these hopes to what we hope for ourselves alone but must entertain a hope that includes the victims, present and past, then theology must be a discursive practice that defends their right to have hope and thus defends the symbolic resources, here apocalyptic, by which alone, it seems, hope might be articulated in a history that offers them so little in which to hope. Yet if it be granted that such a turn to apocalypticism is justified for a theology that attends to the cry of the poor, the question still remains: How can apocalypticism be defended as a credible option for naming God today? How can and should theology get it across to people? After all, granting that much of the modern intellectual distaste for apocalyptic arises from the typically modern urge to reduce everything unruly in religion to more of the same, to erase everything that cannot be reconciled with modern canons of reason (with all the dubious conceptual and social presuppositions that lie behind these canons), is there not also a genuine concern that apocalypticism's dualistic account of history runs the danger of demonizing the other and underwriting awful spasms of violence already too typical of the past several centuries? Should we be in such a rush to abandon prophetic eschatology, with its emphasis on a God who works through already existing historical processes and agents, and a concomitant stress on the importance of responsible human action in history, in favor of an apocalyptic eschatology, with its apparent reliance on supernatural intervention, sapping, so it would seem, the significance of historical praxis?

Perhaps these are some of the reasons behind a continuing tentativeness in Tracy, an unwillingness to embrace fully the apocalyptic hope he has broached. The language is revealing: apocalyptic is not to be "demythologized," to be sure—Tracy is too aware of Metz's (and Ernst Bloch's) critiques of Bultmann to adopt that language. But, he tells us, it must be "deliteralized" to purge it of its penchant for fantastic predictions, violent dualisms, and fanatic self-righteousness. Yet what is left of apocalypticism once it has been deliteralized is a negative content: a "not yet" that cuts off any triumphalist identification of the status quo with the kingdom of God.[19] To be sure, this is a vitally important achievement, particularly in the United States, where such an eschatological reserve with regard to human projects has become the first casualty of the "war on terrorism." But is it enough?

Is not this focus on the "not yet" still Rahner's position, as it was Niebuhr's? To the extent that it allows apocalyptic language at all, does it not make the symbol of the Second Coming and the discourse it unleashes once again a corrective, a negative qualification of positive contents concerning Christian life in history that come from the other Christological symbols? But do not apocalyptic language and symbolism express not only a "not yet," but also a "soon!"? "Come Lord, come!" is a cry made in expectation that it will be answered, answered soon, in history, by a dramatic reversal that can even now be discerned by the apocalyptic visionary and those willing to follow him or her into the extravagant symbolic world constructed to interpret the present that is about to become the novum. This is the classic historical pattern by which apocalypticists respond to a history that seems devoid of hope, especially for a prophetic eschatology that looks for some inner-historical agent who might bring about God's reign. As scholars such as Paul Hanson, John Collins, and Richard Horsley have argued, it is when history turns hopeless, when the prophets' claims about God's sovereignty over history are horrifically challenged by the antiwitness of systemic and pervasive historical evil and suffering, that apocalyptic rhetoric seeks a different pattern for articulating that sovereignty, a new way of claiming the transparency of historical events and processes to God's will.[20] When they do this they have classically resorted to a pattern for interpreting history that is described by Bernard McGinn as "first, a sense of the unity and structure of history conceived as a divinely predetermined totality; second, pessimism about the present and conviction of its imminent crisis; and third, belief in the proximate judgment of evil and triumph of the good, the element of vindication."[21]

The element of vindication, which often includes the resurrection and exaltation of the martyrs who died on the way, entails a positive content: a claim, paradoxically, that God and God's kingdom are *already here,* although here in the mode of advent: God present as the one about to return. This sense of imminent return and vindication is elicited and deployed to marshal resources of patient endurance, watchfulness, and fidelity, as in the parables of Matthew 25. For apocalypticism the "not yet" but "soon" is a modality whereby God's kingdom is *already* here as a reality breaking in upon us, a disturbing modality that necessarily seeks expression in the florid apocalyptic imagery that we moderns find so scandalous. This "already," and not just a "not yet," which, by itself, threatens to become a dispiriting "not ever," is what makes possible a utopian hope that can empower tenacious faithfulness to a vision of God's will for humanity, along with resistance, even to the death, to the gods and idols that represent an inhumane and dehumanizing countervision (of an "antikingdom," as Sobrino names it). It also empowers a prophetic denunciation of global conditions and trends that bring death to God's creation, however necessary and irreversible they appear to those of sound judgment.

DELITERALIZING APOCALYPTIC: TWO STRATEGIES

If this description of what is at stake in the apocalyptic traditions holds water, a "deliteralization" that reduces apocalyptic to a "not yet" does not adequately present the symbol of the Second Coming in its interruptive integrity and positive content, precisely for its creative relation to the other three root Christological symbols for which Tracy so correctly presses us. But then, what kind of deliteralization? For surely Tracy is right that we have had too many instances of catastrophically failed apocalypticisms not to insist on an intellectual and spiritual ascesis for the use of its dangerous but, Metz reminds us, precisely therein salvific, symbolism.[22] Here I can only suggest two possible responses, without being able to work them out fully.

First, the symbol of Second Coming can and should be transformed by its interaction with other root Christological symbols. As Tracy insists, neither a theology nor a Christian life can be built on one of these symbols alone. If the symbol of Second Coming is necessary for an adequate deployment of the other three symbols, then might not the converse be true as well? The other three symbols will also orient the symbol of Second Coming in such a way that the dangers implicit in it are avoided or at least minimized. Redeeming this claim would require nothing less than producing a Christology that results from such a mutual reading of the four Christological symbols. Short of that, let us sketch a provisional outline of how the symbol of Second Coming might inflect and be inflected by the other symbols, relying largely on Jon Sobrino's liberation Christology. The focus will be not only on how the other three symbols are enriched but on how correlating the symbol of Second Coming with the others can remedy three dangers, at least, that are inherent in an exclusive and dysfunction-ally literalistic reading of that symbol and the apocalyptic discourse it un-derwrites: first, that the apocalyptic rendering of history will lapse into a Manichaeism that denies the goodness of creation and the unity of God as sovereign over nature and history; second, that this dualism will lead to a demonization of inner-historical opponents and thus legitimate de-humanizing violence against them; third, that the nonoccurrence of the expected utopian interruption by God will lead to disillusionment and de-spair of salvation in history.

Before proceeding we need a sense of the positive content of the sym-bol of Second Coming, since my argument thus far has been that inter-preting this content in an exclusively negative way, as a "not yet," is inade-quate. I shall proceed on the premise that the symbol of Second Coming is the premier symbol of the kingdom of God. If the symbol of Resurrection conveys God's definitive vindication of Jesus and the disclosure of both true humanity and true divinity in his person and his praxis, then the Second Coming presents the culmination of that self-gift of God's, when Christ "hands over the kingdom to God the Father, after he has destroyed every ruler and every authority and power" (1 Cor. 15:24). This is a plau-sible reading—if not in the light of Mark's Gospel, which conveys with such great force the interruptive and conflictive character of history, and suggests that the only proper response to the "not yet" character of the Marcan Resurrection accounts is to return to Galilee, the place of Jesus's labors, to find him there, in the labor (Mark 16:7),[23] then certainly in the light of Matthew's Gospel. Matthew's is, after all, the Gospel that presents the full apocalyptic scenario, with the elements not just of conflict and cri-sis but of judgment and vindication.[24] For Matthew, particularly in the amazing parables of chapter 25, the response to the apocalyptic "not yet *but soon*" of the presence of God's kingdom is to be watchful and to persist in the radical praxis of feeding the hungry, giving drink to the thirsty, cloth-ing the naked, welcoming the stranger, caring for the sick, visiting the im-prisoned. While the "not yet" of this way of reading the symbol of Second Coming as the symbol of the in-breaking of God's kingdom brings Chris-tianity's anti-ideological reserves into play with regard to existing social-political arrangements, its "but soon" helps us grasp the good news that the unexpected, graced action in history of the God who intervened gracefully and unexpectedly to raise Jesus from the dead is also a possibility and a reality that impinges now on our historical reality as a whole, making possible what appears to be impossible, particularly to the wise ones of sound judgment, for whom history cannot but keep on going the way it has. Finally, then, to articulate the symbol of Second Coming in this way is to appropriate one of the premier themes in liberation theology, the kingdom of God, and to make it operative in Christology. It is thus, I suggest, a way of making the option for the poor in Christian theology, at least on an interpretive-speculative level.[25]

How does including the symbol of Second Coming inflect the other root Christological symbols? First, it introduces a sense of history that, while not denying God's ultimate sovereignty, insists that history is deeply riven by a conflict between God and that which opposes God, so that a theological interpretation of history can and should use categories of kingdom and "antikingdom" (to use Sobrino's way of putting it). For the symbol of Incarnation, then, Incarnation has to mean incarnation in this kind of history. If God is a God of love and life and not a malevolent "idol of death" or a *deus otiosus,* blind or indifferent to the way history really is, then Incarnation will express certainly an ultimate affirmation of and love for creation in its entirety, but prior to that time when all things are one in Christ—that is, now, on this side of the Second Coming—it will reflect a preference, a taking sides in this conflict, articulated in terms of the when, where, and how this incarnation occurs in the concrete in history. To appropriate the symbol of Incarnation, then, is anything but to embrace a cheap nature mysticism; it is to enter into creation, "taking flesh" in it as God did, positioning oneself in history's conflicts so as to act out of the vision of the imminent kingdom and its victory over all that opposes it. While this conflict is not the last word about creation and history, it is pervasive and deep enough to disallow any alleged neutrality or "wait and see" attitude, as the book of Revelation insists in the opening letters to the churches of Asia Minor.

Read this way, the symbol of Incarnation illuminates not only the where and among whom of Jesus's birth, among and preferentially for the poor, but the way that his life unfolded. If one consistently incarnates oneself in history this way, one will be swept up into the conflict of which the Second Coming is the dramatic culmination, but that, according to the apocalyptic script, is preceded by the crisis of God's apparent defeat in history, a defeat conveyed in the New Testament with the symbol of the Cross. In other words, as Sobrino puts it, "[R]eal incarnation in a world of sin is what leads to the cross, and the cross is the product of a real incarnation."[26] The symbol of Cross, interpreted in the light of the historical struggle disclosed through the symbol of Second Coming, becomes a symbol of the *mysterium iniquitatis,* the mystery of why sin seems to have power in history and why those who are faithful to the vision of God's coming reign are so often crushed by that sin. It is also a symbol conveying the depths of God's love, the degree to which God will become one of us, even to the point of sharing in our vulnerability to evil and suffering in history.

Interpreting the symbol of Resurrection through the lens of Second Coming means shifting the focus of the hope it manifests away from survival of the individual after death. Indeed, as Sobrino argues, it shifts the emphasis of resurrection from soteriology to *theo*-logy. Resurrection is not first a statement about our individual salvation from death but a statement about God, a hopeful symbol of God's triumph over the idols of death and a vindication of the proclamation of God as a God of life, which, of course, then has implications for individual mortality, but not apart from all the other ways that death is sinfully present in our world.[27] Proclaiming this even and especially in a history like ours, which, again read apocalyptically, comes to light as a history painfully crucified by death and suffering, the symbol of Resurrection becomes a powerful impetus to live out of a vision of life, not because that is the way history really is, but because that is the way God really is: a God on the side of the crucified in history and not the crucifiers.[28]

On the other hand, the three symbols of Incarnation, Cross, and Resurrection modulate the symbol of Second Coming in crucial ways, ways that are lacking in the dangerous interpretations of the symbol and its accompanying apocalyptic discourse in figures like Hal Lindsey and, more recently, Tim LaHaye. To appropriate the symbol of Second Coming in concert with the symbol of Cross is to specify the way in which God's triumphal victory is achieved: through the cross. God's victory comes not through dehumanizing others and continuing the cycle of violence but by self-sacrifice, by bearing sin. Paradoxically, scandalously to many, God fights the apocalyptic battle in a human way, by becoming vulnerable to evil in history, through solidarity with history's victims.[29] If the symbol of Second Coming relativizes the symbol of Resurrection as the definitive soteriological symbol, the symbol of Resurrection does nonetheless act soteriologically back on the symbol of Second Coming to insist that the decisive victory has already been won in the person, life, and fate of Jesus Christ and that we can experience that victory, indeed in a derivative manner re-present it in our own lives, through the power of the Spirit poured out in the paschal event. As Sobrino puts it, we can in some ways live now as people already risen, as people of the Second Coming.[30] We can live in a hopeful freedom and joy that triumphs over selfishness and cynicism, leading us to become even more fully "incarnate" in history, which means more engaged in the struggle for the kingdom of God. In so doing we penetrate finally to history's deepest reality, carried by a hopeful, Spiritful current in history, however obscure it may be.[31]

This brings us back to the symbol of Incarnation. Incarnation reminds us that however much creation is distorted by suffering and evil, however riven with conflict, it must still be affirmed as good, as the creation of a good God. History is both lovable and beloved as the place of God's unreserved self-gift, a pouring out of God's self that does not hold back, even before the historical reality of the cross. This orients the Second Coming away from a demonization of history, either as a whole or regionally, and lifts up instead an insistence that no matter how deeply history is riven by sin and conflict it is still a history in which God's decisive commitment of love has appeared and been vindicated and that is now defined ultimately by the final victory of the reign of God, impinging even now, a victory that the followers of Jesus are called to make a reality, however partial, in their own lives. In sum, this way of framing the symbol of Second Coming in terms of the three other root Christological symbols rules out a final, Manichaean duality in history (the influence of the symbol of Incarnation), the demonization and dehumanization of others (Cross), and a despairing resignation or cynicism about what we can have and hope for in the present (Resurrection).

A second candidate I would suggest for deliteralizing apocalyptic symbols is less speculative and conceptual and more oriented toward concrete discipleship and spirituality. For the Christological symbols can and should point us back continually to the Gospel narratives out of which they arise and in which they have their historical moorings. They also require the sort of thoughtful elaboration into a theology that will articulate and coordinate, if not totally resolve, the tensions that the symbols together produce.[32] But the symbols have to be seen not just as generative foci for new readings of the evangelical narratives, or as sources that give rise to new speculative Christologies, but as keys to a transformation of one's life now, a transformation of oneself into a follower of Jesus Christ. This process is generally treated these days under the rubric of spirituality and brings with it its own deliteralization of all the symbols, including that of Second Coming. It is here, I would argue, that one can discern a response to the third danger identified above: the problem of disillusionment caused by the failure of apocalyptic hopes and prophecies to find in history, "soon," the Second Coming so ardently longed for.[33]

It is worth noting, after all, that patristic and medieval theology was also concerned with deliteralizing scriptural imagery, moving through the literal to the spiritual senses of Scripture without abandoning or ignoring the literal but contextualizing it in terms of a broader interpretive framework of God's revelatory-salvific action. For them, though, this labor was as much a spiritual exercise, a part of the progression from *lectio divina* through *meditatio* to *contemplatio,* as it was a speculative one. My point is not that we should necessarily return to patristic and medieval readings of apocalyptic texts, since then too the tendency was increasingly to level out the "soon" into a "not yet."[34] Rather, the point is that the academic exercises by which we now treat these texts should be complemented by spiritual ones.[35] This is to follow Tracy's insight that the prophetic, now the prophetic-apocalyptic, must always correlate with some form of the mystical, or Gutiérrez's insight that perhaps today we stand in greater need of a deeper *spirituality* of liberation than we do of more *theology* of liberation. The question then becomes, What sort of spirituality? What spiritual exercises would constitute a sort of modern *lectio divina* oriented by the option for the poor and adequate to the task of reaching the corresponding tropological, moral, and anagogical sense of the apocalyptic texts?

In other writings Tracy has proposed the paradigm of the hidden-revealed God, articulated most powerfully in the work of Martin Luther but discernible as well, Tracy argues, in the work of modern figures as diverse as Rudolf Otto, Simone Weil, Walter Benjamin, and Gustavo Gutiérrez.[36] This is a theological tradition that finds a mystical correlate in a number of important medieval women mystics, including Angela of Foligno and Marguerite Porete, as well as in Meister Eckhart's disciple, Johannes Tauler, with whom Luther was familiar.[37] As suggestive as this proposal is, I propose a somewhat different path through the mystical tradition.

Let us consider instead the deliteralization that comes with the dark night into which, the mystical tradition insists, anyone will be drawn who follows a passionate love of God into this world, be it the contemplative who seeks God's presence in cosmos or interiority or the contemplative *in action* who seeks God's presence by participating in God's work in history.

There is no space here to give even a cursory overview of the history and elements of the mystical tradition that culminates in John of the Cross's famous descriptions of the dark night. Let me only make two related points about it. The first is that the dark night describes not so much a particular experience as a transformation of the person who undergoes it, a transformation that then, to be sure, will have some reverberation in the way he or she experiences self, world, and God.[38] Second, the tradition is grounded in a dialectic inherent to any way of formulating how one will encounter the presence of the Christian God in creation. Since God is its most radical source and ground of being, created being cannot but be transparent to that God. Thus God will be found in the world. Yet to the extent that God radically transcends the world, whatever can be found in the world is not God. Thus the world is not transparent to God. In the mystical tradition this has generally meant that the cataphatic moment that affirms the transparency of the world to God is always accompanied by the apophatic denial of that transparency. Put in somewhat more modern terms, the enlivening sense of presence to God will inevitably always include the painful night of absence. It is not that cataphasis gives way to the (allegedly) real way of experiencing and naming God in apophasis, for, as Michael Sells has pointed out, an apophatic claim, God is "not-x," is in its own way a statement about God that requires its own negating.[39] The two discursive strategies, and the modalities of encountering God that they articulate, are equally necessary. Affirmation and denial, constructed in tension with one another, open up the space within which the mystery of God can be disclosed, a disclosure that entails a transformation of the person that brings about a sharing in the divine life itself.

From here, let us move to the uncontroversial observation that liberation theologies emphasize action at least as much as, if not more than, contemplation as a way to union with God. What happens, then, if we take this basic structure of the contemplative mystical traditions and modulate it into the key of contemplation in action? Then what is at issue is whether or how people find a deep sense of God in the historical events and processes in which they are actively involved, precisely by virtue of that involvement. The foregoing analogy suggests that in one's work in history one will experience a deep sense of communion with God, who is laboring there as well. The spiritual tradition of contemplation in action has labored to identify and articulate this sense of communion. One advocate of such a union, Meister Eckhart, claims that the kind of union with God available in certain kinds of action in the world is superior even to that available in contemplative rapture.[40] Yet given not only the finitude of history but also the presence of sin in history there must, it would seem, also be a moment in which one will inevitably experience not God's hiddenness but the opacity of history to God. This dialectic of presence and absence can be traced in the Bible, particularly in the prophets. In apocalypticism one finds its intensification: a powerful affirmation of God's presence in history lacerated by sin, as history's always imminent, interrupting advent. This affirmation, however, if it is the affirmation of the presence of the biblical God (strictly transcendent to history) in a history realistically affirmed (finite and sinful), will, it would seem, require also an equally strong negation: God is *not* here, or, more terrifying, the God who *is here* so transcends us and our ways of being and acting in history that the "light" of this God's presence is like "darkness" to our reason (here, our practical reason, reason engaged in history).[41] This is an honest admission that God does not become subject to our rational notions of how one ought to act in history to achieve certain ends, that God continues to be the "absolute holy mystery," as Rahner put it, who is, as often as not, experienced in a "dark cloud" or a "night of injustice," as Gustavo Gutiérrez puts it with his insightful readings of John of the Cross and his provocative language of "the dark night of injustice."[42] This does not invalidate the positive discernment now of the imminence of God's irruption into our history, any more than in mystical theology the apophatic denials of the transparency of the created world to God delegitimate or replace the cataphatic affirmations. Both are necessary strategies for any adequate naming of God, whether that naming is rooted in contemplative vision or contemplative action.

This tack differs from the more speculative trajectory offered earlier of moving through the mutual interplay of the root Christological symbols into a Christology that relativizes the different emphases that each offers, including those offered by apocalyptic language, the goal being a speculative Christology. It is a strategy that makes sense and works for someone involved in the spiritual journey of contemplation in action. The controls are not the checks and balances of theological argument but the shaping of a spiritual itinerary by individual discernment, prayerful reading of Scripture, the means of grace, and the companionship of others on the journey. Of course, it involves grace. To be taken into the dark night is always a grace, as John of the Cross so eloquently insists. But alongside the "passive dark night" into which one is drawn by grace there is what John called the "active dark night," in which we dispose ourselves by practices and exercises of self-mortification, placing ourselves in such a way that we might be open for the grace when it is offered. For the transposition of this mystical theology into the tradition of contemplation in action, I would argue that this would mean that one disposes oneself, places oneself in the place of the poor, the marginalized, the victims.[43] It is when one's action in history most corresponds with the action of God, revealed in faith to be an action particularly on behalf of the poor, that one is most likely to experience a genuinely Christian form of contemplation in action, as opposed to a vague reenchantment of the world and one's work proposed by some North American advocates of a spirituality of everyday life, an option that threatens to become a spiritual halo on whatever particular work I happen to be engaged in.[44] In this regard, then, the option for the poor, a practice that demands great asceticism and self-mortification, especially for us, the comfortable, is itself a deliteralizing practice, a spiritual exercise, to the extent that it opens us to the grace of a dark night in which we hold together both the hopeful, apocalyptic imagery of God's active presence in history and the painful sense of God's hiddenness in a history filled with so many crosses.

THE OPTION FOR THE POOR AS A THEOLOGICAL PRINCIPLE

In the foregoing I have argued for the following claims, claims that are interlinked and support one another in a number of ways. First, a contextual theology is not any less a theology, talk about God that respects and draws on the resources of Scripture and tradition and also understands that, however much God discloses Godself in any particular social-historical context, God does not thereby cease being a mystery, indeed, the ultimate mystery of our existence, a fact that must be reflected in our namings of God. Second, looking at history and Christian faith from the perspective of the victims and the marginalized ones of history is an essential feature of any

Christian theology that pretends to "give an account of the hope that is in us" today. Third, such an option for the poor in Christian theology requires a recovery of Christianity's apocalyptic inheritance. Fourth, a recovery of those apocalyptic traditions that both is adequate to their scriptural roots and corresponds to the situation of the poor requires that one interpret them in terms of the symbol of Second Coming, not only as a negative, "not yet" corrective, but as a positive symbol of the in-breaking of the kingdom of God. Fifth, and finally, the sorts of deliteralizations that are necessary if this symbol is to enable a genuinely evangelical disclosure of the God of history can be carried out by a speculative interrelationship of the four root Christological symbols of Incarnation, Cross, Resurrection, and Second Coming from the perspective of the poor and by the spiritual practice of placing oneself actively on the side of the poor. Thus apocalypticism needs the option for the poor as much as the converse.

Of course, this is an ambitious complex of claims, and some have been warranted more or less by appeal to the authority of important modern theologians such as David Tracy, Johann Baptist Metz, Gustavo Gutiérrez, and Jon Sobrino, others with more substantive argument. No doubt more is needed. If nothing else, however, it shows that to make the option for the poor in Christian theology means to make certain fundamental decisions and appropriate certain fundamental parameters about how to talk about God. In other words, while the option for the poor is certainly an option with implications for Christian life both individually and corporately, as well as both politically and spiritually, it is also an option that belongs on the same level as other fundamental options in Christian theologies: opting for the dialectic of grace and freedom, for instance, or for understanding human beings as *simul justus et peccator* (simultaneously justified and accepted yet also sinful). Sobrino, once again, puts the nature of this challenge quite clearly:

> The New Testament contains what one might call *constellations,* components grouped around some central Christian concept in accordance with a logic in faith. Some of these seem to be accorded theologal status more easily than others (such as the elements of the Pauline constellation, though not, of course, exclusive to him: grace, Spirit, freedom, justification, hubris, and the like). The elements of the constellation surrounding the Kingdom—the poor, liberation, structural sin—are generally (with some exceptions) kept on the

ethical and spiritual levels but are not advanced to the theologal one. The "God who justifies sinners" has come to be a theologal and even a dogmatic statement; the "God who has compassion for the poor and the oppressed" does not generally reach this level. The "justification of sinners" has dogmatic roots; not so the "liberation of the poor." The "option for the poor" is qualified, questioned, even when it has not died the death of a thousand distinctions.[45]

No Christian theologian worthy of the name would think of developing any theological theme in a way that ignored the fundamental theological parameters that have arisen out of the long struggle to understand the dialectic between freedom and grace or faith and works, to name just two. These fundamental "constellations," as Sobrino calls them, first came to theological attention out of a need to respond to the needs of the church in a given age. Think, for instance, of Pelagius's and Augustine's concern to better understand the ascesis proper to the Christian life, or Martin Luther's attempt to respond to the epochal question of the late Middle Ages: How do we find a gracious God? Yet the reflection on these themes led to a rich harvest of reflection on Scripture and greater conceptual precision about how to name God and act in accordance with that naming. They thus have come to be a source of fundamental theological parameters that now have to be brought to any new theological research agenda, whether that of understanding the relationship between the new sciences and Christian faith, the relationship of Christian faith to political action in secular democracies, or the relationship of Christianity to the other great world religions. They have reached what Sobrino calls the "theologal level," providing fundamental markers for any authentic Christian approach to God, whether in speculation (theology) or in action (praxis, spirituality).

The challenge facing Christian theologians is to put the option for the poor on a similarly fundamental theologal level. This is not to say that it provides the only parameters constraining, but also enabling, the practice of Christian theology. Other constellations continue to be determinative. It does mean that the option for the poor will continue to be argued over, that there can and should be continual attempts to configure it anew in relationship to other fundamental elements of Christian theology. It means that just as it has taken centuries for the fruits of the high medieval discovery that faith builds on reason to fully emerge, we can expect that it will take generations to explore the nuances that the option for the poor adds to our understanding of God's saving self-disclosure in Jesus the Christ. It means that, like others, it may come to be taken for granted, as at times the fundamental scholastic axiom was, although, as Sobrino suggests, it is at least as difficult, if not more so, to keep in view as, say, the dialectic of sin and grace, of faith and works. Yet we might also expect that just as the latter re-exploded on the scene with a figure like Karl Barth when it was threatened with being forgotten by late-nineteenth-century liberal theology, this option too will continue to irritate and enrich us as long as there are those who suffer in history, making their ineluctable claim on us, and as long as human blindness and sinfulness lead us, to the extent that we surrender to them, to reject or elide that claim.

Notes

This essay began as a response to a paper presented by David Tracy at the conference "The Option for the Poor in Christian Theology" at the University of Notre Dame in November 2002. If while expanding it I have not fully recast it from its original genre of response, this is not only for reasons of utility but out of respect for a theological mentor who provided sure guidance for my own first exposure to political and liberation theology. Whether in agreement or respectful dissent, Tracy's theology has always been a worthy conversation partner for all theologies that attempt to make an option for the poor.

1. Gaspar Martinez, *Confronting the Mystery of God: Political, Liberation, and Public Theologies* (New York: Continuum, 2001).
2. See Gustavo Gutiérrez, *On Job: God-Talk and the Suffering of the Innocent* (Maryknoll, NY: Orbis Books, 1987). This theme was present even earlier. See his foundational work: *A Theology of Liberation: History, Politics, Salvation,* trans. Caridad Inga and John Eagleson, 15th anniversary ed., with a new introduction by the author (Maryknoll, NY: Orbis Books, 1988), 118 ff.
3. Walter Benjamin, "Theses on the Philosophy of History," in *Illuminations,* ed. Hannah Arendt (New York: Schocken Books, 1969), 256.
4. This is a development upon which Gutiérrez himself often remarks. See, for example, "Expanding the View," his introduction to *A Theology of Liberation,* xxi–xxv. See also Gustavo Gutiérrez, *The Truth Shall Make You Free: Confrontations* (Maryknoll, NY: Orbis Books, 1990), esp. 9–11. Gutiérrez is also clear, however, that in whatever way poverty's nature and roots are articulated, socioeconomic analysis continues to be essential if we are to *do anything* about it. See Gustavo

Gutiérrez, "The Task and Content of Liberation Theology," in *The Cambridge Companion to Liberation Theology,* ed. Christopher Rowland (Cambridge: Cambridge University Press, 1999), 19–38, esp. 24–27, 31.

5. See, for example, J. B. Metz, "Theology and the University" and "Religion and Politics on Modernity's Ground," both in *A Passion for God: The Mystical-Political Dimension of Christianity* (Mahwah, NJ: Paulist Press, 1998), 133–36 and 144 ff. respectively.

6. See J. B. Metz, "God: Against the Myth of the Eternity of Time," in *The End of Time? The Provocation of Talking about God,* ed. and trans. J. Matthew Ashley (New York: Paulist Press, 2004), 37 ff., originally published as *Ende der Zeit? Die Provokation der Rede von Gott,* ed. Tiemo Rainer Peters and Claus Urban (Mainz: Matthias-Grünewald, 1999).

7. See Johann-Baptist Metz, "Hope as Imminent Expectation or, The Struggle for Lost Time: Untimely Theses on Apocalyptic," in *Faith in History and Society* (New York: Seabury, 1981).

8. Metz, *Passion for God,* 47.

9. Ibid. For a more recent text, see Johann-Baptist Metz, "Time without a Finale," in Johann-Baptist Metz and Jürgen Moltmann, *Faith and the Future: Essays on Theology, Solidarity, and Modernity* (Maryknoll, NY: Orbis Books, 1995), 79–86.

10. Bloch was also instrumental in Metz's "discovery" of apocalyptic, as can be seen from Metz's dedication of the chapter in *Faith in History and Society* on apocalypticism to Bloch. For a brief overview of the concept of utopia and how it has been received in liberation theology, see José Sols Lucia, *La teología histórica de Ignacio Ellacuría* (Madrid: Trotta, 1999), 170–75.

11. See Gutiérrez, *Theology of Liberation.* On the whole, Gutiérrez adheres more closely to the prophetic strands of the Bible, without following them into their apocalyptic intensification (14–25).

12. Jon Sobrino, *Christ the Liberator: A View from the Victims,* trans. Paul Burns (Maryknoll, NY: Orbis Books, 2001), 41–44.

13. See Jon Sobrino, *Jesus the Liberator: A Historical-Theological View,* trans. Paul Burns and Francis McDonagh (Maryknoll, NY: Orbis Books, 1993), 93–95, 161–62, and "Introduction: Awakening from the Sleep of Inhumanity," in *The Principle of Mercy: Taking the Crucified People from the Cross,* trans. Dimas Planas (Maryknoll, NY: Orbis Books, 1994), 9.

14. See Jon Sobrino, "The Legacy of the Martyrs of the Central American University," in *Principle of Mercy,* 173–85, and "Spirituality and the Following of Jesus," in *Mysterium Liberationis: Fundamental Concepts of Liberation Theology,* ed. Jon Sobrino, S.J., and Ignacio Ellacuría, S.J. (Maryknoll, NY: Orbis Books, 1993), 694–96.

15. For another discussion of this shift on Tracy's part, see Scott Holland, "This Side of God: A Conversation with David Tracy," *Cross Currents* 52 (Spring 2002): 54–59.

16. David Tracy, *The Analogical Imagination: Christian Theology and the Culture of Pluralism* (New York: Crossroad, 1981), 264–86.

17. From an interview with Metz in Mary Maher, "Historicity and Christian Theology: Johannes Baptist Metz's Critique of Karl Rahner's Theology" (PhD diss., Catholic University of America, 1988), 12, 110.

18. From Rudolf Bultmann's 1941 essay "New Testament and Mythology," in *New Testament and Mythology and Other Basic Writings,* ed. and trans. Schubert M. Ogden (Philadelphia: Fortress Press, 1984), 5.

19. This "not yet" has always been at the heart of Tracy's understanding of apocalyptic's contribution; see, for example, *Analogical Imagination,* 266.

20. Thus, as Stephen O'Leary argues, apocalypticism functions "as a symbolic theodicy, a mythical and rhetorical solution to the problem of evil, and . . . its approach to this problem is accomplished through a discursive construction of temporality." Stephen D. O'Leary, *Arguing the Apocalypse: A Theory of Millennial Rhetoric* (New York: Oxford University Press, 1994), 14. Hence it is no accident that theodicy and apocalyptic are so closely interlinked in Metz's work. For Hanson on apocalypticism, see Paul Hanson, *The Dawn of Apocalyptic: The Historical and Sociological Roots of Jewish Apocalyptic Eschatology* (Philadelphia: Fortress Press, 1979).

21. Bernard McGinn, ed. and trans., *Visions of the End: Apocalyptic Traditions in the Middle Ages,* 2nd ed. (New York: Columbia University Press, 1998), 10. For the biblical background to apocalyptic, see John J. Collins, *The Apocalyptic Imagination: An Introduction to the Jewish Matrix of Christianity* (New York: Crossroad, 1984). For further historical material, see Bernard McGinn, ed. and trans., *Apocalyptic Spirituality* (Mahwah, NJ: Paulist Press, 1979), and Bernard McGinn, "Early Apocalypticism: The Ongoing Debate," and Marjorie Reeves, "The Development of Apocalyptic Thought: Medieval Attitudes," both in *The Apocalypse in English Renaissance Thought and Literature: Patterns, Antecedents, and Repercussions,* ed. C. A. Patrides and Joseph Wittreich (Ithaca: Cornell University Press, 1984), 2–39 and 40–72 respectively. A magisterial collection of articles covering all aspects of apocalypticism may be found in John J. Collins, Bernard McGinn, and Stephen Stein, eds., *The Encyclopedia of Apocalypticism,* 3 vols. (New York: Continuum, 1998).

22. See Metz, *Faith in History and Society,* 168 n. 15. It should also be noted, however, that prophetic eschatology is not without its own dangers, as can be seen, for example, from its secularized variant, the ideology of manifest destiny that underwrote European American expansion into the lands of indigenous peoples of North America, or in other "Whig histories of the present," which willingly concede that the fulfillment of history is "not yet" here but can still rest in the more or less smug satisfaction that "our way of life" is securely on the way to it.

23. Thus Sobrino's reading in his epilogue at the end of *Jesus the Liberator,* 273.

24. On the differences between Mark's and Matthew's appropriation of the broad constellation of apocalyptic motifs, see Richard A. Horsley, "The Kingdom of God and the Renewal of Israel: Synoptic Gospels, Jesus Movements, and Apocalypticism," in Collins, McGinn, and Stein, *Encyclopedia of Apocalypticism,* 1:323–39. Indeed, Horsley argues that "the *parousia*—popularly thought of as the 'second coming'—of Christ is really Matthew's construction, at least in the gospel literature" (335).

25. For a discussion of the specificity of the way liberation theology appropriates the theme of the kingdom of God, see Sobrino, *Jesus the Liberator,* 105–34. While Sobrino does not connect the concept explicitly with the symbol of Second Coming, he does define it in ways that clearly show the presence of an apocalyptic scenario: it is a *utopian* element that bears on history now "interruptively," "liberatively" (not "developmentally"); it exists in mortal conflict with an opposing historical force (which Sobrino calls the "antikingdom"); and it represents the hopes of those for whom present history holds the least in which to hope: the poor. For a justification of calling Sobrino's an "apocalyptic" approach to theology, see J. Matthew Ashley, "Apocalypticism in Political and Liberation Theology: Toward an Historical *Docta Ignorantia,*" *Horizons: The Journal of the College Theology Society* 27 (Spring 2000): 28–31.

26. Sobrino, *Jesus the Liberator,* 229.

27. Sobrino, *Christ the Liberator,* 41.

28. Sobrino likes to express this using a play on words: the authentic way to *respond* to the God so marvelously present in the loving act of a real incarnation that leads to the cross is to *correspond* to that God by recapitulating that kind of incarnation in our own lives. He finds a primary scriptural warrant for this in the Johannine tradition, particularly in 1 John 4: see *Jesus the Liberator,* 157 ff., 165–67. "Corresponding to God" is also how he understand "orthopraxis" (190).

29. Sobrino, *Jesus the Liberator,* 244 ff.

30. Sobrino, *Christ the Liberator,* 74–78. This is where the narrative of Luke-Acts, with its portrayal of the post-Resurrection community in Acts, is a decisive "corrective" to the more apocalyptic Marcan account—although at that point Paul's warnings to the Corinthians not to forget the cross becomes equally important.

31. This is, I think, one way of putting the gratuitousness that, on Gutiérrez's reading of Job, is the final and only adequate basis on which to labor on behalf of faith and for justice in history. The sense that one's journey in history, even though full of darkness and suffering, is still a journey in which history "gives more of itself," and the sense that one cannot stop because one feels oneself being led, being carried, is for Sobrino the sense and sensibility for grace that enables one to give a name to the mystery of existence and call it *Abba* (*Christ the Liberator,* 339).

32. See Tracy, *Analogical Imagination,* 281–87. Tracy cites the Johannine and Pauline corpuses as the classic New Testament instantiations of this natural successor to symbolic thought, also listing Hebrews and Revelation.

33. I have developed this argument in somewhat greater length in Ashley, "Apocalypticism," 36–43.

34. See Reeves, "Development of Apocalyptic Thought."

35. Understanding "spiritual exercises" in the sense that they are presented in Pierre Hadot, "Spiritual Exercises," in *Philosophy as a Way of Life* (Oxford: Blackwell, 1995), 81–125.

36. See, for example, David Tracy, "The Hidden God: The Divine Other of Liberation," *Cross Currents* 46 (Spring 1996): 5–16.

37. See Bernard McGinn, "*Vere tu es Deus absconditus*: The Hidden God in Luther and Some Mystics," in *Silence and the Word: Negative Theology and Incarnation*, ed. Oliver Davies and Denys Turner (Cambridge: Cambridge University Press, 2002), 94–114.

38. This is why the "experiences" are not self-validating. One must look at the broader transformation of the person of which they are a part to judge whether they are a part of a genuine spiritual ascent into God or a product of self-delusion, or even a temptation from the devil. For John of the Cross, the key is whether the person is set free to love. This principle has clear implications for a liberation spirituality.

39. See Michael Sells, *Mystical Languages of Unsaying* (Chicago: University of Chicago Press, 1994), 2 ff. See also Denys Turner, *The Darkness of God: Negativity in Christian Mysticism* (Cambridge: Cambridge University Press, 1995).

40. In his sermons on Martha and Mary (Luke 10:38–42): Sermon 2, in *Meister Eckhart: The Essential Sermons, Commentaries, Treatises and Defenses*, ed. and trans. Edmund College and Bernard McGinn (New York: Paulist Press, 1981), 177–81, and Sermon 86, in *Meister Eckhart: Teacher and Preacher*, ed. Bernard McGinn (New York: Paulist Press, 1986), 338–45. For an incisive and nuanced commentary, see Amy Hollywood, "Preaching as Social Practice in Meister Eckhart," in *Mysticism and Social Transformation*, ed. Janet Ruffing (Syracuse: Syracuse University Press), 76–90.

41. Thus the point that Tracy follows, with the "hiddenness" to which Martin Luther alluded at times. See Tracy, "Hidden God," 8–13.

42. See Gustavo Gutiérrez, *We Drink from Our Own Wells: The Spiritual Journey of a People*, trans. Matthew J. O'Connell with a foreword by Henri Nouwen (Maryknoll, NY: Orbis Books, 1984), 83–89, 129–31.

43. *Place* here refers not only or even primarily to geographical location but to the hermeneutical situation that influences one's thought and particularly one's action. See Jon Sobrino, "Theology in a Suffering World: Theology as *Intellectus Amoris*," in *Principle of Mercy*, 27–46, esp. 30–33.

44. For a further discussion, see J. Matthew Ashley, "La contemplación en la acción de la justicia: La contribución de Ignacio Ellacuría a la espiritualidad cristiana," *Revista Latinoamericana de Teología* 51 (September/December 2000): 211–32, and "Contemplation in Prophetic Action: Oscar Romero's Challenge to Spirituality in North America," *Christian Spirituality Bulletin* 8 (Spring/Summer 2000): 6–13.

45. Sobrino, *Christ the Liberator*, 336.

Part Five

POVERTY, CULTURE,
AND COMMUNITY

Chapter 8

CULTURE, THE OPTION FOR THE POOR, AND LIBERATION

VIRGILIO ELIZONDO

All theology is socially and culturally conditioned. There is no culturally unconditioned thought. Hence I begin this presentation with a brief introduction of myself. I am a Mexican American, born and raised in the Mexican section of San Antonio, Texas, during the times when racial and ethnic segregation and degradation were not questioned. Being a white Protestant appeared to be the only way of being a true, a good, and a beautiful human being. All others were considered to be inferior, untrustworthy, and, at best, less than beautiful. The legal system enforced this racist, ethnic superiority, the educational system shaped it, religion legitimized it, and the media promulgated it. By the very fact of being conceived and born, one was either superior or inferior, fully human or of a lesser human group. No matter how much education or wealth one might obtain, one continued to be a poor outcast by reason of conception and birth. Theologically speaking, this was the sin of the world and the blindness of humanity: the inability to see and appreciate the divine image in each and every human being regardless of color, language, class, or ethnicity.

157

TYPES OF POVERTY

I begin by looking a bit into the ambiguity and complexity of poverty. At the basis of all the ambiguities and complexities, poverty means the lack of something. It means not having what one needs. It means not having the basic necessities of life, such as shelter, food, drink, clothing, a space of belonging, and a space of freedom. As a pastor I deal with these different aspects of poverty every day. Certainly the material, economic poverty that many people endure is the most devastating. Frequently I deal with people who do not have money to buy food for their children, and they go to bed hearing them cry because they are hungry; others do not have money for medicine, or the dental work or health care they need, and so forth. Prolonged material poverty leads to disease, weakness, underdevelopment, and early death. Beyond the physical problems, it gives rise to other forms of poverty that are equally destructive of the human spirit.[1]

Psychological poverty is one of the first consequences of material poverty. Because of the dehumanizing circumstances of material poverty, many poor people develop a very low self-image; frequently, they develop incredible inferiority complexes and simply feel that they are less than others in various ways. Since society and especially the media portray the ideal human being as one who has plenty of money, is well dressed, lives in a fancy home, drives a luxury car, and has a perfectly sculpted body, this is the normative model of a good and beautiful human being; the people who do not meet these criteria often feel they are ugly, undignified, and worthless. Consequently, they experience a very low and even negative self-esteem. This is a horrible wound to one's basic humanity, and it affects every level of their behavior.

I also deal with people who are suffering from spiritual poverty because life has no meaning for them. While this type of poverty can be found among all social classes and ethnicities, it is especially prevalent among people who are very successful in the eyes of the world but who, when they reach the top, discover that life becomes meaningless and that their climb to the summit reached by the ladder of upward mobility seems to have no ultimate value or satisfaction.

A few years ago I had a chance to have a very engaging conversation with the Latino pop singer Ricky Martin and found a spiritual depth in him I would not have suspected from his music. Today, most people do not know that Ricky Martin is very personally engaged in working with the discarded street children in India. He said that the more he climbed to the top, the more empty and meaningless his life became. Thanks to a friend, he got engaged working with the orphans and homeless children in Calcutta, and now that is where he spends most of his time. I asked him, "Why don't you do it here?" He laughed and said: "I couldn't do it here. I would be mobbed by fans, but there I am simply a worker. Now my life has meaning—now my life has meaning working with the poorest of the poor and working in an orphanage."

Yet it is not only the rich and successful who suffer from spiritual poverty. Without faith in a greater power, without a sense of transcendence, without a sense of direction or purpose, life can become quite empty, as it does for many people of all ages and backgrounds. I find this type of poverty especially present among young people who fall prey to current fascinations with gadgets, clothing, bodybuilding, the need for constant entertainment, and other externals. I find spiritual poverty as well among young adults whose only ambition is to climb the corporate ladder; I find it among persons whose whole life seems to be limited to superficial, large, and impersonal social gatherings. The lack of meaning and ultimate purpose is one of the great sources of spiritual poverty in many individuals, especially in the developed countries. The modern need for tranquilizers, counselors, and psychiatrists reveals a deeper sickness below the surface.[2] Many have so much materially, yet they experience incredible emptiness that no amount of material goods can satisfy.

There is yet another type of poverty that is deeper and more permanent: existential poverty. To me this is probably the deepest level of poverty and the most destructive. This kind of poverty has nothing to do with material possessions or meaninglessness. It has more to do with the very reality of who people are, where they were born, the color of their skin, the shape of their body, the language they speak, the ethnicity that radiates through every fiber of their being. Maybe people can work themselves out of material poverty, maybe they can discover meaning in life, but people cannot fundamentally change who they are biologically and culturally. I would like to call this existential poverty "cultural poverty," not because any one culture is inferior or poor by nature but because it has been designated as such by the dominant culture in power. Because of who one is, one is labeled as inferior and undignified by the dominant society.[3]

The dominant culture labels others as inferior in many ways: by popular literature, economics, laws, and even brute force. Until very recent times in the United States, the dominant culture—that is, the male white Anglo-Saxon Protestant (WASP)—labeled all those who were not male WASPs as different and inferior simply because they were female, black, Latino, Asian, mestizo/hybrid, Arab, Jew, and others. No matter how much individuals of these ethnic backgrounds succeeded economically, educationally, and professionally, the dominant culture by and large still considered them inferior others, who were different and of a lesser humanity. This discrimination has a way of branding people in the deepest recesses of their being. People end up living with a superimposed identity that penetrates to the depths of their soul and conditions much of their behavior. I call this the great sin of the world: the tendency of the dominant and powerful ethnicities to label others as inferior, uncivilized, backward, unworthy, and undignified and to treat them as such. White Western civilization, for the most part, has championed this type of discriminatory treatment. Since the end of the 1400s, the conquering and colonizing enterprise of Europe and the rise to power of white European immigrants in the Americas, South Africa, Australia, and New Zealand have promoted such biased practices. Not only did these immigrants prosper after stealing lands from native peoples, but they instituted slavery and other legal structures of injustice to protect their own selfish interests. In this conceptualization of reality, only white European males qualified as fully human, decent, dignified, and worthy of trust and respect.[4]

Every culture formulates a normative image of what it means to be human. Basically it involves three components: Who is a true human being? Who is a good human being? Who is a beautiful human being? These three work within us when we meet another person and spontaneously judge ourselves in relation to the other and the other in relation to us. The normative images we have interiorized become so deeply engrained within our subconscious that they furnish the lens through which we see ourselves and others. In other words, our interiorized frame of reference for the true, the good, and the beautiful shapes how we understand what it means to be human, superhuman, or subhuman.

Cultural poverty is the self-depreciation and lack of self-esteem of the people of a subjugated and dominated human group. It reaches into the very soul of those who have to live according to the normative imagery, definitions, and values of others. Because culture is the natural way of being human, one's culture is the place where one feels at home, where one does not have to explain to anyone who one is or why one speaks the way one does.[5] Within one's own culture, all the ordinary things of life such as language, customs, values, food, dress, and religious expression appear quite natural. One may be rich or poor, but at least one knows that one belongs. And in reality no one culture is superior or inferior to other cultures; all cultures are simply particular expressions of being human.

THE ENCOUNTER OF CULTURES

In the encounter of cultures we begin to become aware of cultural difference. In my own culture things are simply the way they are. Some people may like aspects of my culture and others may not; to me they are the ordinary way of being in the world. My culture not only appears natural to me but appears to be nature itself. Ordinary behavior within each person's cultural frame of reference appears quite natural. But in the encounter with other cultures, just as in the encounter with another person, I begin to become aware of differences. This can lead to a beautiful interchange of ideas, values, customs, foods, music, art, and religious expression. Ideally it is an enriching encounter of equals, an encounter of friends that will better each other's lives.

Unfortunately, throughout history the encounter of cultures has been more conflictual than amicable. At times cultural clashes have had brutal consequences. This was certainly the case in the great encounter or clash beginning in 1492, when the Spaniards arrived on the shores of what is today Mexico. In its wake, the great, white, conquering and colonizing European powers subjugated cultures. As a result, people were no longer free to be themselves; they had to live, see, and evaluate themselves according to the imposed norms of the dominant, European culture.[6]

More often than not, when one culture dominates another, it imposes itself by military force and legitimizes itself by its religion. Those belonging to the dominant culture see themselves as agents of civilization and sometimes even perceive their actions as a call from God. In doing so, they set themselves up as the standard of what it means to be created in the image and likeness of God, and it is they who define who is true, good, and beautiful. When this happens, a dominant culture becomes an idol to itself, and the nation begins to make God into its own image and likeness. Religion often further manipulates and justifies the ways of the powerful, which causes the oppression and exploitation of all others. As a result, the dominant European culture virtually eliminated native populations they looked upon as heathens and enslaved others, especially Africans, simply because they defined these people, who were poorer and weaker, as inferior to white people.

Europeans, who saw themselves as the new Israelites, justified the elimination of Native Americans in North America because they looked upon them as the "heathen Canaanites" who did not have a right to the land. Like the Canaanites in the time of Joshua, they were to be wiped out so that the land could be cleared for God's chosen people. Spain and Portugal legitimized the conquest of Latin America because the natives needed to be civilized and evangelized. They were assigned to harsh work for brutal European masters so they could be taken care of, but they had to pay for being taken care of by their death-bearing labor. Africans were brought in to work as slaves, and Asians were brought in to do the work no one else wanted to do. Enslavement of the Africans was justified biblically because the white Christians considered them to be the descendants of Shem, who had been cursed by God to be the slave of his brothers. All this exploitation and brutality was easily justified by white European peoples' idolatry of their own race, with their strict laws of segregation, which preserved the status quo and kept the lesser ones in their place.[7] After all, in their view, God had made white Anglo-Saxons a superior people to rule over all others, and they had the coercive might to impose this mentality upon all others.

This type of unequal encounter continues today in many ways, but especially in the relationship of the dominant society to working immigrants, who are brought in because their work is needed but who are not wanted as human beings; they are used for the prosperity of the country but are not appreciated or respected for who they are. They are brought in only because cheap labor is necessary.

SUBJUGATED CULTURES

What does consistent and brutal subjugation do to the soul? What happens to the minds of people when they experience these unequal encounters and experience themselves as colonized, enslaved, ridiculed, and then have to suffer in silence because there is no possibility of redress? What happens to people when they cannot be themselves but always have to hide themselves and define themselves in terms of the dominant people who have set a new normative image of what it means to be a true, good, and beautiful human being?

Many years ago I found a very fascinating book, *The Colonizer and the Colonized,* written by a Tunisian-born French scholar named Albert Memmi.[8] Though it was published many years ago, its content is still very relevant today. As a native Indian under British colonial rule, Memmi was well educated, even better than many other British people, yet as an Indian he knew that he would never be allowed into the inner circles of British life. He knew that no matter what he accomplished he would never be an equal. He would never fully belong. The book is a profound examination of what this type of segregation and marginalization does to the soul.

In a more contemporary vein, my friend and colleague Daniel Groody wrote a powerful book called *Border of Death, Valley of Life,*[9] which presents the brokenness of undocumented immigrants from Mexico to the United States. He describes how these immigrants are unwanted and ridiculed in Mexico because they are the poorest of the poor. Those who have darker skin because of their indigenous roots are exploited, degraded, and ridiculed for their culture and treated as inferior human beings. Then, because of devastating poverty, they have to leave their home country, where they are already considered inferior and treated harshly, and come to a country that values them only for cheap labor. Groody's book on today's immigrants, and my own books *Galilean Journey*[10] and *The Future Is Mestizo*[11] on Mexican Americans, look at the wounds that marginalized people experience and how such subjugation has affected the collective psyche of a people.

Cultural subjugation is destructive of the human spirit in many ways, and it condemns people to see themselves and everything about themselves as inferior in capacity, beauty, and value. Their language, their customs, their dress, their rituals, in fact everything about their way of life is made to seem inferior and backward, savage and uncivilized, pagan and superstitious. This is cultural poverty—not that the culture is lacking in itself but that it is considered lacking by those in power. The people of a subjugated culture can never appreciate themselves simply as they are; instead, they are forced by the dominant society to see, value, and judge themselves according to the normative image of what it means to be human. The dominant society regulates and imposes the basic norm of what it means to be good, true, and beautiful.

This dynamic of inequality and subjugation among ethnic peoples causes a profound sense of alienation, confusion, meaninglessness, and shame. Of course, there are always exceptions; some will always find ways of resisting and maintaining a healthy self-image in spite of all the assaults. Yet the ordinary person will struggle with the basic question: What is really good? What is really true? What is really beautiful? There is a confusion today especially among the young people in these ethnic groups who struggle to overcome the stereotypes imposed on them by the dominant and powerful of society. They come to feel a sense of meaninglessness because the previous system of meanings and symbols does not have any relevance or meaning to them. There is a deep feeling that many traditions of the past do not make sense anymore, and this results in alcoholism and other problems, as has been the case with many Native Americans.

The most injurious crime of the conquest of Latin America, and there were many horrible things about it, was that the white European *conquistadores* imposed a deep sense of shame of being an *indio,* mestizo, mulatto. Worst of all, they made us ashamed of our native mothers. Many today still experience shame regarding their skin color, their way of life, their way of being, their way of dress, their way of speaking, and their ways of worship. Such rejection brands the soul, in a way worse and more permanent than a branding of the master's mark with a hot iron on the face.

No matter how much people from these mestizo and native groups advance economically or politically, many still regard themselves as socially inferior and inadequate. Even Spanish-language television confirms these stereotypes by negative portrayals of dark-skinned Latin Americans, *indios,* and other persons of color. As a result, many of these people live with an enduring pain that they are never quite fully accepted, respected, or valued.

In the midst of all these dehumanizing social structures, one place where people often can be themselves is in their native places of worship. The black churches of the United States and some Hispanic parish churches, like San Fernando in San Antonio and La Placita in Los Angeles, and regional shrines such as San Juan de los Lagos in South Texas, have played a crucial role in subverting social discrimination. Popular Latin American expressions of faith, usually not appreciated either by the church or by theologians, are the language of affirmation and resistance. In places of worship, people do not have to explain to anyone who they are, or why they pray the way they pray, or why they sing the way they sing.

So popular religious shrines and places are sacred spaces. They are sacred because there the people can experience in their innermost selves that they are what Scripture says: created in the image and likeness of God. In these places they experience the ultimate truth of God and themselves. No one has to explain this experience of God to them because they experience it. They are free to be themselves, so they can celebrate, and indeed they do celebrate.

Therefore these places of popular religion are places of defiance in the face of the mainline or dominant culture. They are places of resistance because people realize that the soul is the one thing that cannot be taken away from them. In these places people celebrate because in spite of everything they are survivors. Such popular religious celebrations are the exterior expressions of their innermost being. The people are there to rise above all the insults and injustices and to celebrate life as they know it. In the celebration people reveal the truth about themselves to themselves in spite of what the dominant society might say about the subjugated cultures. The place of worship is a place of joyful and confident survival, especially in the baptism of infants and first communions of the young. It is a place of survival because the cultures of the poor have babies. The rich cultures do not have babies. For the rich, babies appear to be a burden and a hindrance to pleasure, but for the poor and the struggling they are a welcome blessing, an assurance that life will continue. The old colonizing peoples of Europe show zero or negative population growth, but the babies of the poor are renewing the earth.

Italy is a good example of what is happening in Europe and much of white America. It is a very Catholic country, yet it has negative population growth; more people are dying than are being born. Most of Europe, in fact, has negative population growth, except among the new immigrant populations that are now arriving. When I go to a rich parish in San Antonio, I see hardly any babies around; but I remember that when I was at the cathedral in San Antonio, a cathedral of the poor, frequently there were at least fifty, sixty, or seventy babies crying in symphony. The poor have babies and therefore they will survive.

The Latino population in the United States is a young population, and it is growing rapidly. As we grow in numbers, our responsibility to the whole of society increases. What can be done? What is the response of the subjugated Latino culture? Is it to take our turn in subjugating others? Is it to form new ethnic ghettos? Is it to simply begin forgetting who we are and to become the dominant other—in other words, to commit ethnic suicide? Some people believe this is the way forward, to do what other immigrant groups have done. Will there be some sort of ethnic cleansing? There are many tensions as we search for a new paradigm of how subjugated cultures can find liberation and be the agents of new life not just for themselves but for others as well.

LIBERATION

Of the many options available to subjugated peoples, one of the most compelling can be found in Jesus of Galilee, not so much the Christ of theologians or ecclesial dogmas as the Jesus of the Gospels. The more we Latinos read the Gospels in their own sociocultural context and out of our own social position, the more we discover not only our authentic identity but our mission in the world today. The good news is this: subjugated cultures have a specific, salvific mission in today's world. Jesus was a marginal peasant from the Roman colony of Galilee.[12] He grew up in a small town where I am sure rumors circulated about his mysterious origins, such as who his father was, and he probably struggled not so much with who he was as with who people said he was.

Jesus came out of this context and had an incredible religious experience when he was baptized by John. The baptism of John called for repentance—that is, a change of mind and heart. We do not know what went on before that moment in the life of Jesus. But we do know that with the baptism there was a radical change. He converted from what seems to have been a life of passive acceptance to one of active and visionary activism. All of a sudden he moved from a hidden life to a very public, dynamic, and confrontational life. He began to live and proclaim something beautifully new and exciting but not easily appreciated by everyone. He announced the reign of God, the reign of unlimited forgiveness, compassion, and love that would be the basis of the new human fellowship of radical equality. Out of this reign of God Jesus passed from the reality of a subjugated, dominated, colonized, and segregated culture, with its deep and profound sense of shame, to a powerful sense of self-acceptance, self-assurance, and self-worth. He found his self-assurance in the intimate communion with the one who ultimately counts, *Abba . . . Papacito Dios.*

It was God the Father, the only one who ultimately counts, who recognized him not as trash, not as inferior, not as impure, not as possibly illegitimate, but as his beloved child. The power of being able to recognize one's self as a beloved child, without condition, is one of the most energizing and satisfying experiences any human being can have. It is a healing and liberating experience at the deepest level of existence. It was this experience of the unconditional love of God that allowed Jesus to say, "I AM," regardless of what others thought and said of him. While there are various theological interpretations of Jesus's "I am" statements, I think that such acceptance of love that allows me to claim who I am with grateful pride is the deepest form of liberation one can experience. It frees one from having to explain oneself to anyone, from hiding, and from playing games. One embraces the truth that "I am," *Gracias a Dios,* (thanks be to God). The French have another way of saying it: "If you don't like me, you've got problems!"

Jesus also moved from a culture of retaliation and vengeance to a culture of forgiveness. Only in the forgiveness of the ones who have hurt a person can one find the inner healing and liberation that enables one to be his or her true self. Jesus recognized that forgiveness is the only way to inner freedom.[13] Without forgiveness we will always be dominated, and in many ways controlled, by the very ones who have hurt us.

Jesus went from accepting the status quo to revealing the idols of the dominant society. This got him in trouble with the authorities who profited from the status quo. He revealed how things that were good at one time had become so absolutized that they had become idols and thus enslaved rather than protected the people. I think it is the task of the subjugated minorities to reveal the idols of the dominant society as a service so that they too may be liberated from the idols that demand victims to sustain their style of living: low wages, shady business deals, cheating in contracts, legal tax evasion by the wealthy, especially the large corporations, and so on. The high standards of living of the dominant culture cannot continue without multiple sacrificial victims. Their profits depend on the blood and sweat of poor and defenseless people and nations.

Jesus went from a life that had many ways of segregating people to a new fellowship inclusive of everyone. The minorities today are not looking to simply blend into the system that has previously kept them out. We are searching for a new and more inclusive society where no one will have to suffer the pains of separation that discriminated cultures have suffered in the past. The most beautiful image and powerful activity of Jesus was that of inclusive table fellowship. All the outcasts, all those who had been kept out by the pure and dignified of the dominant society, were now invited to enjoy the table. The irony of the table fellowship of Jesus is that not because anyone is excluded but precisely because everyone is now invited some will not want to come. The joy of the new experience becomes generative of a new movement for humanity.

Jesus moved from the culture of sacrificing others for one's own gain to a new culture of sacrificing self for the sake of others. This new culture would become known as Christianity. It is important to see the sacrifice of the cross not as the one sacrifice of Jesus but as the final moment in the sacrificial process of an entire lifetime, a life that refused to victimize anyone. Jesus sacrificed himself in many ways to redeem and rehabilitate the victims of the world. He was the victim who did not become a victimizer. He always offered something new and surprising. He went from being a victim to being a liberator, a generator of new life. Like Jesus, out of our own suffering today we are called to usher in something new so that all of us together, in new partnerships, may have a better life. Out of the wounds and pains of cultural poverty, new cultures will emerge, and that will be a gift not only to the poor but to all of humanity.

NOTES

1. Gustavo Gutiérrez, *A Theology of Liberation* (Maryknoll, NY: Orbis Books, 1988).

2. Virgilio Elizondo, *God of Incredible Surprises: Jesus of Galilee* (Lanham, MD: Rowman and Littlefield, 2003).

3. Virgilio Elizondo, *Christianity and Culture* (San Antonio, TX: Mexican American Cultural Center, 1999).

4. Robert Ricard, *The Spiritual Conquest of Mexico* (Los Angeles: University of California Press, 1966).

5. Elizondo, *Christianity and Culture,* 18.

6. Ricard, *Spiritual Conquest of Mexico,* 33–35.

7. René Laurentin, *Liberation, Development and Salvation* (Maryknoll, NY: Orbis Books, 1972).

8. Albert Memmi, *The Colonizer and the Colonized* (Boston: Beacon Press, 1991).

9. Daniel Groody, *Border of Death, Valley of Life* (Lanham, MD: Rowman and Littlefield, 2002).

10. Virgilio Elizondo, *Galilean Journey: The Mexican American Promise* (Maryknoll, NY: Orbis Books, 2000).

11. Virgilio Elizondo, *The Future Is Mestizo: Life Where Cultures Meet* (Boulder: University Press of Colorado, 2000).

12. Elizondo, *God of Incredible Surprises,* 25.

13. Ibid., 61–62.

Chapter 9

THE SPIRITUALITY OF SMALL CHRISTIAN COMMUNITIES AROUND THE GLOBE

PATRICK A. KALILOMBE

In this essay I offer some reflections on the way the project of basing the church's life and mission on Small Christian Communities (SCCs) is currently being pursued in Malawi, Africa. It is nearly thirty years since this project was officially adopted by the Catholic dioceses in the Association of Member Episcopal Conferences in Eastern Africa (AMECEA), of which the Episcopal Conference of Malawi is a member.[1] These reflections will bear on questions like the following: In the efforts to implement that project, are we moving in the direction envisioned in those early years, or have we somehow lost the vision and are we moving in a different direction? Did the way the project was originally understood take sufficiently into account the important sociopolitical challenges implied in the task of community building? What are these challenges?

The pastoral project of building Christian communities in Malawi, like similar projects in the Catholic Church, is a logical consequence of the shift in ecclesiological thinking that was made by the Second Vatican Council.

By *ecclesiology* we mean a coherently structured understanding and practice about the church in answer to the questions: What is the church? What is the church for? What form should the church take to function as it should? In this sense, ecclesiology was certainly among the most important areas of theological thinking and practice profoundly affected by Vatican II's program of *aggiornamento* (renewal). The decisive document in this respect was the *Dogmatic Constitution on the Church* (*Lumen gentium*). Documents such as the *Pastoral Constitution on the Church in the Modern World* (*Gaudium et spes*) and the *Decree on the Mission Activity of the Church* (*Ad gentes*) also take up the topic. The decisive principle had already been laid out in the first documents issued by the council. The *Decree on the Apostolate of the Laity* (*Apostolicam actuositatem*) and the *Constitution on the Sacred Liturgy* (*Sacrosanctum concilium*) emphasized that laypeople were equally influential in the life of the church: "Mother church earnestly desires that all the faithful should be led to that full, conscious, and active participation in liturgical celebrations which is demanded by the very nature of the liturgy, and to which the Christian people, 'a chosen race, a royal priesthood, a holy nation, a redeemed people' (1 Pet. 2:9; cf. 2:4–5), have a right and obligation by reason of their baptism."[2]

THE SECOND VATICAN COUNCIL'S SHIFT IN ECCLESIOLOGY

Vatican II shifted the understanding of church away from the predominant model of the church as institution to that of the church as mystical communion, expressed as people of God and body of Christ.[3] The church is not to be seen exclusively, or even principally, as a hierarchically structured institution, in which the hierarchy alone is by right the fully active and responsible representative of Christ in teaching, sanctifying, and ruling, while the rest of the church is mainly passive and dependent. Rather, the church understands itself first and foremost as the one body together representing Christ as prophet, priest, and leader. Admittedly this body consists of diverse but complementary members, each with his or her own place and role, but all the members are to be fully active and co-responsible in fulfilling the common call to build up the life of the whole body and to accomplish its mission in the world. In doing this, they must observe the principle of subsidiarity, each member functioning in his or her proper place so that they all complement each other in the work. Such an ecclesiology was esteemed as important especially for what it does to the laity, who are the most numerous part of the church. It empowers them and enables them to accomplish their calling as the avant-garde in the mission of the church in the world. The Vatican Council's understanding of the church's mission, in fact, means being the sacrament of God's kingdom by being light, salt, and leaven in the world.

This ecclesiology was intended to serve the purpose of church renewal for the whole world. But how exactly and in what areas that renewal would take place depended on the concrete situations in the various parts of the world. Local churches were likely to exploit the various insights of the ecclesiology differently, depending on each one's needs and problems. For example, the Latin American churches, at their Second General Conference at Medellín in 1968, were preoccupied with "The Church in the Present-Day Transformation of Latin America." And it was with that preoccupation in mind that they sought light from Vatican II.[4] They had first to examine the church as it looked at that time, how it structured itself, and how it functioned. For this, they looked at the long history of the church in Latin America, knowing that the past helps to understand the present. To find out whether the situation was satisfactory, they asked themselves: What is the mission of the church? In the light of Vatican II, the church is meant to be an agent of evangelization, to proclaim the good news for contemporary society. What, then, was the situation of Latin America at that time? What were its problems and needs in relation to the coming of God's kingdom? And what kind of ecclesiology would best answer the situation? As a consequence of this study they found out the appropriateness of the council's ecclesiology of church as people of God. From here the Latin American Church resolved to develop its ecclesiology of basic Christian communities or basic ecclesial communities (BECs).

THE ORIGINAL VISION OF SMALL CHRISTIAN COMMUNITIES IN EASTERN AFRICA

The pastoral program of SCCs in Malawi is part of a project of church renewal that was started on the wider level of East Africa in the 1970s. In December 1973, the focus of the conference of AMECEA[5] was "Planning for the Church in Eastern Africa in the 1980s."[6] Nearly a decade after the closing of the Second Vatican Council, AMECEA intended to examine what impact the council was making in the renewal of the African Church and how its message could plan for the church's future, especially in Eastern Africa. At this conference the building of SCCs became a major pastoral policy in the region. This entailed a major shift in ecclesiological emphasis: in the understanding of what the church is, what the church is for, and how the church should function in real life. So momentous was this decision that at the following plenary assemblies of 1976 and 1979, the study conferences concentrated on examining closely this priority of building small Christian communities in Eastern Africa.[7] How did AMECEA conclude that basing the life and mission of the church on SCCs was such a crucial pastoral method? What was their vision of SCCs?

"A Living, Effective, and Self-Reliant Local Church"

The 1973 study conference formulated its recommendation in this way:

> We have to insist on building Church life and work on the basic Christian communities, in both rural and urban areas. Church life must be based on the communities in which everyday life and work take place; those basic manageable social groupings whose members can experience real inter-personal relationships and feel a sense of communal belonging, both in living and working. We believe that Christian communities at this level will be best suited to develop real intense vitality and to become effective witnesses in their natural environment.[8]

The leading idea was to form a church that was not just theoretically universal but at the same time also authentically local and self-reliant:

> While the Church of Christ is universal, it is a communion of small local Christian churches, communities of Christians rooted in their own society. From the Bible we learn that such local churches are born through apostolic and missionary preaching. But they are meant to grow so that with time they become firmly rooted in the life and culture of the people. Thus the Church, like Christ himself, becomes incarnated in the life of the people. It is led by local people, meets and answers local needs and problems, and finds within itself the resources needed for its life mission. We are convinced that

in these countries of Eastern Africa it is time for the Church to be-come really local, that is: self-ministering, self-propagating and self-supporting.[9]

The Result of a Social Analysis of Church and Society

The study conference used social analysis, in line with the recommenda-tions of the Holy See itself. As Pope Paul VI stated, "It is up to Christian communities to analyze with objectivity the situation which is proper to their own country, to shed on it the light of the Gospel's unalterable words and to draw principles of reflections, norms of judgment, and directives of action from social teaching of the church."[10] The participants had indeed set out to analyze the situation in Eastern Africa on two levels: that of the church itself and that of society in general.

A Postmissionary Local Church

In the 1970s the Catholic Church in this region underwent a significant transition. Since its beginning, foreign missionaries had led its develop-ment, but now leadership was passing into the hands of local bishops and institutions. The dominant missionary aim and objective had been to im-plant, or transplant, the church—that is, to set up or reproduce in this part of Africa structures and processes similar to those in the old churches of Europe and America, under the assumption that these forms represented the universal church. Therefore the church, in what it was, did, and wanted to do, imitated what was going on in the churches abroad. This meant that the churches in Africa were not necessarily structured in accordance with the ways of local communities. As a result, they depended less on local expertise and resources than on outside direction and help. This depen-dence was risky. What would have happened if and when the resources from abroad dried up—for example, if missionary workers left and help from abroad was no longer available? Would the churches in Africa not collapse and die?

The main question pertained to how the church should actually func-tion. Should foreign leaders impose their vision on local members, mak-ing it difficult for local communities to run efficiently on their own? As an alternative, we hoped for a church that would structure itself according to the identity of the local members and that could accomplish its mission and program with the resources available to it. From Vatican II the study conference identified the ecclesiology of "people of God" and "body of Christ" as the model that could answer the needs of the Church of Africa. At the same time it recalled the famous missiological formula once proposed by people like Henry Venn and Rufus Anderson, that the aim of missionary work was to build up "self-governing, self-supporting and self-propagating/extending" local churches. Although that formula could not be taken up in all its original historical and ecclesiological implications, it did offer useful insights for the direction in which "de-missionized" young churches should go to offset the dangers of a crippling dependency. Even within the context of the one, holy, catholic, and apostolic communion, local churches needed to strive toward a measure of self-ministering, self-expansion, and self-support. In the concrete situation in which the young churches in Africa found themselves, success in building up such self-reliant ecclesial entities depended on what happened to the ordinary lay members who constituted the vast majority of the church.

De-colonized and Independent Young Nations in Crisis

The study conference later analyzed the wider social, economic, and political context of these East African churches. By 1973 nearly all the nations in the AMECEA region had obtained their national independence. Juridically, and in theory at least, they no longer depended on their former European masters. Now that these nations were freed from colonial domination, oppression, and exploitation, local leaders led and governed their own local communities. Independence meant the dawn of a new era, an opportunity for building up united and harmonious democratic nations of free citizens working hard together to improve themselves and to develop all areas of their common life. The people could look forward to a bright future of peace, dignity, progress, and prosperity. This independence enabled these new nations to embark with enthusiasm on projects of development aimed at improving the life of their people.

But after several years of independence, the study found that things were not getting any better. On the contrary, the situation seemed to be getting worse than during the days of colonialism. The so-called independence was not real. What had actually happened was a deepening of "neo-colonialism," whereby the young nations continued to be dependent on the rich and powerful nations of Europe and America. Domination and exploitation continued in more sophisticated and entrenched ways, including unequal trade patterns and grants and loans that turned into unbearable and impoverishing debts, causing insecurity, destruction, and movement of refugees, especially women and children.

Within the countries themselves there was much polarization among the people. With no peace and no security, there was little hope for genuine development; poverty tended to increase on a national level, but more palpably among the ordinary people. In many countries there was a breakdown in government and leadership. Instead of orderly and peaceful processes for the choice of leaders, there were often running conflicts between ethnic, religious, or regional factions that resulted in a succession of undemocratic governments, usually despotic, corrupt, and oppressive. Here and there the military staged a coup to overthrow a failing civil government with the promise to establish order and good governance. But in almost all such cases the military rule that followed turned out to be worse than the regimes they overthrew. For the people there was not much freedom, peace, or justice; the few people with power and privilege tended to oppress and exploit the majority.

The Church as an Evangelizing Community

From this social analysis the study conference proceeded with its project of planning for the church in Eastern Africa in the 1980s—that is, the appropriate church for the future. The first question was: What should be the mission of the church? The answer here was sought from reflection on the socioeconomic and political state of the newly independent nations. A second question was: What model of church would be in a position to accomplish that mission? Here reflection on the postmissionary local church suggested the answer.

The prevailing situation in the countries of Eastern Africa, as indeed in Africa as a whole, was one of crisis due to a breakdown of social order and sense of purpose. This breakdown took the shape of individual and group egoism, abuse of power and privileges, injustices, violence, and a generalized disregard of human rights. The division was in fact between a few people with power and privileges and the larger group of citizens. This minority systematically dominated, subjugated, disempowered, oppressed, and exploited the majority of the people, resulting in poverty, insecurity, and the loss of hope for any meaningful development. This was clearly contrary to the vision of God's kingdom that Christ had come to establish in the world. What, then, should be the task of Christ's kingdom in such a situation? What kind of good news should it proclaim? Surely not just the possibility of a future salvation for the souls of the people after they died! People needed a comprehensive message of hope even in this present life, the hope that life would change for the better, that they could achieve real freedom, joy, dignity, and power worthy of God's children. The church was being called to act as light, salt, and leaven in society.

What model of church could effectively proclaim that kind of message? How could the church become, in the words of Vatican II, the sacrament of God's kingdom? It should, as a visible community, mirror the wider society around it, precisely because it is made up of members who belong to that society. So rich and poor people, the powerful and the powerless, the young and the old, men and women, and members belonging to different families, ethnic groups, occupations, political parties, and so on should be found within the church. The faith of the community is special: they believe they have been gathered together by God so that they may form the body of Christ, a gathered community that lives by the life of Christ himself and is commissioned to continue his work on earth. This was the vision of SCCs as proposed by the AMECEA conferences. The universal church should be rendered present to the world through such local communities inserted into the wider context of their society.

Twenty-five Years Later: How Are the Small Christian Communities Doing?

When I returned to Malawi in 1998, I was understandably curious to know how this project of building SCCs was doing in the country. At the time of my departure in 1976, the project seemed to be threatened. Dr. H. K. Banda's government had shown signs of suspicion, claiming that the small communities might simply be part of an underground movement of political opposition.[11] Consequently, the church in Malawi had tended to be silent about its intention of pursuing this pastoral program. On the wider AMECEA level, it was clear that the movement of SCCs had been going forward.[12] SCCs had even been officially adopted for the whole of Africa through the Symposium of Episcopal Conferences in Africa and Madagascar (SECAM). Remarkable experiments were taking place in various countries, for example in Tanzania (with Bishop Mwoleka of Bukoba, in the context of President Nyerere's Ujamaa movement), Zaire (Cardinal Malula), Zambia, and other places. It turned out that in Malawi too the movement had not died down after all; in several dioceses there was much talk about forming SCCs designated by different local names.

What exactly was taking place? To what extent were these SCCs an implementation of the original vision of the 1973–76 study conferences? Had the vision changed? The answer could come only after properly conducted research and review. To a certain extent the 1979 AMECEA conference, held in Malawi, had been a review study. Coming three years after the 1976 conference, it was perhaps a bit too early. What developed in the subsequent years? I am not aware that such a review has been made for the Malawi situation after 1979. The best assessment I could find was conducted by Fr. Joe Healey in 1986 for the whole of the AMECEA region, in which he interviewed four Africans: "July 22, 1986 marked the tenth Anniversary of the AMECEA study conference that decided 'systematic formation of Small Christian Communities . . . should be the key pastoral priority in Eastern Africa in the years to come.' While there have been many descriptions and case studies of SCCs in the seven AMECEA countries, there has been relatively little evaluation (assessment, critique, analysis) especially by Africans themselves."[13]

In the report of that research we have reflections from four respondents: a priest, a religious sister, a layman, and a laywoman. They responded to several questions about the state of the SCC project: their successes and achievements, their problems, and their future directions. I find those reflections very enlightening and still useful as points of departure for further reflection on the present Malawian situation. Here they are presented according to my own agenda.

SOME POINTS OF REFLECTION

Has the Vision of SCCs Been Implemented?

The project of SCCs is still being pursued, but with little agreed-upon vision or method. Just as for the AMECEA region in 1986, so also in Malawi today, one of Healey's informants, Fr. Timira, has said: "Certainly there has been a lot of talk about the formation of SCCs, and many Christians have at least heard of it. There are places where parishes have been geographically divided into SCCs and where every Christian belongs to a SCC. There are other parishes where there are only a few model SCCs, and parishes where there are none at all."

The general impression is that, although there is still much talk and activity about the SCCs, the situation is by no means the same everywhere. Although the SCCs were agreed upon as "the key pastoral priority" in all of Malawi, some areas reveal that very little is being done. The affirmation about this being a key pastoral priority seems to exist only on paper, as a theoretical goal. In practice it has not affected overall diocesan pastoral planning. It appears as if it all depends on the local bishop's or the local pastor's personal ideas and feelings. In other words, there is no uniformity; different dioceses approach the forming of such communities in different ways. One person referred to a lack of a clear policy for the systemic formation of the SCCs. He called the process haphazard. This would seem to be true also for Malawi. What has happened, then, to all those clear descriptions and directives from AMECEA? Why have they not made their way down to the churches at the local level? We must look for the answer.

Are SCCs an Imposition from Above?

One of Healey's informants, Sr. Ishengoma, had this to say: "The idea of SCCs seems to be imposed from above and was left to individuals who were ready to cope with this new idea." This is a perceptive and challenging observation. If properly unwrapped and examined carefully, it might alert us to the reasons for the poor performance of efforts to implement the project of SCCs.

One of the main differences between the vigorous BECs of Latin American and the faltering SCCs of Africa is that in Africa the idea of communities has been imposed from above, while the BECs of Latin America arose from the poor people below. I once asked Fr. Jose Marins, the well-known promoter of BECs in Latin America, what he thought of this. In his answer he dismissed the naïve idea that the project of BECs could have sprung spontaneously from the laity at the base. "Such a revolutionary ecclesial praxis could only take shape with a prior indication from above and an ongoing enabling and direction from organic animators: bishops, pastors, community leaders, religious, educators, and so on." The critical factor was not that the idea came from above but that the ordinary people had not been effectively "conscientized" so that they understood and internalized the idea and made it their own. It is not enough to impose SCCs on the people without explaining to them the difference between this "new way of being church" and the way church has been presented and implemented in the past.

In many areas of Africa the project of SCCs had not been properly explained to the people. It had simply been imposed on them, just as so many other things had been in the past. The people did not understand what it was all about. Some wondered what the big idea was about being grouped into communities or what pastors intended to gain by it. As one respondent said, "Many laity do not yet see the SCCs as a felt need and thus do not own it themselves." How can this be explained?

Do Church Leaders Understand and Accept the SCCs and Their Implications?

One of the questions in Fr. Healey's inquiry was: In Eastern Africa do you feel that Catholics are really convinced about, and committed to, SCCs? Bishops? Priests? Religious? Laity? The respondents expressed their views in different ways, which are revealing:

- "Some priests and religious do not yet see the importance of SCCs. They find it difficult for the laity to plan and implement pastoral work without help from the top leaders in the Church. They lack faith in lay people." (Miss Kokunula)
- "The majority of priests do not want changes. . . . The parish priest says 'No' to a suggestion and that's final; a sister or a brother cannot say 'Yes.'" (Sr. Ishengoma)
- "Many bishops accept the pastoral priority, but few seem to have taken definite steps in terms of diocesan pastoral planning and implementation. The priests generally buy the idea but many are not sufficiently informed about SCCs—hence the general lack of commitment. A good number still operate in the old model of church style since they do not clearly know what to do. The laity lack sufficient education and conscientization. Many Christians respond favorably to the pastoral . . . but still suffer from the 'old model of church hang-up' of depending too much on the priests." (Fr. Timira)

These observations raise the question: Have the church leaders clearly grasped the ecclesiological implications of the new system of SCCs, and if so, have they accepted them and decided to include them in their pastoral planning and implementation? The respondents seem to doubt this. This implication of active and co-responsible participation by the laity seems to be the decisive point that either has not been fully appreciated or has not been fully accepted. In many places the clerically dominated church model is still the predominant one. Many leaders in the church apparently have not been able to make the shift toward a new model of the church. They still think and act in line with the previous clergy-centered model.

Consequently the system of SCCs is (mis)understood as just a new refinement of the system of dividing the parish into smaller sections so as to make the pastor's work better organized and more effective. The smallness of the groups, not really communities, into which the faithful are divided is mainly for the convenience of the pastors rather than for building community at the local level.[14]

As a matter of fact, many pastors probably received with enthusiasm the idea of SCCs where previously not much attention had been paid to the importance of organizing pastoral ministry through small groups within the parish. The pastors had been used to handling their apostolate as one homogeneous whole, which made the impact of their ministry rather weak. In such a situation, the idea of dividing the parish into manageable sectors was clearly going to make their work much more organized and effective. Understanding SCCs in this way, simply as a new system of organizing the pastor's field of operation, is certainly different from what the AMECEA project was all about. Still, for those areas, this was already a great step forward, and the church leaders seem to have settled for it.

Have the SCCs Improved the Life of the Church?

Even where the SCCs are being made to function within the traditional priest-centered church perspective, the respondents found that there was some remarkable improvement in the life of the church:

- "SCCs have helped parish priests in preparing the people for sacraments (baptism, marriage), solving family problems, visiting lax Catholics and finding other pastoral solutions. . . . Now there are Bible services where people read and reflect on the gospel, something which was not done before. Helping one another at work, in misfortunes, and celebrations has brought out the life of love among SCCs members and increased cooperation and mutual understanding." (Miss Kokunula)

- "Follow-up actions in terms of works of mercy like helping the poor, or consoling the sick and the bereaved and, in some places, concerted effort towards development, has brought about the contextualization of the gospel message." (Fr. Timira)
- "Personal awareness and involvement in the liturgy, sharing the word of God and applying it to everyday life have taken place." (Sr. Ishengoma)

One advantage is a greater involvement of the laity in the work of the pastor. The SCCs help the priest in preparing people for baptism and marriage; they are involved in dealing with marriage problems and in visiting the sick and the lax members. Within the communities, it is easier to organize and administer contributions from the people. It is also possible to promote collaboration and sharing even in works of mercy and community development. We see also that the SCCs have encouraged the involvement of laypeople in the liturgy, in Bible reading, and in prayer.

However, the respondents remark that these pastors see the SCCs mainly as apostolic groups, implying that the conception does not go much farther than that of a pastoral model. According to this idea, the SCCs are simply a new way of involving the faithful in the programs that emanate from the pastors and are organized and controlled by them. Even though this is a big step forward, it is not really what the AMECEA pastoral program intended to achieve. The program was about building SCCs as the basis for how the faithful would be "church" in their local environment of life and work. Is this the vision being realized?

Major Problems in the Implementation of the SCC Program

The respondents reported some problems that seem to reveal where the SCCs are failing to realize the original vision:

- "There has been over-supervision of the SCCs due to fears, albeit valid, of the dangers of the emergence of 'splinter groups' and 'schisms.' . . . Besides, there seems to be a general lack of participation by men in SCC meetings and other activities. . . . In urban areas, the poorer people show greater vigor and interest in SCCs than the rich. . . . There is still a lot of shyness in sharing the word of God . . . especially on the part of women. In rural areas, the 'timing' of SCC meetings is still a problem." (Fr. Timira)

- "Broken marriages: where husband and wife relationships are not good, it is very difficult to build real SCCs. . . . In some SCCs drinking is a major problem. . . . Superstitious beliefs are in conflict with the Christian way of life. In many cases superstitions have killed the Christian spirit." (Mr. Gichana)
- "Due to family problems there is poor attendance in SCC activities such as the weekly Bible services and community duties." (Miss Kokunula)
- "The idea small has not been understood. That is why we find *Vyama vya Kitume* [apostolic groups] in most parishes instead of SCCs." (Sr. Ishengoma)

While these remarks describe problems, they also put a finger on the main issues and challenges in the project of building the kind of communities that AMECEA was talking about. The pastors' oversupervision of the so-called SCCs is understandable. These pastors do not envision genuinely autonomous responsibility and initiative in determining how their local church will function. For them, such autonomy is dangerous; such communities might turn into sects or splinter groups unless the pastor kept firm control over them. What the laity are going to do, and how they are going to do it, should come from the pastor. He is the one to give all the directives and control what is going on. That is what is normally expected of the apostolic groups that the pastors are willing to form and that they call SCCs. But that is not exactly what the SCC project was about. These pastors will have to take up the challenge and accept a different type of relationship between priest and faithful. It should be a relationship in which the pastor is indeed the animator and the director but in which the faithful are equally active and co-responsible with him for the life and mission of the church.

Challenges in Building up Authentic Small Christian Communities

Building authentic communities is difficult. The objective of the SCC program is to build up members of local churches into alternative communities that are a true mirror of the wider society in which they are found but are at the same time a challenge to it. They are a mirror of society in that the church members come from and are normal participants in that wider society; they share in its culture, its activities and programs, its hopes and aspirations, its joys, its sorrows and problems. But at the same time they are called to be different because, as members of Christ's body, the church, their mission is to act as salt, light, and leaven within that society by striving to live by the tenets of God's kingdom. Through their insertion in society, they bring good news to their society by demonstrating a better way of life and inviting their brothers and sisters to follow in that transformation. That is the objective of forming Christian communities within their local environment.

The remarks made by the respondents reveal some of the typical problems in today's Malawian society. While "there seems to be a general lack of participation by men in SCC meetings," this is because the gender issue is indeed a problem in the society as a whole. The traditional separation of men and women in the assignment of roles and functions may have been a positive thing in the working of society in the past, but times are changing. Some forms of separation are today out of place since they serve as a tool for discriminating against, oppressing, or exploiting women. People tend to hide behind some cultural practices to assert and maintain the superiority of men over women and to find ways of keeping women under control. Thus there are roles and functions—leadership, for example—from which women are excluded even when they could fulfill them as well as or better than men. This pattern of behavior tends to be maintained even within the church. If indeed women tend to be more active in SCCs, one might suppose that this is simply because women are more religious than men. But is that explanation fully satisfactory? Could it not also be because some men hesitate to be part of organizations and activities where women might be in leadership positions? They feel uneasy if they relate and work together in the community without unnecessary distinctions between men and women, young and old.

A similar problem exists in present-day society in the relationship between big people and small people, rich and poor, those in high positions and those in humbler ones, the educated and the noneducated. Society is becoming more and more differentiated along lines of status, occupation, authority, power, and privilege. There are also conflicting distinctions according to tribes, regions, political affirmations, and even denominations and religions, which are obstacles to building up a harmonious, fraternal, and just society. The democratic ideals of mutual respect, solidarity, and unity across all sorts of differences are becoming less and less attainable. This is a challenge for the SCCs. Their experience and practice of community should be an example to the wider society. The remark that "in urban areas the poorer people show greater vigor and interest in SCCs than the rich" is certainly a warning signal. Does it not imply that even in the church there is need to guard against attitudes of discrimination at all levels? The SCCs help show the way toward the building of a nondiscriminatory society.

We read that "due to family problems there is poor attendance in SCCs" and that when there are "broken marriages, where husband and wife relationships are not good, it is very difficult to build real SCCs." This evokes a problem that threatens not just the church communities but also the wider society. Modern life has created special strains on family life. Relations between husbands and wives are often strained and problematic, as are relations between parents and their children. Children are often seen as unruly and undisciplined; they have difficulty respecting authority or obeying elders, with the result of much juvenile crime. All this reveals a deeper and more widespread social disintegration. In the past, when society was composed of smaller, relatively self-contained communities of extended families, clans, and neighborhoods, the cultural norms could maintain a sufficiently stable state of social order and harmony. Modernization has upset much of this social order. We need to analyze the situation so as to understand what exactly is happening in the changed circumstances. Only then can we start restructuring relationships and readjusting behaviors and customs in the hope that a more acceptable moral behavior will result. It is not helpful simply to lament the breakdown of morals; people must learn to deal creatively with social change. When the SCCs become aware of family problems, they should feel challenged to discuss them openly in their meetings so as to come up with workable solutions in line with their faith.

It is significant that the African Synod of 1994 affirmed the evangelization of the family as a critical task of the church in the transformation of modern Africa:

The future of the world and of the Church passes through the family. Not only is the Christian family the first cell of the living ecclesial community, it is also the fundamental cell of society. In Africa in particular, the family is the foundation on which the social edifice is built. This is why the Synod considered the evangelization of the African family a major priority, if the family is to assume in its turn the role of *active subject* in view of the evangelization of family through families.[15]

The African Synod, quite logically, recommends that the church in Africa take as its ecclesial model the church as family of God: "Along these lines, the Special Assembly for Africa affirmed that the goal of evangelization is to build up the Church as the family of God, an anticipation on earth, though imperfect, of the kingdom. The Christian families of Africa will thus become true 'domestic churches,' contributing to society's progress towards a more fraternal life. This is how African societies will be transformed through the gospel."[16]

In the same way the mention of superstitions alerts us to the task of dealing with the problem of the relationship between traditional religion and Christian faith and practice. What are usually called superstitions are in fact a whole complex of beliefs, attitudes, and practices rooted in traditional culture and religion. Beneath them lies a specific worldview, and this complex of beliefs and practices was designed to answer the problems and needs of the individuals, families, and society. Modern Western culture, as well as Christian faith, has come to critique and assess this religious culture. But such a critique cannot be useful and constructive if it is simply an indiscriminate condemnation of traditional religion and culture. Such a condemnation, which has been typical in the past, simply leaves the important issues untackled, so that many African believers are forced to live a double life, both following their so-called Christian faith and observing the beliefs and customs of traditional culture and religions. The African Synod has called for inculturation as an urgent task for the African Church. Inculturation means establishing an honest and respectful dialogue between traditional culture and the Christian faith. Culture is thereby assessed by the Christian faith, not Western culture as such, so that what is true and valid is affirmed as the basis for the people's Christian life, while what is evil is condemned and done away with. This difficult but necessary process should be an ongoing task within the SCCs. The local churches can facilitate the process where a society's life is critiqued and transformed into a new creation in line with the kingdom of God in Christ.

Synodal Process: The Best Tool for Building Small Christian Communities

At the end of the African Synod, church leaders resolved to "take the synod back home" to the local churches, down to the very grassroots. What the bishops had so well laid down as guidelines for the African Church in the new millennium would remain a useless exercise unless the faithful became fully aware of it and owned it. The best way to do this was to organize, in the dioceses, a process whereby all the faithful, bishops, clergy, religious, and laity, could do at their local level what their bishops had done at the wider African level, become informed about the present situation of the church in Africa and of society in general. Then they would be able to discuss the matters together in a synodal process, as the body of Christ meant to live together and walk in oneness along the way of their Christian calling. Each diocese would organize a schedule of meetings, a diocesan synod, that would enable all the faithful to participate actively in a process of mutual information, discussion, and decision making. As a result of this process, which would take whatever length of time it required, even several years, the diocese would be in a position to formulate its pastoral plan and put in place the necessary structures for implementing it.

The pastoral project of SCCs can succeed only through such a process. SCCs are not simply created by dividing parishes into organizational units. They are living organisms that need time and effort to grow together, through a conscious process of mutual knowledge and acceptance, and the will to live and work together as a true picture of the body of Christ.

Notes

1. The decision to begin basing the church's life and mission on SCCs as a deliberate pastoral method was made in 1973 during the AMECEA study conference in Nairobi.

2. Paul VI, *Sacrosanctum concilium (Constitution on the Sacred Liturgy)*, December 4, 1963, no. 14, www.vatican.va/archive/hist_councils/ii_vatican_council/documents/vat-ii_const_19631204_sacrosanctum-concilium_en.html (accessed August 9, 2006).

3. Avery Dulles, *Models of the Church* (Garden City, NY: Doubleday, 1974).

4. Conferencia General del Episcopado Latinoamericano, *The Church in the Present-Day Transformation of Latin America in the Light of the Council* (Washington, DC: Secretariat for Latin America, National Conference of Catholic Bishops, 1973).

5. AMECEA is a service organization for the national episcopal conferences of the eight countries of Eastern Africa: Eritrea, Ethiopia, Kenya, Malawi, Sudan, Tanzania, Uganda, and Zambia. Somalia and the Seychelles are affiliate members. Headquarters are in Nairobi, Kenya. Plenary assemblies take place every three years, followed by study conferences to discuss common pastoral concerns and to look together, in a spirit of collegiality, at some of the major issues facing the church in the region. The organization's aim is therefore collaboration and sharing of various aspects of the Catholic Church's pastoral planning, study, and execution.

6. An overview of this study conference can be found in AMECEA Bishops, "Guidelines for the Catholic Church in Eastern Africa in the 1980s," *African Ecclesial Review* 16 (1974): 1, 2.

7. See the reports on these assemblies that constitute volumes 18 (1976) and 21 (1979) of the *African Ecclesial Review.*

8. AMECEA Bishops, "Guidelines," 10.

9. Ibid., 9–10.

10. Paul VI, *Octogesima adveniens,* May 14, 1971, no. 4, www.vatican. va/holy_father/paul_vi/apost_letters/documents/hf_p-vi_apl_19710514_ octogesima-adveniens_en.html (accessed August 9, 2006). An example of this process is presented by Joe Holland and Peter Henriot, *Social Analysis: Linking Faith and Justice* (Washington, DC: Center of Concern, 1980).

11. My own banishment from the country had been due to such suspicion in regard to the movement of SCCs in the Diocese of Lilongwe, of which I was bishop. See P. A. Kalilombe, "Introduction: My Life, My Faith, My Theology, and My Country," in *Doing Theology at the Grassroots: Theological Essays from Malawi* (Gweru: Mambo Press, 1999), 5–7.

12. Discussions and studies were being reported in the *African Ecclesial Review.* See, for example, Brian Hearne, "Small Christian Communities: Let's Go Ahead!" *African Ecclesial Review* 26 (1984): 262–73.

13. J. G. Healey, "Four Africans Evaluate SCCs in E. Africa," *African Ecclesial Review* 29, no. 5 (1987): 266.

14. This was the point I was trying to make in my doctoral dissertation; see P. A. Kalilombe, "From 'Out Stations' to 'Small Christian Communities': A Comparison between Two Pastoral Methods in Lilongwe Diocese" (PhD diss., Graduate Theological Union, Berkeley, 1983).

15. John Paul II, *Ecclesia in Africa* (Nairobi: Paulines, 1995), no. 80.

16. Ibid., no. 85.

Part Six

POVERTY, RACE,
AND GENDER

Chapter 10

THE FEMINIST OPTION FOR THE POOR AND OPPRESSED IN THE CONTEXT OF GLOBALIZATION

MARÍA PILAR AQUINO

Commitment to the alleviation of human suffering, and especially to the removal of its causes as far as possible, is an obligation for the followers of Jesus. . . . Our task here is to find the words with which to talk about God in the midst of the starvation of millions, the humiliation of races regarded as inferior, discrimination against women, especially women who are poor, systematic social injustice, a persistent high rate of infant mortality, those who simply "disappear" or are deprived of their freedom, the suffering of peoples who are struggling for their right to live, the exiles and refugees, terrorism of every kind, and the corpse-filled common graves of Ayacucho. What we must deal with is not the past but, unfortunately, a cruel present and a dark tunnel with no apparent end. . . . How are we to speak of the God of life when cruel murder on a massive scale goes on in "the corner of the dead"? How are we to preach the love of God amid such profound contempt for human life? . . . These are our questions and this is our challenge.

—Gustavo Gutiérrez, *On Job: God-Talk and the Suffering of the Innocent*

The powerful voices of the life-giving forces of history are necessary in these times if one is to continue believing that the Christian faith has some hope to offer those who day by day around the world have in sight only "a cruel present and a dark tunnel with no apparent end." To continue to sustain the struggles for a different world that offers a viable future of well-being and joy, one needs spiritual strength that nourishes and cultivates a conviction that will not succumb to cowardice or to indifference in the presence of the vast desolation, violence, and injustice experienced worldwide.

At the time of this writing, several events took place that showed me the pertinence of the topic addressed in this essay. Two accounts from the same issue of the *L. A. Times* (November 9, 2002), complete with telling photographs, challenge us to work toward a different world of hope and justice.[1] One is a story on Catholic approaches to globalization and ethics that focuses primarily on a forum on the subject then being held at Loyola Marymount University. Pictured are thousands of marchers in Washington, D.C., protesting the exclusionary tendencies of the current globalization model. The photograph highlights how this massive movement is fashioning an alternative agenda in pursuit of global justice. The photograph depicts banners and signs with slogans like "Globalize Justice," "No Oil War," "Save Our Planet," "Stop Washington's War," and "Another World Is Possible!" The last of these is the slogan of a growing and influential movement called World Social Forum, which seeks to participate in the deliberations about the dynamics of the present model of globalization and to intervene in its transformation with the intent of making it equitable, all-inclusive, and democratic.[2] The second story reports on the controversy over the discovery of sexual abuses committed by U.S. Catholic priests against minors, young men, and women. This story is accompanied by photographs of two Catholic bishops who represent opposing positions. On one side stands Bishop Robert Brom from San Diego, who advocates revising and improving the existing systems of accountability for the clergy so that they answer responsibly to the concerns of both the church and society. On the other side stands the former bishop of Boston, Cardinal Bernard Law, who allowed the abuse of power and its cover-up to continue without remedy. This topic raises numerous questions concerning the role and function of the Roman Catholic hierarchy, and of the entire church's identity and function in the world.

The feminist option for the poor and oppressed in the context of globalization is central, urgent, and in need of more scholarship and more visibility. Published in a local paper in South Bend, Indiana, a full-page photograph appears to affirm this need. The page is completely covered with the faces and silhouettes of sixty-one women.[3] Its most impressive aspect is that it publicly presents a tragedy that societies, churches, and religions prefer to silence. All of these women are archived on a listing of women who either have been murdered or have disappeared in this region, and the circumstances under which they lost their lives continue to be unknown because the perpetrators of these crimes are unknown and unpunished. Any justice for these women, even that of a proper and dignified burial, is still a pending debt. This newspaper also includes a report on the front page concerning another massive mobilization of European social movements in Florence, Italy, to show their opposition to the current globalization model and the present wars due to their harmful effects on the world's poor people and on the environment. All these events, though apparently unrelated, provide the background for my concerns related to the option for the poor.

These events speak of something more than mere human contingency. I believe that the marches organized worldwide for agendas of social justice, respect, dignity, and human rights, the new awareness of a need to critically evaluate the social role and function of churches, and the re-emergence worldwide of campaigns to eradicate sexual violence against women are all visible signs of the life-giving (dynamic/vigorous) forces of history that are bringing forth new possibilities and hope for humanity and the world. These dynamic forces express the renewed energies of people who are challenging the idea that transforming the present set of circumstances is impossible and are seeking to contribute to the design of a world free from the threat of violence and oppression. In these dynamic though still tenuous and fragile forces and renewed energies I have been able to see the signs of the presence and activity of Divine Wisdom in our midst. Before such a re-creating presence, through the grace and friendship of Divine Wisdom, we are given the possibility of entering into a new stage because it is time to reaffirm hope in the realities that are beginning to emerge. The option for the poor comes to strengthen the new processes that are aimed at creating a different world.

I propose to emphasize some of the many contributions that Gustavo Gutiérrez has made to the theme of the option for the poor and the oppressed and to express the great admiration and the profound respect and love that I have for him. As a way of honoring his work, I will avoid the conventional themes that specialized studies present in a repetitive form about poverty, women, and globalization and instead take a different route.[4] To understand better the significance and magnitude of the option for the poor and the oppressed as it has been formally systematized by Gutiérrez since 1967,[5] it is necessary to know something of the tragedy lived by the Peruvian people. Only from this vantage point can one understand why Gutiérrez affirms that "to be with the oppressed is to be against the oppressor. In our times, and on our continent, to be in solidarity with the 'poor,' understood in this way, means to run personal risks, even to put one's life in danger."[6] Also one can better understand why, for Gutiérrez, the option for the poor and the oppressed can only be solidarity, protest, and a clear affirmation, against all skepticism, that another world is possible. Without this option we would be abdicating our right to challenge the dynamics of the existing globalization model that continues to take us through a dark tunnel with no apparent end. And from the Peruvian context one can better understand the meaning and impact of a *feminist* option for the poor and the oppressed in the new context of globalization. Consequently, I will first briefly present the history of the horror lived by the Peruvian people. Then I will argue that the full impact of the option for the poor and the oppressed can be better appreciated from the standpoint of feminist struggles and that the feminist option for the poor and the oppressed raises possibilities and proposals that are most necessary for contributing to a radical transformation of the present reality. Finally I will explore what this option entails for the work of the churches in the new contexts set forth by globalization.

CONFLICT, HOPE, AND THE STRUGGLE FOR JUSTICE

Gutiérrez's account of the tragic experience of the Peruvian people is one example of the dramatic cry for justice, human dignity, and human rights expressed in all his writings from beginning to end. But his cry envelops all oppressed peoples in their struggle to transform the horror of social injustice that manifests itself in systemic violence, indiscriminate repression, the destruction of persons, and the concealment of truth. The immense suffering that they experience is presented in all its intensity in Gutiérrez's words, and it appears before our eyes so that we may not be exempt from responsibility. The inhumane atrocities committed against people who are struggling for their fundamental right to life are vividly confronted in his writings. For him, "[T]he truth is that only when we face these facts is it possible to pass a Christian judgment on them and give guidelines for rising above them. . . . [T]he theology of liberation seeks to provide a language for talking about God. It is an attempt to make the word of life present in a world of oppression, injustice, and death."[7] This is a truth that Gutiérrez has not wanted to hide or silence. On the contrary, as a wise prophet and a religious visionary he sends forth a strong call to every person who values the critical-ethical humanistic tradition so that we may all take an active role in the struggle to eliminate the causes of such atrocities. From the perspective of the Christian tradition, according to Gutiérrez, no church can escape its responsibility to actively work for justice, respect of human rights, and the people's democratic participation in every decision that affects their lives. The basic reason the church is obliged to work for justice is that "the cargo of inhuman, cruel death with which all of this misery and oppression is laden is contrary to the will of God of Christian revelation, who is a God of life. . . . [S]ocial injustice, which plunders the masses and feeds the wealth of the few, the denial of the most elementary of human rights, are evils that believers in the God of Jesus can only reject."[8]

When Gutiérrez speaks of "the option for the poor and the oppressed," he is referring to the deliberate choice that every person and the entire Christian community ought to make to transform the horror of social injustice, which is damaging and destroying oppressed humanity throughout the world. If this option is not taken, the possibility of struggling for justice and human rights disappears, and the inhumane conditions under which marginalized human beings survive continue undisputed, without a remedy in sight.

For the Peruvian people and for all who feel their pain, August 28, 2003, will remain marked forever as a day of mourning and prayer. On that day the final report of the Truth and Reconciliation Commission of Peru (TRC) was presented to the world.[9] This magnificent report documents and exposes the tragedy lived by thousands of Peruvian women and men who fell victim to the massive violence perpetrated by state agents, paramilitary groups, and terrorist organizations from 1980 to 2000. Even though the number of dead reported by the final report is estimated at 69,280, it does not include the numerous crimes occurring before or after these years. Further, as the president of the TRC noted, statistics "unfortunately do not express the real gravity of the acts. The numbers do not suffice to illustrate the victims' experience of suffering and horror."[10] According to the final report, the atrocities committed against the defenseless population included massacres, extrajudicial executions, assassinations and kidnappings, forced disappearances, torture and other serious injuries, violations of the collective rights of Andean communities and natives of the country, and other crimes and grave violations of human rights.[11] The gravity of the human rights violations is manifested in the systematic or generalized practice, reiterated and persistent, of sexual violence, rape, and sexual abuse against Peruvian women.[12] According to the final report, "[T]he women affected by sexual violence were, generally, women from low-income sections of the population, Quechua-speaking farmers, widows—that is to say, those considered most vulnerable,"[13] and the Ayacucho department presented the greatest number of sexual violations and rape in the context of crimes and massacres. Even though the TRC recognizes that "sexual violence is present in the daily life of women, in times of peace as well as in times of armed conflict,"[14] during the time period investigated by the TRC it took diverse forms cruelly perpetrated against women solely for being women: sexual abuse, rape, forced unions, sexual servitude, forced abortions, forced recruitment and sexual captivity, pregnancies resulting from rape, sexual assault and molestation, forced nudity, and multiple instances of sexual abuse.[15] All this has occurred amidst grave conflict caused by social injustice. Sexual violence has been perpetrated "as a demonstration of the perpetrator's power,"[16] "as a method of torture employed for the purpose of obtaining information or self-incriminating confessions,"[17] and "as a kind of intimidation, punishment, or reprisal."[18] Further, all these abuses and atrocities (*ultrajes* and *vejaciones*) against women have occurred "in the context of absolute impunity."[19] This is the context that explains the kinds of questions Gutiérrez raises when he says, "In Peru, therefore—but the question is perhaps symbolic of all Latin America—we must ask: How are we to do theology *while Ayacucho lasts?* . . . How are we to proclaim the resurrection of the Lord where death reigns, and especially the death of children, women, the poor, indigenes, and the 'unimportant' members of our society?"[20] The Peruvian background allows us to better understand Gutiérrez's repeated calls for greater attention to the degrading, inhuman, intolerable, discriminatory, unjust, and unacceptable situation that women experience.[21]

From an ethical-political perspective, the TRC seeks both to expose the atrocities committed so that no one can claim ignorance or historical innocence before such acts of violence against dispossessed humanity and to make it possible for society to prevent them from happening again by eradicating their causes.[22] Silence, acquiescence, lack of interest, denial, withholding of information, and concealment of the truth of the acts only lead to collaboration in the violation of basic human rights and to a sustained repetition of social conflict. A new and just social order can be inaugurated if people confront the truth of the acts, take responsibility for them, and actively participate in eradicating the factors that impede the realization of that order. In the preface to the final report, the president of the TRC states that "this report exposes, then, two scandals: that of massive murder, disappearance, and torture, and that of indolence, ineptitude, and the indifference of those who could have impeded this catastrophe but did not do so."[23] Churches and theologies also must accept their share of responsibility, as they could have used their resources and religious power to contribute with greater efficacy to the interruption of this human catastrophe. Yet neither the Roman Catholic Church, nor all the other churches, nor any theology makes enough of an effort to impede it.

Another reason proposed by the TRC for examining the events endured during those years of anguish is that the memory of the flagrant injustices committed might restore dignity to those who have died "before their time"[24] and keep similar events from being repeated in the future. The commission understands that to establish social harmony (convivencia social) and build a peaceful future, it is indispensable to launch a multidimensional process of social reconciliation through the restorative action of justice, the reestablishment of the dignity and fundamental rights of every person, the construction of a democratic-participative citizenship, the elimination of poverty, and the explicit acknowledgment and respect of the dignity and rights of women.[25] For the TRC, "[T]he reconciliation process is made possible, and is made necessary, through the discovery of the truth about what happened in those years. . . . [I]f truth is a prior condition for reconciliation, justice is, at the same time, its condition and its result."[26] In this way, the commitment to justice, to an integral rehabilitation of people, and to a just social order sustained in truth appears as a key condition for preventing the reemergence of another human catastrophe like the one endured in Peru and for making possible the emergence of a new reconciled humanity.[27] This commitment acquires a sense of urgency when we speak about eliminating sexual violence and sexual abuse against women. As Virginia Vargas, the prominent feminist sociologist from Peru, aptly noted in her reflection on the work of the TRC, "[W]ithout justice for these abuses there will be no real justice."[28]

In the specific context of the processes of truth and reconciliation, Gutiérrez has made an immense and courageous theological contribution. His influence on the work of the TRC is manifest, especially in the final report's section on the significant role that the Catholic Church and the evangelical churches played in the conflict.[29] In addition to gathering, through various quotations, Gutiérrez's reflections, and his public denunciations and protests against kidnappings, attempted murder, and massacres, the final report includes his trenchant observation that "[b]lindness to reality is leading us to a kind of collective suicide."[30] Speaking of the atrocities that render defenseless the vast majority of marginalized peoples, Gutiérrez acknowledges that "[t]here are no words to express the reaction that those crimes provoke. Our immaturity as a nation makes it difficult for us to confront real challenges with efficacy; it is more likely that we are being broken by their virulence. . . . One of the more tragic consequences of the situation in which we are currently living is the skepticism it produces regarding the possibilities of building a renewed country."[31]

In this situation, and in the forum of theological activity, what Gutiérrez did in presenting liberation theology as an "option for the poor and the oppressed" was affirm, against all skepticism, that collective suicide is not our destiny, that a world without violence is possible, and that the hope for change has a place in this world. This hope is rooted in the constant struggles of the people in civil, social, and feminist organizations to bring about radical changes in the existing social order, greater justice, peace and well-being, and rights and dignity for all people. The option for the poor and the oppressed is about eradicating "the scandalous reality of poverty"[32] in a way that transforms social reality and liberates everyone.

Gutiérrez has insisted in all of his writings that social injustice is the creator of poverty and exclusion. It tramples on human dignity, denies basic human rights, and, in its theological formulation, is contrary to the will of God; it is a sin because it severs the friendship relationship between humanity and God and among ourselves.[33] That is why the believer who finds spiritual sustenance in the experience of Christian discipleship must struggle against social injustice: it is commitment, it is solidarity, it is protest, it is a human and Christian duty, and it is an affirmation of hope that a new reconciled humanity and a world without social conflicts is possible here on earth. If we are to live in accord with God's purpose for the world, as persons and as a community, we are obliged to help repair injustices and prevent conflict through a sustained re-creation of the theological arguments and of the theological, religious, and spiritual resources that strengthen our commitment. In the words of Gutiérrez: "[T]he practice of justice is required of the disciples of Christ."[34] Only in this way can religion and theology help stop negligence, indifference, silence, and complicity before the human catastrophes that are testing Christian hope. This is much more urgent in the new scenarios set up by globalization.

THE FEMINIST STRUGGLE FOR JUSTICE: CONFLICT AND HOPE

The term *feminist* sharpens the focus and emphasizes that the full impact of an option for the poor and oppressed can be better appreciated from the perspective of participation in the feminist struggles within the new contexts affected by globalization. This option should not by any means be understood as averse to or divorced from worldwide feminist struggles, movements, theologies, and spiritualities. In my opinion, theological perspectives that forsake this option are inconsistent with the purpose and implications of liberation theology as they have been initiated and developed by Gutiérrez. Liberation theology emerged from the struggles for justice and validates efforts toward recognition of human dignity and rights. Drawing on the Christian tradition, it argues in favor of historical emancipation and works toward the goal of genuine participative democracy and liberation for all humanity. Feminist struggles have the same purpose and involve the same commitment toward the radical transformation of the world. The following are three reasons why it is important to specify and make explicit what is feminist about the option for the poor.

The Majority of the Poor and Oppressed Are Women

There exists today overwhelming evidence for the urgency of bringing to center stage the struggles for the dignity and rights of women in the working agenda of societies, churches, and religions.[35] In the theological arena, this evidence amply validates the wake-up call given by Elisabeth Schüssler Fiorenza twenty years ago when she said, "[I]f liberation theologians make the 'option for the oppressed' the key to their theological endeavors, then they must articulate that 'the oppressed' are women."[36] The immediate consequence must be changes in theological discourse, which tends to be abstract in its understanding of the locations, the subjects, and the actors of theological reflection. Theological discourse that begins from and speaks about the crucified majorities, the suffering peoples, the great masses, or the poor is insufficient if it does not specify that these majorities are women. As noted by the 2002 Report of the United Nations Population

Fund, "[W]omen are disproportionately represented among the poor. . . . [M]ore women than men live in poverty, and the disparity has increased over the past decade, particularly in developing countries. . . . [W]omen continue to be disadvantaged relative to men in basic rights and associated status."[37] Similarly, a study initiated and sponsored by the World Council of Churches on how churches and ecumenical organizations could respond with greater efficacy to reduce poverty indicates that "women are the poorest of the poor, or form the majority of the poor or are especially vulnerable. . . . [W]omen and children make up the largest proportion of the world's poorest people."[38] Whether in Guatemala, Peru, Mexico, or the United States, among the majorities of poor people that are women, indigenous women in particular have a slim chance of escaping poverty and exclusion.[39] Further, the 2002 final report of Human Rights Watch notes women's particular vulnerability to human rights violations: "Our monitoring showed that violence and discrimination remained pervasive components of many women's lives. Governments both actively violated women's human rights and failed to prevent abuses by private actors."[40] This same world organization acknowledges that "millions of women throughout the world live in conditions of abject deprivation of, and attacks against, their fundamental human rights for no other reason than that they are women. . . . Abuses against women are relentless, systematic, and widely tolerated, if not explicitly condoned."[41] What was true for Peru also holds worldwide: sexual violence, rape, and sexual abuse against women reach horrific dimensions in the context of grave social conflict. In the case of Sierra Leone, the human rights organization WITNESS documents that "[c]ountless atrocities were committed during Sierra Leone's recent, decade-long civil war, with women particularly targeted for violence. . . . Women young and old were beaten, mutilated, raped, and killed by child soldiers and their adult commanders. For the rebels, sexual violence became a weapon to be used against the civilian population, as a demonstration of its power and impunity. . . . Until WITNESS' involvement, the deliberate and widespread targeting of women for abduction and rape during the conflict remained a largely untold story."[42]

This situation affecting women on the global level is so grave that the 2003 final report of the United Nations Development Programme speaks of taking up, as a global priority, the rising situation of "the missing women," in reference to "females estimated to have died due to discrimination in access to health and nutrition."[43] In this context one can better

understand the summary judgment made by Dora María Téllez concerning the situation of women in Nicaragua, which also applies to all women
in our communities: "[T]he general condition of women is worse than
that of men. . . . [T]he health situation of women is not good."[44] In this
context as well, one can better understand why Ivone Gebara has articulated the option for the poor as "an option for the poor woman."[45] In the
same way, Schüssler Fiorenza has been consistent in pointing out that feminist liberation theologies understand this option as "the option for poor and
oppressed *women,* because the majority of the poor and exploited today are
women and children dependent on women for survival."[46] Thus the feminist option for poor and oppressed *women* not only radicalizes the starting
point of theological reflection but also leads to a significant shift in the
way we understand the end of theological activity.

To speak of a feminist option for poor and oppressed *women* allows
for a more critical understanding of the causes that maintain and multiply
the dehumanization of majorities in the world and offers a better grasp of
the tasks that lie ahead of us with regard to eradicating such causes. As I
will suggest shortly, what is feminist in this option clarifies and deepens
the liberating function of theology in the present circumstances that we
must confront.

Critical Feminism Provides a Radical Analysis of Injustice

Several specialized studies are consistent in indicating that social injustice
is at the root of violations of women's fundamental dignity and rights,
whether sexual violence, dehumanizing poverty, or any other form of
exclusion.[47] In every part of the world, this injustice acquires grotesque
dimensions when it is examined through the lens of situations in which
women are forced to live. According to the Inter-American Development
Bank, the true magnitude of the inequalities affecting women in Latin
America has barely begun to be known.[48] The system in which we find
ourselves is hostile to women's aspirations of justice and well-being. Social injustice is the primary cause of the social conflicts that are ripping
apart entire societies, and these conflicts have had atrocious effects on the
lives of women.[49] According to Gutiérrez, followers of Jesus are obliged
to commit themselves to the alleviation of human suffering, and especially
to the removal of its causes as far as possible. Further, since to attack the
root of these evils it is necessary to identify and transform the innermost

causes of social injustice, Christians are obliged to commit to radical change. The notion that we need a radical transformation of the causes of social injustice appears throughout Gutiérrez's writings.[50] For him, only this radical transformation can lead us to overcome the social conflicts so that we may help bring forth a new world according to God's designs and put "the universe back on its feet by establishing a just order."[51] Gutiérrez's call for radical transformation takes on enormous significance in the present world circumstances. But a critical radical approach that is feminist would indicate that to know what needs to be transformed one must analyze and call things by their names.

Conventional approaches to the present situation and a critical feminist understanding differ in their ability to name these causes and determine their effects on the world's majorities. While conventional studies sum up the multidimensional processes of the contemporary world in the term *globalization*[52] or *neoliberal globalization,*[53] a critical feminist analytical framework exposes the *kyriarchal*[54] characteristics and interstructuring of those processes as they evolve within what I have been calling a *kyriarchal globalization* that validates and multiplies *kyriarchal relationships of domination.* Because of the kyriarchal articulation of the current neoliberal globalization, the patterns of social disparity and of sexual violence against women are bound to be repeated and multiplied again and again in every society, culture, and religion of the world.

Conventional discussions of the current globalization model generally omit that this is a kyriarchal globalization and that kyriarchal relationships of domination are necessarily embedded within it. This omission is possible because the analytical activity lacks the feminist theoretical-political tools that would allow it to render an account of the causes of exclusion and sexual violence against women. For example, as the United Nations Economic Commission for Latin America and the Caribbean (ECLAC) has pointed out, the term *globalization* has a mere analytical use to explain and describe the multidimensional, ambiguous, and complex nature of the financial, economic, ecological, political, social, and cultural processes that are both influencing the entire world and increasingly affecting human relationships in domestic, local, national, and regional terms. But ECLAC indicates that the actors involved in the shaping and implementation of these processes participate in them on clearly unequal terms because "developed-country governments, together with transnational corporations, exert the strongest influence, while developing-country governments and civil society organizations hold much less sway."[55] According to numerous studies, one major characteristic of neoliberal globalization is its asymmetric and unequal nature because of the enormous disparities in power between the key actors of these processes and because of access to the benefits that globalization can provide. For ECLAC, "Globalization has not only engendered growing interdependence; it has also given rise to marked international inequalities. Expressed in terms of a metaphor widely employed in recent debates, the world economy is essentially an 'uneven playing field,' whose distinctive characteristics are a concentration of capital and technology generation in developed countries and the strong influence of those countries on trade in goods and services."[56]

Because of this inequality, the great majorities of the world, women and those who depend on them, are excluded from the table that defines social agendas, from design of social dynamics, and from the potential benefits of globalization. At the same time, if this model of globalization is governed by the values of profit, greed, and global domination, then there is no place for the notion of respect for human dignity and human rights. Acknowledgment and respect for the dignity and rights of women are not priorities for anyone in this system of globalization, and the situation is likely to continue to the extent that studies continue to ignore women's dignity and rights because the current model of globalization is shaped by kyriarchal domination. Those who do not even bother to know what life is like for those living beyond the commodities of the so-called "First World" may find it disturbing that this situation of scandalous disparities has become so glaring that even the World Bank, one of the key actors in shaping the current kyriarchal globalization model, has become afraid of the monster it created. Recently, the president of the World Bank stated that "[i]t is time to take a cold, hard look at the future. Our planet is not balanced. Too few control too much, and too many have too little to hope for—too much turmoil, too many wars, too much suffering. The demographics of the future speak to a growing imbalance of people, resources, and the environment."[57] This judgment only confirms that in today's world so many disparities, so many frustrated aspirations, so many social conflicts, so many humanitarian catastrophes, and so many violations of human rights have occurred, through the deliberate action of powerful elites who have created for themselves a world based on profit and domination, that for excluded humanity they have created "a cruel present and a dark tunnel with no apparent end."

The critical feminist theologies of liberation insist that successful radical transformation requires a radical analysis of the causes of this situation. The starting point for such an analysis is the feminist option for the poor and oppressed majorities of the world. A critical feminist analysis radicalizes the search for a new remodeling of the global agendas by taking as its central axis of thought and action the commitment to the struggles and aspirations of excluded women, who as majorities of humanity continue to affirm that another world is possible. But for this to occur, we must identify the deep roots of social injustice. No radical transformation can occur without transforming the material conditions that keep women marginalized within kyriarchal societies, cultures, and religions. A critical feminist analysis shows that the results of kyriarchal globalization are consistent with its nature and cannot render anything else because it is a system of domination that creates social injustice, which necessarily leads to grave social conflicts. From this analytical starting point, it is necessary to state clearly that the present model of globalization has been shaped according to social models based on kyriarchal traditions, systems, ideologies, and practices, within which social relationships serve the interests and goals of domination and control. For women who are the majorities of the world, these relationships operate in a way that is hostile to our interests for emancipation, justice, and well-being. From the perspective of a critical feminist framework, following Schüssler Fiorenza, the practice of naming and transforming the radical causes of social injustice is made possible through a "critical systemic analysis of domination."[58] This type of analysis opens the door to reconceptualizing the function of theological activity within the new contexts of kyriarchal globalization: "A critical feminist theology of liberation . . . aims to change entirely structures of alienation, exploitation, and exclusion. Its goal is to transform theoretical and theological-religious knowledge and sociopolitical systems of domination and subordination. Such a feminist theology understands itself as a critical theology of liberation because its critical systemic analyses and its intellectual practices for the production of religious knowledge seek to support struggles for wo/men's liberation around the world."[59]

Very few Latin-American male liberation theologians have taken the time to enter into serious dialogue with feminist theological discourses. Gutiérrez is one of the few exceptions, and I dare say that this is because he is indelibly marked by his religious commitment to heal and overcome the unspeakable tragedy of sexual violence lived by the poorest women of his community. His contribution certainly serves to support the feminist struggles for the systemic transformation of kyriarchal globalization toward what, using the terminology coined by Schüssler Fiorenza, I have suggested calling a *radical democratic-emancipatory globalization*.[60] This transformation is demanded by the feminist option for the poor and the oppressed majorities of the world, who are women and those who depend on them.

Feminist Theology Calls for a Shift from Silence to Word

"From Silence to Word" is the title of an article by Virginia Vargas on the work of the TRC of Peru.[61] Vargas seeks to repair the damage caused by silence about sexual violence and sexual abuse of women. This Peruvian feminist author is launching a great challenge to the Christian community worldwide—that we abandon cowardice, expose these realities, and actively embrace a commitment to alleviate and remedy the damage. Though the TRC has judged this reality "a violation per se of human rights" and a "crime against humanity [*crimen de lesa humanidad*]," even now it is relegated to oblivion and invisibility by a majority of states, societies, cultures, and religions.[62] This reality of silence is evidenced everywhere and is particularly severe in situations of armed conflict. According to Human Rights Watch, "[U]ntil recently many viewed violence against women as an inevitable, if regrettable, consequence of war. This attitude guaranteed impunity for perpetrators, effectively silencing women who suffered gruesome sexual and physical abuses."[63] Vargas explains that this reality continues to be "naturalized and invisible, in the home sphere, in private life, in public life, in politics, in personal and collective dealings. It is the first and most unquestionable form of revealing power relationships, and, internalized, it grows within them. These are the most open wounds of exclusion that women bear, because exclusion is multiple and experienced as natural."[64] As an expression of domination and control of men over women, sexual violence against women continues to be ignored and unquestioned principally due to the validation rendered to such domination by the kyriarchal systems in all spheres of human existence. According to recent studies conducted by the World Health Organization (WHO), "[T]he 'private' nature of this sort of violence often treats it not as a crime, but as a family matter, or as a normal part of life."[65] Therefore, such violence is sustained and multiplied by the perpetrators with impunity. Gutiérrez indicates that one of the greatest obstacles to transforming this reality is "its almost hidden character in habitual, daily life in our cultural tradition—to the point that when we denounce it, we seem a little strange to people, as if we were simply looking for trouble."[66] In my view, part of our ecclesial and theological duty is to denounce it, make it visible, and remove all obstacles to its eradication. This is a duty for Christians because its existence is contrary to the will of God and, according to Christian revelation, we cannot accept it.

A deliberate commitment from churches and theologies to end sexual violence against women is urgent because for many women, including me and my family, it is a reality that touches our personal lives. Millions worldwide are faced with this calamity. WHO reports that although sexual violence extends worldwide and constitutes a severe problem as a violation of human rights and public health, "[i]n most countries there has been little research conducted on the problem. . . . [T]he relationship between these sources and the global magnitude of the problem of sexual violence may be viewed as corresponding to an iceberg floating in water. . . . In many countries, data on most aspects of sexual violence are lacking, and there is a great need everywhere for research on all aspects of sexual violence."[67]

Gutiérrez observes, "[W]hen faced with a situation of this magnitude, neutrality is impossible and it calls for our active participation. . . . [P]assivity or indifference would be neither ethical nor Christian."[68] Regarding churches and theologians' active participation against sexual violence toward women, it is important to recognize that the naming of this reality, that is, the shift from silence to word, has been made possible only through the struggles initiated and developed by feminist theologians. In fact, the activity against this violence by the great majority of priests and male theologians is insufficient and mediocre. In my opinion, feminist theologies have taken up the challenge raised by this reality and have exposed the fact that sexual violence against women is not a private affair; is not acceptable, and should not be validated by Christian discourse.[69] On the contrary, the causes of this reality ought to be analyzed rigorously, exposed critically and systematically, and, above all, transformed radically. Moreover, feminist liberation theologies insist that this transformation is an indispensable component of the struggle against kyriarchal systems that make invisible, naturalize, maintain, and multiply sexual violence against women. To produce such transformation, one must make a deliberate and explicit full turn toward feminist epistemology and critical-emancipatory feminist hermeneutics.

More than twenty years ago I had the privilege of participating in one of the famous summer courses in the Centro Bartolomé de las Casas offered in Lima, Peru. In the course syllabus, which I keep to this day, Gutiérrez indicated that the theological activity in the church "seeks to understand what the word of God says to us today in order to transform our personal and community life, ordered towards the advancement of salvation history."[70] For me, Gutiérrez's teaching continues to be alive today because that sense of purpose attributed to theological activity has not changed. In fact, we act in a way contrary to the work of Divine Wisdom in our milieu if our theological activity does not use the power of religious and theological language for the transformation of the world. This is why the function of theological reflection continues to be critical reflection and creative naming of all activity that leads us to make this world a reality that conforms better to the reality of Divine Wisdom. According to Christian revelation, this reality speaks of a new humanity finally reconciled and of a new world founded upon justice, equality, peace, freedom, and abundance of life. The tasks of transformation are to bring together this reality and our own so that full citizenship, respect for the inviolable dignity of women and men, affirmation of the inviolable character of human rights, individual and collective well-being, and genuine joy become possible for everyone. Precisely because all these conditions are historically and literally inviable in today's kyriarchal globalization, no one who subscribes to Christian discipleship is exempt from the tasks involved in transformation. Consequently, I believe that the primary function of theological activity in the present circumstances is that of contributing its conceptual and institutional resources to the shift from present-day kyriarchal globalization toward a radical democratic-emancipatory globalization. In Gutiérrez's thought, to participate in the struggles to transform the radical causes of scandalous situations of social injustice lived by the majority of humanity is to affirm "a permanent demand of Christian love";[71] it is to participate actively in the eradication of sin in the world and consequently to bring forth God's reign, "which has come in its fullness into history and embraces the totality of human existence."[72] The presence of the reign of God in the reality of the world finds expression in the full restoration of justice.

Theological activity from the standpoint of a feminist option for the poor and oppressed majorities of the world, for emancipation from systemic kyriarchal domination, leads one to recognize and interpret critically where the presence and activity of Divine Wisdom occurs today in our milieu. This Christian option—which in reality is a demand, a duty, and an impelling urgency—allows one to find and name the presence and activity of Divine Wisdom in the life-giving forces of history, that is, in sociopolitical and ecclesial movements, in critical liberating religious discourses, in emancipatory visions, and in global struggles to radically transform every kyriarchal relationship of dominance. These life-giving forces are the ones that today are clearly affirming hope that things can change and confirming visions of a different, alternative world.

I wish to suggest that the feminist option for the majorities of poor and oppressed women, geared toward liberation from kyriarchal domination, not only engenders greater Christian hope but also actively nourishes the emergence of a radical democratic-emancipatory globalization with visions of change and hope. On the basis of the struggles supported by this option, we now have an open possibility of rejecting pessimism, of leaving behind indifference, and of confirming that visions of change do have an effect on the world. We now know that situations of grave social conflict can be resolved and prevented. We also know that while kyriarchal globalization makes sexual violence against women invisible, the strength of the feminist struggles around the world exposes that another type of globalization is already on the way. The signs of this new hopeful process are arising everywhere. For example, the National Feminist Committee of Nicaragua affirms that, in the context of globalization, "better living is a right" and the issue of the rights of women has become "a shield of struggle."[73] In a recent study on globalization and development, ECLAC acknowledges that "feminist internationalism had a decisive influence, throughout the twentieth century, on the recognition of women's equal rights."[74] Human Rights Watch similarly notes how women's movements have sought to change national agendas in order to shift from silence to word: "The international women's human rights movement functioned as the antidote to government complacency and lack of commitment. In every arena, women's rights activists challenged governments' cursory commitment to women's human rights."[75] The former president of Amnesty International greets with optimism the participation of this organization in the emergence of new networks for social change, observing that "the indivisible links between socio-economic and political rights have been mirrored in the emergence of a new network of protest movements. . . . A global solidarity movement to address the negative consequences of globalization is in the making."[76] It is also important in this context to take into account and to positively value the UN's commitment to promote a world agenda of equality and rights for all women: "Women's equal participation with men in power and decision-making is part of their fundamental right to participate in political life, and at the core of gender equality and women's empowerment."[77]

NEW TASKS FOR CHURCHES AND THEOLOGIES

In this new context, in which there increasingly appear signs that another world is possible and that we can put the universe back on its feet by establishing a just order, I wish to propose some ideas that may serve to continue the theological deliberations about what is entailed in carrying out a feminist option for the majorities of poor and oppressed women in the world.

To Work for Liberation and against the Kyriarchal Powers of Evil. To understand today what the obligations and tasks of the entire Christian community are, it is necessary to analyze critically how the kyriarchal powers of evil operate, how they are manifested, and what effects they have. This supposes that the follower of Jesus Christ makes a conscientious choice to confront the reality of the world as expressed in the aspirations and struggles of the global movements that are erupting today as new signs of the times. A contribution to the advancement of salvation history implies a clear option to renounce pessimism, indolence, and indifference in the face of the scandalous magnitude of social injustice that increases and multiplies social conflicts. Churches cannot evade their radical commitment to liberation from the kyriarchal powers of evil because the liberation-salvation vision is engraved in the Gospel of Jesus Christ and as such demands that churches become accountable to themselves and to the world.

To Work for the Dignity and Rights of Women and against Complicit Silence. The feminist option for the majorities of poor and oppressed women demands that churches confront and repair the atrocities committed all over the world against the dignity and the rights of women through sexual violence, rape, and sexual abuse. In my opinion, because of the sin of omission to exorcize the ghost of silence that conceals this global reality, no religion or any church can claim ignorance before this situation of immeasurable proportions. Neither can any claim innocence because kyriarchal religions, churches, and theologies have contributed significantly to the religious validation of systems that accept the degradation and humiliation of women. These systems radically reject the presence of Divine Wisdom in the world and directly contradict the liberating truth of the Christian tradition. To repair this damage, the church's power elites can and should fulfill their obligation to transform the kyriarchal relationships of domination that define their existence. The churches also can and should intervene in the implementation not only of mechanisms that eradicate the sexual abuses perpetrated by priests and pastors but also of mechanisms that end sexual atrocities against women.

To Work for the Transformation of the World and against the Negation of Hope. The transformation of the world in the present circumstances occurs through active participation in the global and local struggles for a radical democratic-emancipatory globalization. At the core of this plural movement for social change grows the hope that another world is possible, a world without violence, without war, without totalitarianism, and without social injustice. As one can see in the work of truth and reconciliation commissions, the World Social Forum, and international movements for justice, many Christian communities are involved in these struggles, and they become a confirmation of hope. The extensive theological work of Gutiérrez has given support and inspiration to this search for alternatives. Churches and feminist theologies of liberation in this context can and should continue participating with our plural resources, contributing to validate religiously, theologically, and politically the visions of change and hope that are on the way. The adoption and further development of critical-transformative feminist theory, analysis, epistemology, and hermeneutics are indispensable for illuminating the path. By her sovereign will, her grace and power, we are called to this by Divine Wisdom, *Sabiduría Divina,* who dwells within the world's struggling humanity, the poor and oppressed women who hunger and struggle for justice, well-being, and liberation.

Notes

1. Larry B. Stammer, "Globalization: A Challenge for Ethicists," and Religion News Service, "Bishops and Abuse Crisis: The Buck Stops Where, How?" both in *Los Angeles Times,* Religion section, November 9, 2002, B16.

2. See World Social Forum, "Mobilization for Global Justice," www.globalize this.org/ (accessed August 3, 2006).

3. "Unsolved Homicides/Disappearances of Michiana Females," *South Bend Tribune* (South Bend, IN), November 10, 2002, A11.

4. I am in debt to my friend in hope, Dora María Téllez, a prominent Nicaraguan scholar, political analyst, and historian, for suggesting and inspiring me to take this route. She is a renowned Sandinista commander, the President of the Sandinista Renewal Movement (Movimiento Renovador Sandinista or MRS), and she also inspires my own commitment to a spirituality of justice for the poor. See Alianza MRS, "Alianza Partido Movimiento Renovador Sandinista," http://alianzaherty2006.com/ (accessed September 27, 2006).

5. Gutiérrez first used the expression "an option for the poor and the oppressed" in a course entitled "The Church and Poverty" that he presented in Montreal in 1967. See Roberto Oliveros, *Liberación y teología: Génesis y crecimiento de una reflexión, 1966–1976* [Liberation and Theology: Genesis and Growth of a Reflection] (Lima: Centro de Estudios y Publicaciones, 1977), 98–99; Julio Lois, *Teología de la liberación: Opción por los pobres* [Theology of Liberation: Option for the Poor] (San José, Costa Rica: Departamento Ecuménico de Investigaciones, 1988), 34; James B. Nickoloff, ed., *Gustavo Gutiérrez: Essential Writings* (Maryknoll, NY: Orbis Books, 1996), 4.

6. Gustavo Gutiérrez, *A Theology of Liberation: History, Politics, and Salvation,* rev. ed. (Maryknoll, NY: Orbis Books, 1993), 173.

7. Gustavo Gutiérrez, *The Truth Shall Make You Free: Confrontations* (Maryknoll, NY: Orbis Books, 1990), 75, 81.

8. Gustavo Gutiérrez, "Option for the Poor," in *Mysterium Liberationis: Fundamental Concepts of Liberation Theology,* ed. Ignacio Ellacuría and Jon Sobrino (Maryknoll, NY: Orbis Books, 1993), 237.

9. Comisión de la Verdad y Reconciliación de Perú (CVR) [Truth and Reconciliation Commission of Peru (TRC)], *Informe final* [Final Report], 10 vols. (Lima: CVR, 2003). For the report in translation, and for further information about the commission's mandate, findings, and recommendations for restoration and reconciliation, see the CVR/TRC's home page, "Comisión de la Verdad y Reconciliación," www.cverdad.org.pe/ (accessed December 12, 2003).

10. Salomón Lerner Febres, *Discurso de presentación del informe final de la Comisión de la Verdad y Reconciliación* (Lima: Comisión de la Verdad y Reconciliación, 2003), also available at the CVR/TRC Web site, www.cverdad.org.pe/informacion/discursos/en_ceremonias05.php (accessed February 22, 2004). See also Salomón Lerner Febres's preface to the CVR's *Informe final,* 1:13–17.

11. CVR, "Introducción," in *Informe final,* 1:23.

12. CVR, "1.5. Violencia sexual contra la mujer," in *Informe final,* 6:263–384, 303, 363, 374.

13. Ibid., 6:375.

14. Ibid., 6:302.

15. All these forms of sexual violence against women, and others not mentioned here, are shown, widely documented, and described in "1.5. Violencia sexual contra la mujer" of the CVR's *Informe final.*

16. Ibid., 6:337, 375.

17. Ibid., 6:375.

18. Ibid., 6:284, 375.

19. Ibid., 6:284, 275, 302–3, 370, 372, 376.

20. Gustavo Gutiérrez, *On Job: God-Talk and the Suffering of the Innocent* (Maryknoll, NY: Orbis Books, 1987), 102.

21. Gustavo Gutiérrez, *The Power of the Poor in History: Selected Writings* (Maryknoll, NY: Orbis Books, 1983), 102, *We Drink From Our Own Wells: The Spiritual Journey of a People* (Maryknoll, NY: Orbis Books, 1984), 10, "Option for the Poor," 237, *Truth Shall Make You Free,* 56, 70, and *Theology of Liberation,* xxii.

22. Gutiérrez, *Power of the Poor,* 92, and *Theology of Liberation,* xxix.

23. Salomón Lerner Febres, preface to the CVR's *Informe final,* 1:13. Mr. Febres served as president of the CVR.

24. Gutiérrez, *Power of the Poor,* 77.

25. See the CVR's outstanding chapter on the foundations of reconciliation, "Fundamentos de la Reconciliación," *Informe final,* 9:13–104 (ch. 1).

26. Ibid., 9:13.

27. Due to the purpose of this essay, I have focused my reflection on the Peruvian TRC. However, in the past two decades, a significant number of countries have experienced similar atrocities, and more than twenty-five countries have implemented their respective commissions. In other cases, the United Nations has implemented international criminal tribunals. Among the most prominent and well-known truth and reconciliation commissions are those of South Africa, Guatemala, El Salvador, Argentina, East Timor, Sierra Leone, and Chile. The theological communities around the world have given insufficient attention to the work of these commissions, as well as to the impact and ramifications of this work for the contemporary processes of social reconciliation. For a comprehensive list of the truth and reconciliation commissions in the world, see the following Web sites: United States Institute of Peace (www.usip.org/library/truth.html); Truth Commissions Project: Strategic Choices in the Design of Truth Commissions (www.truthcommission.org/); INCORE Guide to Internet Sources on Truth and Reconciliation (www.incore.ulst.ac.uk/cds/themes/truth.html); Comisiones de la Verdad en América Latina (www.derechos.org/koaga/iii/1/cuya.html); and Asociación Pro-Derechos Humanos (www.aprodeh.org.pe/sem_verdad/enlaces.htm). See also the prominent studies by Priscilla B. Hayner, *Unspeakable Truth: Confronting State Terror and Atrocity* (New York: Routledge, 2001), and Martha Minow, *Between Vengeance and Forgiveness: Facing History after Genocide and Mass Violence* (Boston: Beacon Press, 1999).

28. Virginia Vargas, "From Silence to Word: The 'From Denial to Acceptance' Seminar of the Peruvian Truth and Reconciliation Commission," in *Reconciliation*

in a World of Conflicts, ed. Luiz Carlos Susin and María Pilar Aquino (London: SCM Press, 2003), 22.

29. CVR, "3.3. La Iglesia Católica y las iglesias evangélicas," in *Informe final,* 3:239–342.

30. Ibid., 3:263.

31. Ibid., 3:269.

32. Gutiérrez, *Power of the Poor,* 118, 139, and *Theology of Liberation,* 165–68.

33. Gutiérrez, "Option for the Poor," 238.

34. Gutiérrez, *Truth Shall Make You Free,* 162.

35. It is highly significant that the final reports for 2004 of the two most prominent human rights world organizations are focused on eradicating sexual violence against women. See, for example, Amnesty International, *It's In Our Hands: Stop Violence against Women* (London: Amnesty International Publications, Peter Benenson House, 2004), also available at www.amnesty.org/actforwomen/ (accessed July 26, 2004); LaShawn R. Jefferson, "In War as in Peace: Sexual Violence and Women's Status," Human Rights Watch World Report 2004, www.hrw.org/wr2k4/ and http://hrw.org/wr2k4/download.htm .

36. Elisabeth Schüssler Fiorenza, *Bread Not Stone: The Challenge of Feminist Biblical Interpretation* (Boston: Beacon Press, 1984), 44.

37. United Nations Population Fund, *The State of World Population 2002: People, Poverty and Possibilities: Making Development Work for the Poor* (New York: United Nations Population Fund, 2002), 8, 26, also available at www.unfpa.org (accessed November 18, 2003).

38. Michael Taylor, *Christianity, Poverty, and Wealth: The Findings of "Project 21"* (Geneva: World Council of Churches Publications, 2003), 7.

39. Inter-American Development Bank, Sustainable Development Department, "About Social Exclusion, Mission Statement," March 25, 2003, www.iadb.org/sds/ (accessed February 23, 2004).

40. Human Rights Watch, "Women's Human Rights," in *Human Rights Watch World Report 2002* (New York: Human Rights Watch, 2002), 536, 545, also available at www.hrw.org/wr2k2/women.html (accessed December 15, 2003).

41. Human Rights Watch, Women's Rights Division, "Women's Rights," www.hrw.org/women/ (accessed May 24, 2004).

42. WITNESS, *WITNESS Annual Report 2003* (New York: WITNESS, 2003), 4, also available at www.witness.org under "About Us: Reports" (accessed December 14, 2003).

43. United Nations Development Programme, "Priority Challenges in Meeting the Goals," ch. 2 of *Human Development Report 2003, Millennium Development Goals: A Compact among Nations to End Human Poverty* (New York: Oxford University Press, 2003), 18, also available at www.hdr.undp.org/ (accessed February 29, 2004).

44. Dora María Téllez, "Nicaragua: Entorno económico y social," in *Gobernabilidad democrática y seguridad ciudadana en Centroamérica: El caso de Nicaragua,* ed.

Andrés Serbin and Diego Ferreyra (Managua: Coordinadora Regional de Investigaciones Económicas y Sociales, 2000), 52–53.

45. Ivone Gebara, "Option for the Poor as an Option for the Poor Woman," in *Women, Work and Poverty,* ed. Elisabeth Schüssler Fiorenza and Anne Carr (Edinburgh: T. & T. Clark, 1987), 110.

46. Elisabeth Schüssler Fiorenza, *Discipleship of Equals: A Critical Feminist Ekklesia-logy of Liberation* (New York: Crossroad, 1993), 255.

47. United Nations Population Fund, *State of World Population 2002,* 5, 8, 28; World Health Organization, "Sexual Violence," ch. 6 of *World Report on Violence and Health* (Geneva: World Health Organization, 2002), 174, also available at www. who.int/ (accessed February 16, 2004).

48. Inter-American Development Bank, "Gender Wage Gaps," July 16, 2003, www.iadb.org (accessed September 13, 2003).

49. María Pilar Aquino, "Towards a Culture of Reconciliation: Justice, Rights, Democracy," in Susin and Aquino, *Reconciliation,* 126–34.

50. Gutiérrez, *Truth Shall Make You Free,* 132, "Option for the Poor," 239, and *Theology of Liberation,* 17.

51. Gutiérrez, *We Drink From Our Own Wells,* 11.

52. Víctor E. Tokman, *Hacia una visión integrada para enfrentar la inestabilidad y el riesgo* (Santiago: United Nations, 2003), 1–45, also available at www.eclac.cl (accessed February 23, 2004).

53. On the meaning of *neoliberalism,* see Pedro Montes, *El desorden neoliberal* (Madrid: Trotta, 1999). See also the outstanding critical study of the world neoliberal globalization of markets by Franz J. Hinkelammert, *Cultura de la esperanza y sociedad sin exclusión* (San José, Costa Rica: Departamento Ecuménico de Investigaciones, 1995).

54. This is a feminist analytical category coined by E. Schüssler Fiorenza. According to her, "the neologism *kyriarchy-kyriocentrism* (from Greek *kyrios* meaning lord, master, father, husband) seeks to express this interstructuring of domination and to replace the commonly used term *patriarchy,* which is often understood in terms of binary gender dualism. I have introduced this neologism as an analytic category in order to be able to articulate a more comprehensive systemic analysis, to underscore the complex interstructuring of domination, and to locate sexism and misogyny in the political matrix or, better, patrix of a broader range of oppressions." Elisabeth Schüssler Fiorenza, *Rhetoric and Ethic: The Politics of Biblical Studies* (Minneapolis: Fortress Press, 1999), 5.

55. ECLAC, "Globalization: A Historical and Multidimensional Perspective," ch. 1 of *Globalization and Development* (Brasilia: ECLAC, 6–10 May, 2002), 17, also available at www.eclac.org (accessed February 23, 2004).

56. ECLAC, "Inequalities and Asymmetries in the Global Order," ch. 3 of *Globalization and Development,* 75.

57. James D. Wolfensohn, "A New Global Balance: The Challenge of Leadership," President of the World Bank Group Address to the Board of Governors,

Dubai, United Arab Emirates, September 2003, p. 13, also available under "News and Events, Speeches" at www.worldbank.org (accessed February 23, 2004).

58. Elisabeth Schüssler Fiorenza, *Jesus Miriam's Child, Sophia's Prophet: Critical Issues in Feminist Christology* (New York: Continuum, 1994), 12–18.

59. Ibid., 12.

60. On this feminist conception of globalization, see María Pilar Aquino, "The Dynamics of Globalization and the University: Towards a Radical Democratic-Emancipatory Transformation," in *Toward a New Heaven and a New Earth: Essays in Honor of Elisabeth Schüssler Fiorenza,* ed. Fernando F. Segovia (Maryknoll, NY: Orbis Books, 2003), 385–406; Schüssler Fiorenza, *Rhetoric and Ethic,* 44–55.

61. Vargas, "From Silence to Word," 17.

62. CVR, "1.5. Violencia sexual contra la mujer," 6:265, 269, 272, and others.

63. Human Rights Watch, Women's Rights Division, "Women and Armed Conflict; International Justice," www.hrw.org/women/conflict.html (accessed December 13, 2003).

64. Vargas, "From Silence to Word," 18.

65. WHO, "Gender and Women's Health: Gender-Based Violence," www.who.int/gender/violence/en/ (accessed September 12, 2003).

66. Gutiérrez, "Option for the Poor," 237.

67. WHO, "Sexual Violence," 149, 150, 174.

68. Gutiérrez, *Truth Shall Make You Free,* 75.

69. See, for example, Mary John Mananzan et al., eds., *Women Resisting Violence: Spirituality for Life* (Maryknoll, NY: Orbis Books, 1996); Elisabeth Schüssler Fiorenza and Mary Shawn Copeland, eds., *Violence against Women* (Maryknoll, NY: Orbis Books, 1994).

70. Gustavo Gutiérrez, "Syllabus: Qué es hacer teología," *Jornada de Reflexión Teológica* 13 (1983).

71. Gutiérrez, *Truth Shall Make You Free,* 79.

72. Gutiérrez, *Theology of Liberation,* 171.

73. Comité Nacional Feminista, "Posicionamiento ante el IX Encuentro Feminista Latinoamericano y del Caribe," in *Feminismo y globalización: Apuntes para un análisis político desde el Movimiento,* ed. Martha Yllescas and Sofía Montenegro (Managua: Comité Nacional Feminista, 2003), 64.

74. ECLAC, "Globalization," 56.

75. Human Rights Watch, *Women's Human Rights: Human Rights Watch World Report 2002,* 536, see Human Rights Watch, "Women's Human Rights."

76. Pierre Sané, foreword to *Amnesty International Report 2001* (New York: Amnesty International Publications, 2001), 3, also available at www.amnesty.org (accessed August 8, 2003).

77. United Nations, "United Nations Millennium Declaration," September 6–8, 2000, www.un.org/millennium/ (accessed April 25, 2006).

Chapter 11

POOR IS THE COLOR OF GOD

M. SHAWN COPELAND

I am the God of your father, the God of Abraham, the God of Isaac,
and the God of Jacob. . . . I have seen the affliction of my people who are in Egypt,
and have heard their cry because of their taskmasters; I know their sufferings.

—Exodus 3:6–7

Philip said to [Jesus], "Lord, show us the Father, and we will be satisfied." Jesus said
to him, "Have I been with you all this time, Philip, and you still do not know me?
Whoever has seen me has seen the Father. How can you say, 'Show us the Father'?
Do you not believe that I am in the Father and the Father is in me?"

—John 14:8–10

In the current context of widespread and persistent global poverty, injustice, and exploitation, Christian theology, in its effort to incarnate integrity and authenticity, can no longer ignore the cry of the poor, excluded, and despised for life. Gustavo Gutiérrez brings us face to face with a new future:

> Our task is to find the words with which to talk about God in the midst of the starvation of millions, the humiliation of races regarded as inferior, discrimination against women, especially women who are poor, systematic social injustice, a persistent high rate of infant mortality, those who simply "disappear" or are deprived of their free-

216

dom, the sufferings of peoples who are struggling for their right to live, the exiles and refugees, terrorism of every kind, and . . . corpse-filled common graves.[1]

In other words, Christian theology must learn to speak about the God of Jesus of Nazareth who preferentially identifies with and walks with the poor, excluded, and despised.

With the statement "Poor is the color of God," I mean to take seriously that God's preferential love for the poor offers a disclosive moment in which the Divine Being manifests Godself to us through the poor. These millions of actual children, women, and men are a crucial symbol of the presence of the incarnate particularity of Jesus of Nazareth in our world. Moreover, if to see them is to see Jesus of Nazareth, and if to see him is to see the God on whom he stakes his whole life (John 14:9), we may say in fear and trembling, in hope and in humility, *If seeing the poor is seeing God, then poor is the color of God.*

Of course, this proposal is controversial. On the one hand, to say that God becomes one with the poor and accompanies them with preferential love raises questions for those of us who are not poor and who may be the cause of their misery. But such extravagant expenditure of divine love forms an invitation to us—an invitation to self-examination, to remorse, to repentance, to healing, to change both personal and social. On the other hand, it is difficult for us to envision and embrace a "poor god." After all, the attributes of omnipotence, omniscience, sovereignty, and beauty contradict the concrete condition of the poor as powerless, dispossessed, and unfulfilled.

I will amplify this thesis in four steps. First, if poor is the color of God, we must consider the poor: Who are they? What constitutes the condition of poverty? How can we measure and understand poverty? Answers to these questions will uncover something of contemporary poverty; unsurprisingly, these answers resonate with the same disquiet found in the social vision of the Hebrew prophets (Amos 8:4–8). Next, we shall draw out from the Gospel of Luke a picture of Jesus's social stance—that is, the response that he made in his teaching and ministry to the question of how persons and groups ought to live together.[2] To do this, we will make use of relevant events, sayings, and parables. Luke's Gospel is particularly relevant since scholars argue that it was written for an economically mixed community, more than likely including affluent and well-to-do households as well as slaves, freeborn, and freed persons. Moreover, the New Testament scholar Sharon Ringe maintains that Luke is more inclined to "talk *about* the poor," and to talk *"to* the well-to-do" concerning their responsibilities for the poor within (social) structures that still maintain some in poverty.[3] Luke's project, she concludes, may prove "especially important and especially challenging for those of us who want to live lives of justice-seeking discipleship in privileged parts of the world."[4] Third, we shall take up the relation between our response to Jesus and our response to the poor. The call to discipleship is a call to a praxis of solidarity and compassion with the poor. Jesus teaches us much about the Holy One of Israel whom he calls *Abba,* Father. The final step attempts to say something of this God, to clarify what it means to say that being with the poor is being with God and that being with God is being with the poor.

THE POOR AND THE CONDITION OF POVERTY

What is poverty? Poverty is the chronic inability to meet basic vital needs such as food, clothing, shelter, medicines, and adequate schooling. Poverty looks back at us from the vacant eyes of the child resigned to drink unclean water. Poverty looks back at us from the strained face of a parent who buries an infant dead from malnutrition. Poverty is the anguish and terror of sickness in old age, the raw rage of youth yearning for life. Poverty is violence and despair; it is fear and silence and powerlessness in the face of the future.

What is poverty? The World Bank has estimated that in 1999, 1.2 billion people worldwide (or 23 percent of the population of the developing world) had consumption levels below $1 a day and 2.8 billion lived on less than $2 a day.[5] The social critic Thomas Pogge writes:

> Worldwide, 34,000 children under age five die daily from hunger and preventable diseases. . . . Two out of five children in the developing world are stunted, one in three is underweight and one in ten is wasted. . . . One quarter of all children between five and fourteen, 250 million in all, are compelled to work, often under harsh conditions as soldiers, prostitutes, or domestic servants or in agriculture, construction, textile, or carpet production. . . . [Moreover,] the assets of the top three billionaires are more than the

combined GNP of all least developed countries and their 600 million people.[6]

Such poverty results from the intensification and extension of acquisitive materialism and growing international inequality between rich and poor peoples and nations. Thus "the poor person," Gustavo Gutiérrez declares, "is the product, or byproduct of an economic and social system fashioned by a few for their own benefit."[7]

Where is poverty? Poverty lurks in the rise in unemployment in Western Europe, Italy, France, and Germany, where rates stand approximately at 10 to 12 percent.[8] Poverty shadows India, which, between 1993 and 1998, paid the World Bank $1.475 billion dollars more than it received.[9] Poverty brutalizes sub-Saharan Africa through famine. Poverty stalks the United States, where, since 1975, the real value of the minimum wage has fallen by 25 percent; where to afford to rent a two-bedroom home at the nationally weighted Fair Market Rent (FMR) a worker would have to earn $14.66 per hour, which is nearly three times the federal minimum wage and still more than double the highest minimum wage among states that have enacted higher minimum wages.[10]

Who are the poor? Even though poverty has become more visible, the poor are still hidden in shelters, hotels, and nursing homes and buried in public cemeteries. The poor are the poorest of the poor. Among Dalit and Adivasi families who live in the poorest states of Bihar, Uttar Pradesh, and Orissa in India, 85 percent have no electricity.[11] The poor are children who cannot breathe because of vermin-induced asthma. The poor are mothers who chain-smoke to stave off hunger. The poor are fathers who weep in shame because they cannot protect their families.[12] They stand and wait in lines—to fill out forms, to eat soup, to bathe, to sleep. The poor are brought to resignation; they have no options.

Who are the poor? The poor in the Gospels are those children, women, and men who are trampled on in their need, who are cheated and exploited because they have no reserves. The poor in the Gospels, echoing Amos 8:4–6, are those whose lives and labor are bought and sold in loans with exorbitant interest rates. The poor are without privilege, without status. While the poor may be understood to form an economic category, this group also includes those whom tradition has marked as outcast through physical infirmity or ritual impurity. Like the biblical Hagar, the poor in every time and place seek the hope-filled face of survival that is God.[13]

The Social Stance of Jesus

According to the Gospel of Luke, Jesus of Nazareth inaugurates his ministry in the small synagogue of his hometown. Jesus takes the scroll from the attendant and reads: "The Spirit of the Lord is upon me, because he has anointed me to preach good news to the poor. He has sent me to proclaim release to the captives and recovering of sight to the blind, to set at liberty those who are oppressed, to proclaim the acceptable year of the Lord. . . . Today this scripture is fulfilled in your hearing" (Luke 4:18–19, 21; cf. Isa. 61:1–2; 58:6).

The Lukan narrator tells us that the gathered worshipers react with pleasure and pride: "All spoke well of him and wondered at the gracious words which proceeded out of his mouth; and they said, 'Is not this Joseph's son?'" (Luke 4:22). But Jesus's evocation of Elijah stings, and neither the cautious nor the cynical are willing to tolerate it. What was appreciative wonder sours into anger and an attempt at violence: "They rose up put him out of the city, and led him to the brow of the hill . . . that they might throw him down headlong" (Luke 4:24–29). Thus, from the outset of the third Gospel, Jesus is identified with prophecy and the fatal destiny of prophets. Moreover, his ministry and miracles signal the in-breaking of the reign of God: He was sent to those who were poor, excluded, and despised, who were wounded and impaired, who were brokenhearted. To these children, women, and men who were without choice or future, Jesus announced the comfort and coming of the reign of God, and he pledged that God was *for* them and *with* them. Indeed, the poor *(hoi ptochoi)* were at the center of his ministry. The poor included not only children, women, and men who were materially impoverished but those who were socially or religiously outcast, those physically impaired with blindness, paralysis, leprosy, or deafness. The poor included those who were oppressed or displaced through political occupation or ritual impurities, those who were broken in heart and spirit from isolation and persecution (Luke 4:18, 6:20–22, 7:22, 14:13, 21).

For the women and men drawn to this prophetic ministry, Jesus offered a new and compelling "way" of being God's people (Luke 8:1–3). He challenged his followers to live Jubilee traditions in the here and now.[14] These women and men were to place the poor at the center of their hearts and lives. Poor, excluded, and despised children, women, and men were to be loved and cherished, healed and embraced, nourished by the proclamation of the good news of the reign of God. Those drawn to Jesus's "way" were to follow him, to risk all, to turn away from anyone and anything, no matter how dear, that might distract them from this mission (Luke 14:26–28). Through word and deed, Jesus taught his disciples to center themselves in and on the God whom he knew and loved with all his heart, all his soul, all his strength, and all his mind (Luke 10:25–27; 11:1–13). He enjoined them to love others—particularly, poor, excluded, and despised children, women, and men—concretely and without reservation, to act on behalf of these "little ones" for restoration to God and to community (Luke 10:29–37).

Luke presents Jesus as having definite concern for the poor, excluded, and despised (Luke 4:38–39; 7:11–17; 8:43–48; 7:36–50). But Jesus was not indifferent to the rich. This Gospel shows Jesus in the company of persons from a wide range of social class backgrounds, accepting dinner invitations and hospitality from the wealthy (Luke 6:29–32; 14:1–7; 19:1–10) and, on occasion, healing them or members of their households (Luke 7:1–10; 8:40–56). In his study of this Gospel, Richard Cassidy concludes that Luke's Gospel underscores "universalism [as] the striking feature of Jesus' social stance."[15] But what does the rabbi from Nazareth think of riches and the use of possessions?

Opposition to Acquisitiveness.   In Luke 12 we find a large crowd gathered to hear Jesus. Suddenly, a man calls out to him asking for help in gaining a rightful share of an inheritance. Jesus replies: "Take care! Be on your guard against all kinds of greed; for one's life does not consist in the abundance of possessions" (Luke 12:15). He follows this retort with a parable of a landowner who, fortunate in the abundance of his harvest, pulls down his barns to build larger ones. The man does not merely store grain; he hoards it. Proud and smug, he believes that he has fortified himself against all misfortune. The man says to himself: "Soul, you have ample goods laid up for many years; relax, eat, drink, be merry." But God said to him, "You fool! This very night your soul is being demanded of you. And the things you have prepared, whose will they be?" Jesus concludes with a warning: "So it is with those who store up treasures for themselves but are not rich toward God" (Luke 12:16–21). The parable treats the consequences of conspicuous accumulation. The landowner not only has enough to meet present needs but has more than enough—surplus. To be "rich toward God" would have meant that he shared this surplus with the poor. In hoarding what was perishable—grain, he loses what is most perishable—his soul.

Admonition to Simple Living.   The parable of the "rich fool" is followed by a series of instructions that sketch a "way of life" in which possessions are decentered and desire is redirected to "the way" that Jesus taught. This "way" is oriented toward the reign of God; with that commitment, all that is needful will be provided. Jesus commands all who would follow him to sell their possessions and give the money to the poor. Then he encourages them to seek their heart's desire, the "unfailing treasure in heaven . . . for where your treasure is, there your heart will be" (Luke 12:22–34).

Opposition to Materialism.   In his encounter with a rich ruler, Jesus levels another warning about attachment to economic security, possessions, and social status. A wealthy man, prominent in the town (perhaps his name is known by Luke's community), asks Jesus a profound and searching question: "What must I do to inherit eternal life?" Keeping the law, Jesus tells him, is the way to eternal life. But the man has kept the commandments faithfully, so he is looking for something more. Jesus looks at him and says, "There is still one thing lacking: Sell all that you own and distribute the money to the poor, and you will have treasure in heaven; then come, follow me." "When the man heard this, he grew sad; for he was very rich" (Luke 18:18–22).

Here is a man who has everything and wants more. But the more that he desires requires that he relinquish what he has, and he cannot strip himself of his possessions and property. He fears loss of economic security, self-esteem, and social standing. In a commentary on this pericope as told in Mark, George Soares-Prabhu writes that whatever this man may own in terms of material possessions or "moral merit, he lacks . . . the freedom which comes to those who have experienced that God is good. To experience this he must give all that he has to the poor and follow Jesus."[16] Here is a man who cannot empty his hands to seize the freedom for which he yearns and that Jesus offers. Instead, he capitulates to the demands and codes of his social class.

Opposition to Exclusions.   With the parable of the Good Samaritan (Luke 10:25–37), Jesus challenges the narrow definition of neighbor love by showing the potential of a renewed and open heart. With the story of the Great Banquet (Luke 14:12–24), he shows just how unrestricted that love must be. Here God's reign is symbolized as a great feast; the pains of hunger, isolation, and sadness are supplanted by plenty, companionship, and rejoicing. God sets a table for the "little ones," those children, women, and men who usually are denied access to restorative moments of human encouragement and celebration, to the material benefits of culture and society.[17]

In parables and instructions on the use of possessions, Jesus advances a distinctive prophetic praxis on behalf of the reign of God.[18] This praxis is at once historical and eschatological, ethical and moral, social and religious, personal and communal. It narrates and dramatizes images and stories of reversal and transformation, "invert[s] the usual ways of thinking about power and authority," and demands personal conversion and new solidarities.[19] Jesus invites all who would follow him to abandon loyalties to class and station, family and kin, culture and nation in order to form God's people anew. Above all, Jesus challenges us to break with the security of achievement, wealth, and status to "trust solely in God's providential care."[20]

RESPONDING TO THE POOR IS RESPONDING TO JESUS

The Gospels enact how a response to the poor is a response to Jesus and his invitation to discipleship. Following Jesus means following him to the poor. The Sermon on the Plain (Luke 6:20–26) and the story of Zacchaeus (Luke 19:1–10) provide good examples.

The Beatitudes or Sermon on the Plain.   Arguably, some of the most consoling and most discomfiting language that Jesus employs is found in the Beatitudes or Sermon on the Plain (Luke 6:20–26):

> Then he looked up at his disciples and said:
> "Blessed are you who are poor,
> for yours is the kingdom of God.
> Blessed are you who are hungry now,
> for you will be filled.
> Blessed are you who weep now,
> for you will laugh.

Blessed are you when people hate you, and when they exclude you,
  revile you, and defame you on account of the Son of Man. Rejoice
  in that day and leap for joy, for surely your reward is great in
  heaven; for that is what their ancestors did to the prophets.
But woe to you who are rich,
for you have received your consolation.
Woe to you who are full now,
for you will be hungry.
Woe to you who are laughing now,
for you will mourn and weep.
Woe to you when all speak well of you, for that is what their
  ancestor did to the false prophets."

We should recall that Jesus lived in a land occupied by a conquering
foreign power. The social and psychological anxiety this produced can
scarcely be imagined. Certainly, the poor, excluded, and despised were no
strangers to hunger, grief, and oppression. Yet even in the midst of political repression and social upheaval some classes and individuals profited
from the occupation; some collaborated and betrayed family and friends.
Some religious leaders squandered the power of office and position to gain
security and affirmation. The reversals that are implicit in these sayings
echo with the traditions of Jubilee. Surely, the possibility of change, of
overturning a repressive order, was "good news" for the poor. On the other
hand, to men and women of privilege, "the Beatitudes doubtless brought
more threat than comfort."[21] What would happen to them in a "new"
order of things? What infidelities and betrayals would be made public?
The key to their transformation lies in their willingness to surrender the
securities of the "old, established order" and acknowledge the coming
"reign of God."

Zacchaeus.   The chief tax collector of Jericho, the wealthy Zacchaeus,
was curious to see Jesus. The Gospel describes him as short in stature, so
to see the rabbi from Nazareth he positioned himself in a sycamore tree
along the route Jesus would take. Unexpectedly, Jesus looked up and saw
Zacchaeus and, despite the disapproval of the crowd, made himself a
guest in Zacchaeus's house. Perhaps Zacchaeus was grateful to be seen for
who he truly was, a son of Abraham (Luke 19:9). Perhaps he had been
uncomfortable with his situation as a tax collector collaborating in and

benefiting from Roman domination. We do not know. What we do know is that Zacchaeus reversed his life; offered an opportunity for transformation, he took it. Zacchaeus responded to Jesus by responding to the poor: "Half of my possessions, I will give to the poor; and if I have defrauded anyone of anything, I will pay back four times as much" (Luke 19:8). He discovered that following Jesus meant following him to the poor. Willingly and publicly, Zacchaeus pledged to give half of his wealth to the poor and to compensate at a substantial penalty the money he had extorted from his neighbors. Unlike the rich ruler, Zacchaeus, when offered the opportunity to discover a new and richer life, chose it.

Jesus invites his disciples in every age to be present to him by being present to the poor. And, if we would be present to the poor in our own time, we too must change our way of living, of being in the world. Yet to stand with and beside the poor, to work in solidarity with poor women and men, we cannot be innocent about poverty. Gutiérrez teaches us that this solidarity may "manifest itself in specific action, a style of life, a break with one's social class."[22] And the surest way to be with the poor is to struggle against poverty: a praxis of compassionate solidarity is an expression of Christian love and a protest against poverty. It is an "act of love and liberation" lived in authentic imitation of Jesus of Nazareth through which we "take on the sinful human condition to liberate humankind from sin and all its consequences."[23]

THE GOD OF JESUS

The God whom Jesus discloses in his person, his teaching, and his praxis is a God of solidarity and compassion. The God of Jesus bathes the unclean and impure, holds the cripple, comforts the brokenhearted. The God of Jesus of Nazareth is a God who loves the poor, excluded, and despised.

The God whom Jesus shows us is a God who extends the Sabbath so that it serves the lives of those whom God has created. The God whom Jesus reveals is a God whose household has room for all. The God whom Jesus reveals is a God so eager with love for us that God is driven to become incarnate; our God has a "passion for human beings."[24]

Poor is the color of God because God in Jesus has taken up the cause of poor, excluded, and despised persons as a divine cause. Poor is the color of God because to see Jesus is to see his God, his Father (John 14:8–10).

Poor is the color of God because God has made the liberation of poor, excluded, and despised persons a divine goal. To say that poor is the color of God is to say that God has made the condition of the poor, excluded, and despised God's own. This affirmation is grounded in biblical witness: God elects or chooses a poor and despised people (the enslaved Hebrews), takes up their cause, and promises their liberation and flourishing. To say that poor is the color of God means that God is one with, for, and on the side of the poor, excluded, and despised. Poor is the color of God because God, in Jesus of Nazareth, in an act of divine love, took on the existence of the poor and became one with them, emptying himself of all the riches and sovereignty of divinity, becoming a vulnerable God of the poor.

What does it mean to say that poor is the color of God or that being with the poor is being with God? What might it mean to say that broken and impoverished children, women, and men even manifest God to us in such a way that they make God present to us and for us, not only in this time and place, but always (Matt. 26:11)?

Poverty is uncertainty in the ordinary circumstances of life—uncertainty about how to pay the rent, how to pay medical bills, how to eat on a regular basis. The poor, Rosemary Haughton writes, "have always been the beloved of God in the very simple sense that being poor means being vulnerable and therefore divine love finds it easier to break through."[25] And God does—in the streets of Los Angeles and Roxbury, in the favelas of Sao Paulo and Lima, in the prisons of Columbia and Zimbabwe, in the mines of Bolivia and Russia. In these places and many more, God calls to us to open ourselves to the poor, who are as a doorway by which to step into the life and hopes of God. For being with the poor—excluded and despised children, women, and men—is being with God. Poor is the color of God because being with the poor is being with God.

NOTES

1. Gustavo Gutiérrez, *Essential Writings,* ed. James B. Nickoloff (Maryknoll, NY: Orbis Books, 1996), 318.

2. I borrow the phrase *social stance* from Richard J. Cassidy, *Jesus, Politics, and Society: A Study of Luke's Gospel* (Maryknoll, NY: Orbis Books, 1978).

3. Sharon H. Ringe, "Luke's Gospel: 'Good News to the Poor' for the Non-Poor," in *The New Testament: Introducing the Way of Discipleship,* ed. Wes Howard-

Brook and Sharon H. Ringe (Maryknoll, NY: Orbis Books, 2002), 65; see also Cassidy, *Jesus, Politics,* 32–33.

4. Ringe, "Luke's Gospel," 64.

5. For the latest statistics on global poverty, see World Bank, "Poverty" (under "Data," "By Topic"), http://web.worldbank.org/WBSITE/EXTERNAL/DATASTATISTICS/0,,contentMDK:20394878~menuPK:1192714~pagePK:64133150~piPK:64133175~theSitePK:239419,00.html (accessed August 7, 2006).

6. Thomas W. Pogge, "The Moral Demands of Global Justice," *Dissent* 47 (Fall 2000): 37–38.

7. Gustavo Gutiérrez, "The Irruption of the Poor in Latin America and the Christian Communities of the Common People," in *The Challenge of Basic Christian Communities,* ed. Sergio Torres and John Eagleson (Maryknoll, NY: Orbis Books, 1981), 109.

8. Amartya Sen, *Development as Freedom* (New York: Anchor Doubleday, 1999), 95.

9. Arundhati Roy, *The Cost of Living* (New York: Random House, 1999), 29.

10. National Coalition for the Homeless, *Welfare to What II,* June 2001, available from the National Coalition for the Homeless, 1012 Fourteenth Street NW, Suite 600, Washington, DC; 202–737–6444, www.nationalhomeless.org.

11. Arundhati Roy, *Power Politics* (Boston: South End Press, 2001), 59.

12. For a penetrating account of the suffering of children, women, and men who are homeless and poor, see Jonathan Kozol, *Rachel and Her Children: Homeless Families in America* (New York: Fawcett Publications, 1988).

13. For a recent treatment of the biblical Hagar as a point of departure for womanist theology, see Delores S. Williams, *Sisters in the Wilderness: The Challenge of Womanist God-Talk* (Maryknoll, NY: Orbis Books, 1993).

14. N.T. Wright, *Jesus and the Victory of God* (Minneapolis: Fortress Press, 1996), 295.

15. Cassidy, *Jesus, Politics,* 24.

16. George Soares-Prabhu, "Anti-Greed and Anti-Pride: Mark 10:17–27 and 10:35–45 in the Light of Tribal Values," in *Voices from the Margin: Interpreting the Bible in the Third World,* ed. R. S. Sugirtharajah (Maryknoll, NY: Orbis Books, 1995), 125.

17. Sharon H. Ringe, *Jesus, Liberation, and the Biblical Jubilee* (Philadelphia: Fortress Press, 1985), 58.

18. Wright, *Jesus and the Victory,* 243, 280.

19. Ringe, *Jesus, Liberation,* 13.

20. Soares-Prabhu, "Anti-Greed and Anti-Pride," 125.

21. Ringe, *Jesus, Liberation,* 54.

22. Gustavo Gutiérrez, *A Theology of Liberation: History, Politics, and Salvation* (Maryknoll, NY: Orbis Books, 1988), 172.

23. Ibid., 172.

24. Rosemary Haughton, *The Passionate God* (New York: Paulist Press, 1981), 6.

25. Ibid., 326.

Chapter 12

THE OPTION FOR THE POOR IN THE CONTEXT OF GLOBALIZATION

A Feminist Vision

MARY CATHERINE HILKERT

Building on María Pilar Aquino's insights from an earlier chapter, I would like to reflect on the connections between poverty and gender in a globalized economy in which the inequities between rich and poor grow more and more vast and in which women and children remain the poorest of the poor. In particular, I want to highlight three of the theological implications of the reality that Aquino identified for our reflection and discussion. First, the faces of women deprived of basic rights fully reveal the face of the poor and the excluded to whom theology is accountable. Any option for the poor must address this reality and must account for this fact in a sustained manner. Second, liberation theologians must be explicit regarding the transformation of the church's dominant structures and theologies. Third, male and female theologians have the responsibility of consciously ending our contribution to the systems, theories, and theologies that multiply dominance in society and in the churches if we are to contribute to the genuine flourishing of humanity and of the earth.

THE FACES OF WOMEN AS THE FACES OF THE POOR

The faces of women fully reveal faces of the poor, but many of us have yet to make the connections between poverty and patriarchy. As Aquino pointed out, the statistics confirm that around the globe women are the poorest of the poor. The United Nations General Assembly held a special session in June 2000 on gender equality, development, and peace for the twenty-first century.[1] Significant progress was reported in many areas since the time of the Beijing Conference, which identified "the persistent and increasing burden of poverty on women" as one of the twelve areas of critical concern requiring the special attention of the international community. Nevertheless, at the beginning of the new millennium, it remains the case that

- The majority of the 1.5 billion people living on one dollar a day or less are women, and the gap between women and men caught in the cycle of poverty continues to widen.
- Women earn on average slightly more than 50 percent of what men earn.
- Women living in poverty are often denied access to credit, land, and inheritance, and their labor goes unrewarded and unrecognized.
- Women living in poverty lack adequate access to health care, nutrition, education, and support services.
- Women's participation in decision making at home and in the community is minimal.
- Women lack the resources to change their situation.[2]

To concretize those statistics and bring the focus close to home, we need only turn to the local and national newspapers. As Aquino noted, a recent article in the South Bend, Indiana, paper carried a full page of photos of unsolved homicides and the disappearances of women of diverse ages, races, and ethnic groups, the vast majority of whom were presumed to be victims of domestic violence.[3] Women for whom pictures were not available were portrayed by the same anonymous silhouette, which rendered them once again invisible.

In the minds of most of my undergraduate students, the faces that come to mind when we talk about liberation theology are the faces of the poor without attention to gender. Yet the faces that come to mind when we talk about feminist theology are the faces of privileged women of the dominant class, race, and ethnicity in this culture. We have yet to make the connections between poverty and patriarchy, between sexism and racism, between violence against women and the devastation of the earth. Each of these forms of injustice involves the systematic and structural denial of the full dignity and inherent worth of human persons or of God's beloved creation. One group that holds power in a social system assigns value to another group to the detriment of the other and in a way that keeps the other in a subordinate position.[4] As Shawn Copeland has noted, we will not be able to discover what it means to be human until we stand in solidarity not only with the poor but more specifically with the forgotten subjects of history, the "exploited, despised, poor women of color."[5] That solidarity entails a recognition of the humanity of the other, both as "fully human" and as "other," and a willingness to be in mutual relationship with the other. One way of specifying the preferential option for the poor is to ask ourselves: Are we, as the church, committed to justice for poor women, and specifically for poor women of color? That question brings us to a second challenge from Aquino's chapter, namely the need for transformation of the church's dominant structures and theology.

TRANSFORMATION OF THE CHURCH'S DOMINANT STRUCTURES AND THEOLOGY

There is no question that poor women, and those who, like Gustavo Gutiérrez, have lived and ministered with them in the church of the poor, have found good news of liberation and radical hope in the person and praxis of Jesus, in the Gospel, in the prophetic heritage of the church's social teaching, and in authentic Christian discipleship. But we have not heard the proclamation of that liberating Word from the voices of women, and specifically from the voices of poor women of color. We have not heard them preach the good news of salvation they discover in the very Scriptures that have been used to perpetuate patriarchal and homophobic biases. Nor do the struggles and joys of poor women of color serve as the starting point for our theological reflection, let alone for official church teaching, or as a criterion of their validity.

In speaking of the poor, the Puebla document recognized that women are doubly oppressed and marginalized, even though the section was moved to a footnote in the final text: "The poor do not lack simply material goods. They also miss, on the level of human dignity, full participation in sociopolitical life. Those found in this category are principally our indigenous peoples, peasants, manual laborers, marginalized urban dwellers and, in particular, the women of these social groups. The women are doubly oppressed and marginalized."[6]

In 2001 the U.S. Catholic bishops issued a "Call to Solidarity with Africa," noting that Africa is quickly becoming the primary place of poverty in the world. The document recognizes that "African women bear a disproportionate burden of poverty, lack of health care, and little political empowerment."[7] It calls attention to the severity of the HIV/AIDS crisis in Africa as well. But it was the organization African Women Religious Leaders, meeting in Kenya in June 2002, that made explicit the connection between the two. Muthoni Mwithiga, the keynote speaker at that meeting, insisted that commitment to the African orphans of AIDS and to dealing with the HIV/AIDS crisis "requires an adjacent commitment to gender disparity, sexuality, and the need for empowering African women."[8]

Poor women of color are, of course, included in the church's social teaching, as are all women, but the struggles, hopes, and experience of women are all too often relegated to the footnotes. One of the reasons that the church's call for justice to women, and to poor women precisely as women and not only because they are poor, is not heard more clearly was identified by the bishops themselves. In the document from their 1971 synod, *Justice in the World,* they affirm that "[e]veryone who ventures to speak to people about justice must first be just in their eyes."[9] Preaching justice for women is undercut when the word of healing and truth is rarely proclaimed by women in the name of the church, at least not from the pulpit at Eucharist. The affirmation that Jesus took on the fullness of humanity and shared our lot in every way becomes incredible to women when ecclesial documents say that, if the role of Christ in the celebration of the Eucharist were not taken by a man, "it would be difficult to see in the minister the image of Christ."[10] Communities of the poor have witnessed the image of Christ in women who have lived and died in their midst. Yet those same women who were their pastors and faithful friends could not minister the Eucharist or speak the reconciling words of the church's sacrament of reconciliation in the name of the church, even when that meant that those communities would be deprived of the church's sacramental ministry. The prayer of the church does indeed form the faith of the church. When our ritual roles of leadership are limited to males and when only male images and language for God are permitted in liturgical texts and public prayer, we are being formed in the belief that men have a fuller capacity for imaging the divine than do women. But even more is at stake: our very understanding of who God is and where God is to be found in our midst.

How can the church be a community that encourages women to say no to domestic violence, to sexual exploitation, and to social injustice when women's voices, especially women's voices that challenge the dominant structures and theology of the church, are rarely audible, much less authoritative, in the circles in which official church teaching is defined? Nowhere is this more true than in areas of sexual morality, where women are those most directly affected.

A church in which only ordained males can speak with authority, whether in granting absolution and proclaiming our faith in the death and resurrection of Jesus or in interpreting the faith of the church and declaring prophetic social teaching, will not be able to proclaim the full baptismal equality and dignity of women with credibility. The anthropological claim that all persons are created in the image of God undergirds all of our social teaching, including the preferential option for the poor. But that very equality and dignity is called into question when men define what constitutes women's unique feminine roles, vocations, and responsibilities and when women's subordinate roles in the ecclesial community are legitimated on the basis of divine revelation.

THE CALL TO CONVERSION ADDRESSED TO THEOLOGIANS

The call of conversion addressed to the church involves all of us, but it requires something different from each of us according to our different social and ecclesial locations. In addition to calling for change on the part of the hierarchy, Aquino rightly calls for male and female theologians to reflect on our own participation in structures of inequality and dominance and our own exercise of power and responsibility. That is a particular challenge to those of us who are women who hold and exercise a degree of power within academic or ecclesial systems or both. Feminist theology is too often perceived as privileged white women's theology because we who are feminist theologians have too often failed to recognize our own biases and the limits of our worlds, our words, our concerns, our relationships, our circle of solidarity, and, ultimately, our vision of the reign of God. Perhaps the warnings to two of the pioneers of Catholic feminist theology can stand as a challenge to us all as we try to dwell in what Catherine of Siena called the "cell of self-knowledge" so that we may come to realize the many conversions that will be demanded of us if we are truly to share God's preferential option for the poor and the excluded.

The first passage comes from an open letter that the black lesbian feminist poet Audre Lorde wrote to Mary Daly over twenty years ago, one of the first public challenges to white feminists. Lorde's charge was that white feminists, by reducing all difference to gender and ignoring our own racism, were perpetuating the same kind of structures of domination and exclusion we were trying to critique. As Lorde wrote to Daly,

> [T]o imply that women suffer the same oppression simply because we are women is to lose sight of the many varied tools of patriarchy. It is to ignore how those tools are used by women without awareness against each other. . . . Did you ever read my words, or did you merely finger through them for quotations you thought might valuably support an already conceived idea concerning some old and distorted connection between us? . . . [B]eyond sisterhood is still racism.[11]

The final challenge is to women in academia, but the charge extends to all of us who hope to speak and live in solidarity with the poor, including poor women of color. The poem "Academic Women," from the feminist poet and social activist Renny Golden, concludes Elisabeth Schüssler Fiorenza's introduction to her volume on feminist biblical hermeneutics, *Bread Not Stone,* and is a reminder to us all.

> Rainbow fish precious, picked from the catch.
> You swim through their corridors, upstream.
> you've done their task and ours,

double labor familiar as laundry.
We quote from your books,
claim you before men
who tell our bodies they're all we got.
Sisters, light dazzles when it's pure.
Beacons: remember you illumine someone's way.
Their seduction is naming you stars . . .
brilliant, singular, without purpose.

When you speak of the common woman, the poor woman
get the accent right.
Consider the net enfolding you.
Outside we are thousands.
Unless you swim in our waters,
you'll miss the depth.
From time to time, you will have to mention us,
but you won't get it right.[12]

NOTES

1. UN Department of Public Information, "Women 2000: Gender Equality, Development, and Peace for the Twenty-First Century," 2000, fact sheet, www.un.org/womenwatch/asp/user/list.asp?ParentID=4002 (accessed May 24, 2006).

2. Ibid.

3. "Unsolved Homicides/Disappearances of Michiana Females," *South Bend Tribune,* November 10, 2002, A11.

4. See M. Shawn Copeland, "The Interaction of Racism, Sexism, and Classism in Women's Exploitation," in *Women, Work, and Poverty,* Concilium 194, ed. Elisabeth Schüssler Fiorenza and Anne Carr (Edinburgh: T. & T. Clark, 1987), 19–27.

5. M. Shawn Copeland, "The New Anthropological Subject at the Heart of the Mystical Body of Christ," *Proceedings of the Catholic Theological Society of America* 53 (1998): 30.

6. John Egleson and Phillip Scharper, eds., *Puebla and Beyond* (Maryknoll, NY: Orbis Books, 1979), no. 1135.

7. U.S. Conference of Catholic Bishops, "A Call to Solidarity with Africa," November 14, 2001, www.usccb.org/sdwp/africa.htm (accessed May 24, 2006).

8. Muthoni Mwithiga, Keynote Speech, Meeting of African Women Religious Leaders, quoted in "Women of Faith and the Orphans of AIDS Crisis in Africa:

Agents of Delivery," Nairobi, Kenya, June 9, 2002, www.wcrp.org/RforP/womens%20program/women_nairobi_preassembly.html (accessed May 24, 2006), 1.

9. Synod of Bishops 1971, "Justice in the World," in *Catholic Social Thought: The Documentary Heritage,* ed. David J. O'Brien and Thomas A. Shannon (Maryknoll, NY: Orbis Books, 1992), 295.

10. *Inter Insigniores,* "Vatican Declaration: Women in the Ministerial Priesthood," *Origins* 6 (February 3, 1977): 522.

11. Audre Lorde, *Sister Outsider* (Freedom, CA: Crossing Press, 1984), 67–70.

12. Renny Golden, "Academic Women," in *Struggle Is a Name for Hope: Poetry,* ed. Renny Golden and Sheila Collins, Worker Writer Series 3 (Minneapolis: West End Press, 1983), 20; quoted in Elisabeth Schüssler Fiorenza, *Bread Not Stone: The Challenge of Feminist Biblical Interpretation* (Boston: Beacon Press, 1984), xxiv–xxv. Reprinted here by permission of West End Press.

Part Seven

POVERTY, LITURGY,

AND POPULAR RELIGIOSITY

Chapter 13

THE PLACE OF THE POOR
IN THE EUCHARISTIC ASSEMBLY

CASIANO FLORISTÁN

For a long time the poor have not found their appropriate place in the eucharistic assembly, either because they are relegated to the last places or because they have taken refuge in various forms of popular religiosity that are less clerical, more egalitarian, and more free. Nevertheless, contemporary base communities in Latin America and immigrant Catholics in parishes and communities in the First World, to use two examples, demonstrate that the poor flourish when they are treated as brothers and sisters without discrimination. This represents an accomplishment of vibrant communities and renovated parishes that have made their own the option for the poor. To examine the situation of the poor with regard to the Eucharist, I will analyze it as a meal celebrated in a fraternal assembly, where Christian agape is shared and grace is celebrated with the privileged presence of the poor.

THE EUCHARIST, CHRISTIAN MEAL

Exegetical and historical research on the Eucharist in the past decades insists on emphasizing the symbolic aspect of the meal to understand it in depth. To eat, affirms Luis Maldonado, "is, above all, a human act; but it is also—it can be—a numinous, sacred act; finally it can become an evangelical act."[1] Eating is one of the most common acts of human beings. It shapes human experience and religious rites. It is necessary for sustaining life, which is sacred. Even the way we season and prepare food shapes part of our culture.

Of course we do not eat alone; eating is basically a social act. We eat with our brothers and sisters and friends in groups or in community. When eating is done in community, it is a sign of communion. Along with our daily meals are festive banquets, wedding receptions, fraternal dinners, and ancestral religious agapes. Food and drink are part of living together as human beings and part of our religious rites.

Two of the most important primordial necessities of human beings are food and drink. Eating and drinking nourish life; they enable one to celebrate with friends or brothers, to unite in intimate communion, to share feelings and festivities. The meal, a natural symbol of the intimacy and joy of friendship, is a sacrament of life and wisdom.

Food and drink took on special importance in the ancient Near East, which was prone to spells of famine and drought. Consequently one of the government's functions was to make sure subjects were well nourished, a responsibility that was not always fulfilled. Being destitute was another term for being hungry and thirsty.

Unlike Stoic and Gnostic texts, which describe approaching God through fasting and various corporal mortifications, the Bible takes seriously the human needs of the body. Of course, we must provide food for the stomach and the person as a whole. *Hunger* and *thirst,* therefore, are ambivalent terms in the New Testament, where we also hear of phrases like the "hunger and thirst for justice." At the beginning of his public life Jesus was hungry in the desert, and he died on the cross saying, "I am thirsty." He was tempted in both instances. Satisfying others' hunger and slaking their thirst are acts of mercy, which are taken into account in God's judgment, where Jesus is dressed with the clothing of misery.

Through taste one perceives the flavor of food. Let us remember that taste *(sabor)* and knowledge *(saber)* come from the word *wisdom (sabiduría),* perceived in two ways: as food and as knowledge. The Eucharist could be called a morsel and a drink within the context of a meal. Tasting God is finding a delicious knowledge of God.

Bread and wine, which are basic elements of Mediterranean towns, are obtained through an elaborate process, starting from the grains and the grapes that emerge from the earth, by action from the sun and the rain, as stalks of wheat and grapevines. They are the gift of the earth and the work of human hands. The grains are crushed and the grapes are pressed. The bread and wine are symbols of solids and liquids, body and blood, nature and history, culture and cult, dispersion and unity, work and celebration, sustenance and inspiration, masculinity and femininity, and the hunger and thirst of the poor. Wheat and grapes become flour and grape juice and finally bread and wine through a long and complex process of grinding and pressing, baking, cooking, boiling, and fermenting. The bread and wine represent the totality of the universe.

It has been rightly said that to eat together is the essence of Christianity. Communitarian agape, as a shared meal, is a central element of Christian churches, called Eucharist by Catholics, offering by the Orthodox, and holy supper by Protestants. Exegetes and historians give various reasons to justify Christian agape. Vatican II affirms that "no Christian community is built up which does not grow from and hinge on the celebration of the most holy Eucharist."[2] "The Eucharist," claims M. Díaz Mateos, "is the central activity of the church, but that activity appears to most people as a cultic act, ritual and sacred, not as a familiar and communitarian act, as eating can be."[3]

According to the Old Testament, union with God is achieved through nourishment. Deuteronomy reminds us that the poor, immigrants, widows, and orphans should be welcomed to the sacrificial meals. According to the prophets Elijah and Elisha, the people will be filled in the fullness of messianic times, characterized by the banquet of the poor, where food will abound and drink will be exquisite. A "feast of rich food and choice wines, juicy, rich food and pure, choice wines" will be offered to "all nations" (Isa. 25:6–8).

God wants everybody to eat and to share food so that there will be a solidarity among people concerning the goods and provisions of this world. "Many will come from the east and the west, and will recline at the table of the kingdom of heaven with Abraham, Isaac, and Jacob" (Matt. 8:11). Jesus says, "I confer a kingdom on you, just as my Father has conferred one on me, that you may eat and drink at my table in my kingdom" (Luke 22:29–30b). Therefore, "Blessed is the one who will dine in the kingdom of God" (Luke 14:15). God wants solidarity in the sharing of food and goods.

Christian life does not consist in celebrating rituals. We should not forget, says Paul's letter to the Romans, "that the kingdom of God is not food or drink, but justice, peace, and joy in the Holy Spirit" (Rom. 14:17). Nonetheless, all meals had a sacred character in Jesus's time. Hence they were accompanied by a prayer of thanksgiving. God is not only the Lord of history but also the owner of the earth and all of its goods. He is the host of every meal. God desires that we all eat and share meals, that we have solidarity with each other concerning the food and the goods of this world.

It is as necessary to feed everyone else, especially the poor and socially or religiously marginalized, in other words, the Third World, as it is to feed oneself; it is an evangelical imperative. Without the sharing of food and drink, natural signs of creation elaborated by human beings, there is no Eucharist. Moreover, the Eucharist is a fraternal agape that makes present Christ's charity, completely given in person. At the end of his life, he gives himself in the form of bread, broken and shared, sacrament of his body; the sharing of the cup is an efficacious sign of his blood.

As J. M. Castillo notes, "Justice was not required in fact, from the outset, as a condition, or as a consequence, and much less as constitutive of the Eucharistic celebration."[4] The Eucharist is frequently associated with devotion and adoration, not with justice or solidarity. It has been improperly suggested that the Eucharist is the "bread of the angels" or "food for the soul," understood from the perspective of an exaggerated spiritualism. It has been reduced to a mere act of duty, alienated subjectively and objectively by its distance from transformative social and political praxis.[5] The alienation of the bread and wine from the context of a meal "runs the risk," says Leon Dufour, "of ignoring the influence that nourishment and a meal have on the Eucharistic rite as such."[6]

In the Bible, food and drink are fundamental signs of God's love that unites itself with humanity. Bread and wine are goods of creation. They are portions of the cosmos and the work of human hands. They are not, before or after blessing, petrified, static things; rather, they are dynamic— that is, they keep a relationship, they are a communication, a communion in Christ. In what is called the consecration, which happens in the context of the eucharistic prayer, there exists a change of functions, of meaning and purpose. The natural signs of bread and wine, which point out the love of God in creation, are changed into Christian symbols that express the liberating and saving love of Christ. Instead of the substance of the cosmos, the Lord of the cosmos is symbolically and really present. The bread and the wine were symbols of the humanized cosmos; after the blessing they are signs of the resurrected Lord, the fullness and aspiration of all of humanity and of the whole cosmos.

All those present eat the same eucharistic bread and drink from the same sacred cup. They eat and drink in one and the same communion, expressing a *koinonia*. They participate in the bread and wine of human fraternity and divine filiation. The sign of union comes, not from the grains of wheat gathered in the bread, or from the bunches of grapes pressed into one drink, but from the unitive function that the consecrated, broken bread and the overflowing cup for the salvation of all possess.

Naturally the relation of the Christian to creation is not abolished any more than the bread and wine are annihilated. This Eucharist simultaneously belongs to this history and to the future. The bread and the cup give the fruit of the paschal act of Christ: the death to sin and the resurrection to life. They give this fruit as an anticipation. The Eucharist announces not only the death of Christ until he comes but also a foretaste of the joyful banquet of the poor in the new heaven and the new earth. Thus in the Eucharist there is a cascade of meanings.

The sacramental reality of the body and blood of the Lord is founded upon the symbolic reality of the bread, the wine, and life. The concrete reality of human beings is our body and our blood, but the bread and wine are necessary conditions for human life. A person cannot live without eating and drinking. The bread and wine, considered in their unity, are the source of earthly life given by God in God's own unity of flesh and blood. Furthermore, the bread and wine are given in a single act. The breaking of the bread and the blessing of the cup are the symbols of a banquet. God gives life with the bread and the wine that sustain it. The blessing of the bread and the wine repositions the meal within a new life of total communion at the new table of the kingdom of God, where the invitees eat the same and are equals. God and Jesus become present when food and drink are shared equally among all brothers and sisters.

DEMANDS OF FRATERNITY

In many well-established cultures and religions, brothers and sisters are those who proceed from the same parents, due to the blood relationship, or from certain friends, due to the relationship of choice. Relationship then, takes place in the family or among people intimately connected by friendship. Effectively, our true brothers and sisters are not only those of the same family but also the friends with whom we have established a deeper level of connection. To fraternize means, therefore, to have friendship and solidarity, above all with those who are outside our circle, in order to live with them in peace, without tension, threats, or violence.

To understand the meaning of the word *fraternity* we must take into account the cultural and religious tradition we inherited. In the Judaism of Jesus's day, *brother* meant one who professed the same religion. The term also referred to a proselyte or candidate who was about to enter Judaism or to someone who formed part of the same rabbinic group or school of apprentices who in time would become teachers. In contrast, *neighbor* referred to a person who lived in Israel without being an Israelite. Hence the daring, almost scandalous, teaching of Jesus of Nazareth that one should treat the helpless neighbor like a brother, with the greatest example being the Good Samaritan. The New Testament demands that we love our brother and our neighbor. However, it is not enough to simply call those in one's community one's brother or sister; it is necessary to live authentically in fraternity.

Evidently, the Christians of the first communities treated each other like true brothers and sisters in virtue of their spiritual fraternity, which exceeded the natural fraternity. According to the council of Jerusalem, brothers were also Christians who came from pagan towns. All the members of the community were believers, and all were baptized, both men and women. The Christian fraternity derived from the fatherhood of God and from the extraordinary fact that Jesus became everyone's brother, especially the poor with whom he identified himself. Jesus Christ was the first-born of the multitude of brothers and sisters.

Probably the word *brother* is the most frequently used word in our vocabulary that has also lost the most meaning. Until a few years ago, the sermons of many preachers in the parish pulpits invariable began with the words "My dear brothers," even though these words sometimes did not correspond with reality. In the sixteenth century, *fraternity* meant a group of lay brothers, such as the one to which Erasmus belonged, who banded together to live the evangelical demands of Christianity.

Today it is incomprehensible that we worry only about those who are our own, belonging to our own team, ethnicity, language, or nation, without giving importance to a universal vision, or that we continue to cling to our own kin without sharing anything important with others, out of fear of newcomers, the poor, and those of another skin color. It is unacceptable for the Christian community to discriminate against the poor for being poor and not to consider them brothers. For St. Paul, according to J. D. Crossan, the terms *brothers* and *sisters* meant "people who share."[7]

The French Revolution produced the slogan "Liberty, equality, fraternity," in which *fraternity* can be understood as equality among all human beings, in freedom. This slogan has its roots in the Gospel. Since Vatican II and the democratization of society, we have begun to call again *brother* that person who participates in the Eucharist and has a commitment to social justice. The search for fraternity in so many spheres of society points out the need to live as brothers and sisters. The exemplary ethos of modernity is an ethos of equality, liberty, and fraternity, in the service of the fraternity of all human beings.

THE MEALS OF JESUS

"Jesus was crucified," says Robert. J. Karris, "because of how he ate."[8] Without Jesus's meals we cannot understand the kingdom of God, whose image is an open and egalitarian banquet. That image scandalized Jewish and Roman societies of the day, which were classist and xenophobic. The lordship of Jesus is a response to the most profound human needs, one of which is to satisfy hunger. Consequently, God judges us, according to St. Matthew, by the way we treat the poor.

In the Gospels the meals of Jesus with all types of people are very important. Jesus's meals were viewed by the Jewish ruling class with suspicion and hostility. He was accused of being a "glutton and a drunk, a friend to publicans and sinners" (Matt. 11:19; Luke 7:33–34) and of "embracing sinners and eating with them" (Luke 15:2; Mark 2:15). Let us recall that the Jews were prohibited from eating with pagans (Acts 10:28, 11:3). This unequal society, structured in a selfish and hierarchical way, was condemned by Jesus. Luis Maldonado notes, "Jesus did not accept distinctions in rank, in social honor, which are, in reality, divisions and discriminations."[9]

An understanding of the Eucharist begins not only with the Last Supper but also with other, previous meals in which Jesus took part. The Eucharist gathers, remembers, and actualizes meals of friendship and discipleship that Jesus celebrated with his disciples during his mission; the reconciliation banquets with repentant sinners, publicans, and people of ill repute; the distribution of the multiplied bread to the hungry; the Passover meals celebrated during his earthly life; the final, farewell supper before his death; and the joyful banquets with the glorified Christ after his resurrection.

The multiplication of the loaves, mentioned six times by the four evangelists, a unique case in that sense, constitutes a sign that should be interpreted socially and eucharistically. Christ, who is the bread of life, satiates the hungry multitude by multiplying the barley loaves, which, according to Dufour, are the bread of the poor.[10] By distributing this bread in the desert, Jesus is teaching his disciples to distribute it with generosity and abundance.

In the multiplication of the bread, Jesus performs five acts from the eucharistic tradition, narrated by the synoptics: he takes the bread, raises his eyes to heaven, and blesses, breaks, and distributes the loaves. In the multiplication of the loaves, according to John's Gospel, the people ask for bread (the poor want to be fed and have that right), and the identification of the bread with the person of Christ in a sacramental perspective is also present (the Eucharist demands a distribution of bread because it is the communion of the body of Christ in the community of brothers and sisters). When Jesus multiplied the bread, he indicated that the messianic age had already arrived.

The Last Supper of Jesus is the outcome of the conflict-ridden narratives of all the meals described in the Gospels. John the Evangelist does not describe to us the development of the Last Supper, nor does he record the words of Jesus over the bread and wine. He narrates the washing of the feet within the supper (John 13:1–15), as if the meal were reduced to this act of service. Before the stunned gaze of his disciples, in the middle of his farewell dinner, Jesus washes their feet. The teacher and lord assumes the acts of a slave (someone not Jewish) or of a woman (a wife to her husband and a daughter to her father), persons who offered this type of service in the patriarchal society within which Jesus lived. The narrative insinuates a new model of behavior, opposed to the social use of master above slave and of man above woman.

The disciples do not understand it, and Peter becomes irritated. The act of washing the feet demonstrates an inversion of social status, since Jesus, who was teacher and Lord, plays the part of a servant like a slave or a woman. He performs this prophetic gesture of washing the disciples' feet as a symbolic anticipation of his death and as an example of total service and of access to the fraternal banquet that is the foundation of the new community. "By situating the washing of the feet at an unexpected moment and emptying it of its ordinary function," affirm A. Destro and M. Pesce, "Jesus necessarily transforms it into a highly symbolic act."[11] In an indirect way, Jesus, by becoming a slave, condemns slavery.

THE CHRISTIAN AGAPE

Exegetes and historians give various rationales for the Christian agape. Some believe that a Christian agape is a continuation and an actualization of the meals of Jesus. Others explain Christian agape in relation to Greco-Roman communitarian banquets characterized by the religious experience of the community, proper to certain associations.[12] Christian banquets symbolized unity and friendship, equality among all, and utopia.

From the beginnings of the church, Christian fraternity among the baptized integrated into its being members of different social or religious origins, while the communities of the Pharisees, Essenes, and pagans defended segregation and discrimination. The Jews of Jesus's time did not admit pagans to the community table because meals were considered an intimate gesture of the chosen people. This did not occur among the first Christians. The very presence in these early communities of Hebrews who were descendants of Judaism and Hellenists who came from paganism, along with rich and poor, created the first tensions and internal disputes.

Women, slaves, and baptized pagans were present at the eucharistic meals, alongside and therefore equal to men, free persons, and Jewish converts to the Christian faith. According to the expression of some exegetes, these were open meals. Everybody ate the same. Those who had more donated more, and those with the least or nothing at all did not feel ashamed. Bringing to the common table what each one could assured everyone of a weekly dignified meal, where the majority were poor.

"The community shared all the food that was available," affirms J. D. Crossan, "which symbolized and ritualized, but also carried out and materialized, the equal justice of the Jewish God."[13] Some historians of early Christianity, such as R. Jewett and J. D. Crossan, talk about various shared meals, among which the most outstanding are the patronal and the communitarian.

Patronal meals were primitive meals of communities, where some members were relatively rich and influential and acted as everyone's host. They took place in rich and spacious homes. There were, however, two dangers: those who had more sometimes tried to use their hospitality to gain positions of power, and tensions could arise between the poor who had nothing and the rich who contributed almost everything, as seen in the Corinthian community. With freer schedules, the rich would arrive early, while the poor, the workers, and dependents would arrive late. St. Paul did not tolerate such a situation: everything must be shared among everyone.

The communal meals were the fruit of mutual support, where the members were all poor. Participants would gather in modest places. Each one would bring what he or she could. This would require labor on everyone's part. Perhaps for this reason St. Paul did not tolerate that anyone live in idleness due to a lack of will. If a baptized person does not want to work, he said, let him not eat: he is not a brother. Brothers and sisters are people who share everything, festivities and labors, with joy and generosity, without discrimination. "In the context of the shared meals," says R. Aguirre, "Jesus questions the hierarchies active in his society and proposes alternative values."[14]

The early agape, at least in the Corinthian community, degenerated into disorder, which St. Paul denounced. Due to the gluttonous feasts that would occur at times, the agape was prohibited in the fourth century and disappeared completely in the sixth century. This constitutes a considerable pastoral loss. The Christian communities today are trying to restore it.

After the third century the term *brother* was restricted to priests and monks. Laypeople—illiterate, ignorant, and of little light, as they were considered—did not merit the generous and glorious title. Naturally, there have also been, throughout the centuries, modest Christians who have known how to share and have behaved as brothers.

Since the beginning of Christianity, then, the Eucharist was a group meal and a service at which people mutually helped each other. The breaking of bread in the Lord's Supper was understood as a communion (*koinonia*) and participation. The *koinonia* is the total Christian communion, expressed in the collection, a sign of fraternal love among churches and peoples; in the communication of goods and the holding of goods in common, so as to overcome private property and express the principle that everything belongs to everyone because the reign of God demands it; in the affective and spiritual relationship among the believers, with the apostles, and with God; and in the manifestation of the communal spirit, constitutive of the Eucharist.

Called in the New Testament the "Lord's Supper" (1 Cor. 11:20) or the "breaking of the bread" (Acts 2:42), the Eucharist was, from its beginnings, a fraternal sign of believers who shared all at one meal and a form of giving thanks to the Father, Jesus Christ, and the Holy Spirit. "Because there is one loaf, we who are many are one body, for we all partake of the one loaf" (1 Cor. 10:17). In the Eucharist we become the community of the Lord.

A characteristic of the early church, according to the Gospel of Matthew, was fraternal correction, a difficult and demanding exercise that disappeared all of a sudden. Correcting others or being corrected surely produced tensions and heated disputes among the brothers of a community. Fraternal correction disappeared probably for the same reasons as the fraternal agape of the Sunday celebration; both led to irritations and fights because some were not willing to hold possessions in common, to sit and eat with everyone at the same table, and to be corrected by others.

In all of this, special attention must be given to fraternal welcome. To welcome someone is to offer him or her hospitality. It is proper for an association, group, or community to offer hospitality when receiving a new member. A Christian welcome is the act by which a community receives the converted person, whether a catechumen beginning the journey of Christian initiation or a newly baptized believer. It is ritualized by a hug, a kiss, a handshake, or some other fraternal sign.

From the beginning of the church, such gestures of welcome were foundational to pastoral ministry (Rom. 15:7). In the beginning deacons offered such hospitality, but it disappeared with time. Today it has again become a necessary service. Naturally, there are communities and parishes in which everyone knows and welcomes everyone else. But in other, larger gatherings, such hospitality is necessary, especially to foreigners, shy people, disabled people, and poor people. The service of hospitality takes place at the entrance of the church to greet, receive, and welcome those who arrive. This helps integrate them better into the assembly.

THE EUCHARIST IS CELEBRATED IN COMMUNITY

At the end of the 1970s, just after Vatican II, a sort of group mysticism arose that was based on the communitarian phenomenon of Christianity.

Its origin was due, on the one hand, to the new awareness of the church as *communio* in its double sense, community of believers and community of churches, and, on the other, to the offer of personal participation of the Christian laity, with preference to the poor and marginalized, not to mention the formation of educational, psychological, labor, and political groups.

Church means the community of Christians. Consequently, ecclesial life is alive to the extent that the communitarian aspect of Christianity is vibrant. But the communitarian aspect grows and matures when communion is lived—that is, communication and participation with others and with God at one table, at one meal. Evidently, the Christian community of the future could have different levels and varied forms of expression. We must create incarnated or inculturated forms of Christian community. Sectarian-type communities—those that seek proselytes, are turned in on themselves, believe themselves owners of the truth, look down on other people, and live alienated from the poor—are dangerous.

The original fact of Christian liturgy, and thus of the Eucharist, is a being together in close-knit assembly. *Ekklesia* means a convocation or an assembly. Without the gathering of believers in an assembly there is no genuine Christian Eucharist. What is decisive in the eucharistic celebration is not the locale, the obligation, or the presider but the Christian sacrament of the assembly, to the extent that the believers who are gathered by the strength of the Word listen, sing, pray, and eat in solidarity, without discrimination.

The assembly, a term retrieved after Vatican II, is the principal sign of the church, to which are added the baptized believers. Together they form a unity through the Eucharist. As the epistle to the Galatians affirms, "There is neither Jew nor Greek, there is neither slave nor free person, there is not male and female, for you are all one in Christ Jesus" (Gal. 3:28). The assembly is a social group that comes together periodically for an interchange of communication, with the objective of coming to some decisions, according to the order of the day or of the meeting, and for a common agape and Eucharist. It should have features constitutive of any and all human assemblies: orderly presiding, fluid communication, an educational dimension, appropriate rhythm, shared acts, and belonging or affiliation among its members.

At the Sunday Eucharist, men and women believers gather with their personalities, their culture, their problems, and their aspirations, which should be taken into account and respected. They all have the right to be welcomed, especially the poor, marginalized, and oppressed. Together they go beyond their differences, though without ignoring them. The community gathered as an assembly to eat is the first sign of the Eucharist. Consequently, the Eucharist is always a communitarian act and a shared meal, where there is no room for distinctions according to social class.

Jesus compared the kingdom of heaven to a wedding banquet, at which the food is plentiful, exquisite, and gratuitous. When the guests do not arrive, excusing themselves for various reasons, the host in the parable invites the "poor, cripples, blind, and lame" who are found "on the outskirts of the city" (Luke 14:21b–23; Matt. 22:9–10). This way of understanding nourishment or the sharing of a table, notes J. D. Crossan, rejects "economic discrimination, social hierarchies, and political distinctions."[15] Jesus was accused of being a glutton, a friend of publicans and sinners—that is, he was accused of abolishing distinctions and discriminations.

Having the faithful, presided over by a presbyter, sit around a table in a circular or semicircular fashion facilitates the cohesion of the assembly. "Word, table, and community," affirms M. Díaz Mateos, "are the components of Christian identity that we celebrate in the sacrament of the bread. Good health and the dynamism of the faith of the church are based on this triad. The three mutually enrich each other, they complement and need each other."[16]

Nevertheless, those responsible for the church often forget the Lord's example that "this man welcomes sinners and eats with them" (Luke 15:2) and invites the "poor and the crippled, the blind, and the lame" (Luke 14:21) to the great meal of the kingdom. We have not followed the urging of James's letter to make no distinctions in the assembly between "a man with gold rings on his fingers and in fine clothes" and "a poor person in shabby clothes" (James 2:2). It seems as if the early Christian communities from the beginning had problems with discrimination between the rich and the poor. It is not easy to introduce to the assembly the blank slate of equality.

THE PERSPECTIVE OF THE POOR

The most complete document of the New Testament about the poor and poverty is the Gospel of Luke, in which all of Mark's passages on the theme and most of Matthew's can be found. The letter of James harshly criticizes the rich and takes up the cause of the poor. It denounces differentiating in the assembly between rich and poor when offering seats (James 2:2–4). To think less of the poor is the equivalent, according to Paul, of "despising the church and shaming those who are without" (1 Cor. 11:22). Not only are personal differences annulled in the agape, but functions are inverted. Jesus himself says, "Let the greatest among you be as the youngest, and the leader like the one who serves" (Luke 22:26).

Luke and the writings of the New Testament in general speak more of the poor than of poverty, understanding the poor to be the needy ones who because of their economic destitution require help.[17] The Gospel of Luke focuses more than others on Jesus's meals and presents the most eucharistic allusions.

According to the Bible, as R. Fabris notes, "The poor person is the one who is deprived of the essential goods to life, dignity and human liberty."[18] "Poverty in the Bible," adds Gustavo Gutiérrez, "is a scandalous state that threatens human dignity and, consequently, is contrary to the will of God."[19] The term *pauper* (poor) in the Vulgate means "little"; it represents those who have few resources and, at the same time, lack freedom, since the opposite of the poor is not only the rich but the rich and powerful.

The term *poor* in the Bible, besides being a social or economic category, represents a spiritual and religious category. The poor are for Luke the privileged recipients of the good news. Throughout the whole Bible, it is clear that God exalts the insignificant ones. God loves the poor precisely because their misery reveals an absence of justice. God is their lawyer. In a word, the poor are vicars of Christ because in them is a mystery and a sacrament. The idea that the condemned ones of the earth should be vindicated runs throughout the entire history of Christianity because it understands God as vindicator of the poor. In fact, evangelical protests against injustice and in favor of the poor have never been lacking in the church, even in the face of opposition by certain hierarchically minded members who are friends of honors and riches.

The poor are the recipients of the good news because they lack health or salvation and because God, being just, has wished it this way. In other words, the Gospel is good news for the poor because it proclaims liberation, since, for people of faith, to know God is to practice justice (Jer. 22:16). In reality, Jesus's entire ministry was good news for the poor. As C. Escudero Freire writes,

The poor are, in the plan of God, the recipients and beneficiaries of God's kingdom that Jesus proclaims and realizes. Jesus liberates them from the clutches of the powerful and restores them to their condition as free beings; the rich, on the contrary, remain marginalized from the kingdom, imprisoned in their own wealth, without the capacity to value human rights and without the capacity to understand the offering and urgency of the kingdom of God. The condition of the rich is desperate; it remains, nevertheless, the possibility, although difficult, of their conversion: "I will give you a new heart and place a new spirit within you, taking from your bodies your stony hearts and giving you natural hearts" (Ezek. 36:26).[20]

According to the Acts of the Apostles, the idea of the early church is not poverty but fraternal love, a norm of love, or of charity, that is translated into sharing what one has and is, according to the total communion based in Christ. That is why the Acts affirm that "all who believed were together and had all things in common" (Acts 2:44). The first Christians put all their goods in common not to make themselves poor but to ensure that in the end no one would be poor. The ideal for Luke is not poverty but detachment from riches and fraternal charity, which means sharing. Therefore, we must love the poor more than poverty. In other words, inequality among people is unjust; God wants equality for all.

The irruption of the poor in society and the Christian perspective on the poor as a theological locus have taken a Copernican shift within the post-Conciliar church itself, especially in the formulation and acceptance of the option for the poor, a decision that was incorporated into the magisterium of the church with the adjectives *preferential* and *nonexclusive.* Many believe, with serious biblical reasons, that this option is key for reading the Gospel, that it is central to the Christian faith, and that it occupies a central place in theology. Ignacio Ellacuría stressed that "the preferential option for the poor is a mark of the true church, on a level with those used to defining it as one, holy, catholic, and apostolic."[21] Therefore, it is not strange that the theme of the poor has become such a disputed issue.

Gutiérrez reminds us that in the 1950s and 1960s the poor became present in the social and political arena and that when they arrived they came with the burden of poverty. This development coincided with the convocation of Vatican II.

In 1962, a short time before the beginning of the council, John XXIII spoke of "the Church that is and wants to be for everyone, and especially the Church of the poor."[22] The Latin American Episcopal Conference (CELAM) at Medellín in 1968 spoke of giving "effective preference to the poorest and neediest sectors, and to those segregated for whatever reason."[23] According to Puebla (1979), the Medellín conference made, in 1968, "a clear and prophetic option for and solidarity with the poor."[24]

In fact, the expression *option for the poor* was coined by liberation theologians in 1970. Its meaning was generalized around 1973, and it was sanctioned by Puebla in an important chapter of its resolutions, actually entitled "The Preferential Option for the Poor." John Paul II has made the phrase his own in various discourses.[25] It was also defended in the document of the Congregation for the Doctrine of the Faith about some of the problems of liberation theology, under the expression already consecrated, "preferential option for the poor."[26]

The adjective *preferential* was officially introduced by Puebla to demonstrate that this option does not contradict the universality of Christian salvation. The preferential option can also be translated into terms of solidarity, and, of course, it has a prophetic dimension. The Episcopal Conference of Santo Domingo adds that it is "neither exclusive nor excluding." A nonexcluding preferential option means, according to Jon Sobrino, "that no one should feel excluded from a church with that option, but that no one lacking that option can expect to be included in the church."[27] According to John Paul II, "The option for the poor holds a special primacy in the exercise of Christian charity."[28] Last, the church must convert herself to the poor—in other words, give priority to a liberating evangelization with the goal of being a credible and authentic sign.[29]

A Human Hunger, a Divine Banquet

Four hundred years before Christ, the Greek playwright Aristophanes wrote in his comedy *Ecclesiazusae (Women in Parliament)* the following: "I want all to have a share of everything and all property to be in common; there will no longer be either rich or poor; no longer shall we see one man harvesting vast tracts of land while another has not ground enough to be buried in, nor one man surround himself with a whole army of slaves while another has not a single attendant; I intend that there shall only be one and the same condition of life for all."[30] Some exegetes are of the opinion that Luke, who was thoroughly familiar with Greek culture, when describing in three summaries the Jerusalem community, took Aristophanes' words into account.

"All who believed were together," says Luke, "and had all things in common; they would sell their property and possessions and divide them amongst all according to each one's need" (Acts 2:44–45).

> The community of believers was of one heart and mind, and no one claimed that any of his possessions was his own, but they had everything in common. With great power the apostles bore witness to the resurrection of the Lord Jesus, and great favor was accorded them all. There was no needy person among them, for those who owned property or houses would sell them, bring the proceeds of the sale, and put them at the feet of the apostles, and they were distributed to each according to need. (Acts 4:32–35)

Jesus was critical of a Jewish cult that was excessively sacralized and overly legalistic, that excluded the poor and the incurably sick, and that marginalized both from the God of the kingdom and the kingdom of God. In accordance with the New Testament, the celebration of the Eucharist is the work of the heart, the true locus of the cult, and the fruit of justice, which is the sacrament of the kingdom of God. This is why the earliest Christians celebrated the one God made fully revealed in Jesus Christ, present where two or three are gathered in his name, committed to the solidarity of the kingdom of God, and concretized in the preferential option for the poor.

In the early church, Christians celebrated the Eucharist preceded by a meal. The double, and only, table was that of the poor and of the Lord, an outpouring of the commandment of justice and love. The loss of the agape or meal that preceded the Lord's Supper (1 Cor. 11:17–34) and the overshadowing of the conflictive meaning of the Eucharist have notably influenced the ritualization of the eucharistic celebration, which has been emptied to a great degree of its social content. By contrast, John's narratives about the distribution of the living bread among the hungry multitude and the washing of the feet help us to understand the Eucharist as a sacrament of solidarity.

"Communitarian meals," affirms P. Schmidt-Leukel, "appear to be one of humanity's preferred possibilities to commemorate and celebrate the social nature of its being and its connection with the general interrelatedness of life. What is even more painful is the awareness that, despite all the achievements of civilization, we still live in a world where a great number of people are hungry and are excluded from the universal community of those invited."[31]

Although some religions privilege fasting as a means to reach union with the divine, the fundamental Christian gesture of entering into communion with God occurs at a communal meal that wealthy and poor disciples share in solidarity with each other and in the dangerous and unsettling memory of Jesus. Jesus wished to be remembered by his disciples mainly in the human act of eating and in the fraternal act of sharing. With a little bread and wine we celebrate the Eucharist. Blessed and consecrated, the bread and wine are transfigured into the body and blood of Christ.

In its origins, the Eucharist was a group meal and a service of mutual help. It was first celebrated in the context of an agape, with a communitarian sharing of bread and wine, transfigured by giving thanks. The Christian community is manifested in the act that all its members eat of one bread and drink of one cup, a sacrament that anticipates the banquet of the Reign of God.

NOTES

1. Luis Maldonado, *Eucaristía en devenir* (Santander: Sal Terrae, 1997), 12.

2. "Presbyterorum Ordinis: Decree of the Life and Ministry of Priests," in *Vatican Council II,* ed. Austin Flannery (New York: Costello, 1996), no. 6.

3. M. Díaz Mateos, *El sacramento del pan* (Madrid: PPC, 1997), 119.

4. J. M. Castillo, "Donde no hay justicia no hay eucaristía," *Estudios Eclesiásticos* 52 (1977): 556.

5. See E. Dussel, "El pan de la comunión, signo comunitario de justicia," *Concilium* 172 (1982): 236–49.

6. Leon Dufour, *La fracción del pan: Culto y existencia en el Nuevo Testamento* (Madrid: Cristiandad, 1983), 51.

7. J. D. Crossan, *El nacimiento del cristianismo* (Santander: Sal Terrae, 2002), 430.

8. Robert J. Karris, *Luke: Artist and Theologian* (New York: Paulist Press, 1985), 47.

9. Maldonado, *Eucaristía en devenir,* 66.

10. Leon Dufour, *Diccionario del Nuevo Testamento* (Madrid: Cristiandad, 1977), 135.

11. A. Destro and M. Pesce, *Cómo nació el cristianismo juánico: Antropología y exégesis del Evangelio de Juan* (Santander: Sal Terrae, 2002), 81.

12. See M. Klinghardt, "'Tomad y comed; este es mi cuerpo': Ágape e interpretación del ágape en el cristianismo primitivo," in *Las religiones y la comida,* ed. P. Schmidt-Leukel (Barcelona: Ariel, 2002), 39–44.

13. Crossan, *El nacimiento del cristianismo,* 424.

14. R. Aguirre, *La mesa compartida: Estudio del NT desde las ciencias sociales* (Santander: Sal Terrae, 1994), 124.

15. J. D. Crossan, *Jesús: Biografía revolucionaria* (Barcelona: Grijalbo Modadori, 1996), 84.

16. Díaz Mateos, *El sacramento del pan,* 228.

17. The term *poor* is found thirty-four times in the New Testament, twenty-four times in the Gospels and ten specifically in the Gospel of Luke. The word *poverty* appears only three times and *poor person* once (2 Cor. 8, 9). Cf. H.-H. Eser, "Pobre," in *Diccionario teológico del NT,* ed. Lothar Coenen (Salamanca: Sígueme, 1983), 3:380–85.

18. R. Fabris, *La opción por los pobres en la Biblia* (Estella: Verbo Divino, 1992), 21.

19. Gustavo Gutiérrez, *Teología de la liberación: Perspectivas* (Salamanca: Sígueme, 1972), 369.

20. C. Escudero Freire, *Devolver el evangelio a los pobres* (Salamanca: Sígueme, 1977), 273.

21. Ignacio Ellacuría, "Las iglesias latinoamericanas interpelan a la iglesia de España," *Sal Terrae* 70 (1982): 221.

22. John XXIII, radio message, November 11, 1962, quoted in Andrea Riccardi, "The Great Expectations of the Ecumenical Council," www.vatican.va/jubilee_2000/magazine/documents/ju_mag_01051997_p-46_en.html (accessed August 8, 2006).

23. Conferencia General del Episcopado Latinoamericano (CELAM) II (Medellín, Colombia, 1968), "Poverty," no. 90, in *Medellín Conference: Final Document. The Church in the Present-Day Transformation of Latin America in Light of the Council,* 2 vols. (Bogotá: General Secretariat of CELAM, 1970–73).

24. CELAM III (Puebla, Mexico, 1979), *Puebla Conference: Final Document. Visión Pastoral de America Latina: Equipo de Reflexión, Departamentos y Secciones de CELAM* (Bogotá: CELAM, 1979), no. 1134.

25. See, for example, John Paul II, "El discurso a los Cardenales y a la Curia Romana, el 2 de diciembre de 1984," *Ecclesia* 2204 (1985): 14

26. Congregation for the Doctrine of the Faith, "Instruction on Certain Aspects of the 'Theology of Liberation,'" August 6, 1984, www.vatican.va/roman_curia/congregations/cfaith/documents/rc_con_cfaith_doc_19840806_theology-liberation_en.html (accessed August 8, 2006).

27. Jon Sobrino, *Puebla: Serena afirmación de Medellín* (Bogotá: Cristología, 1979), 38.

28. John Paul II, "Sollicitudo rei socialis," December 30, 1987, no. 42, www.vatican.va/holy_father/john_paul_ii/encyclicals/documents/hf_jp-ii_enc_30121987_sollicitudo-rei-socialis_en.html (accessed August 8, 2006).

29. CELAM III, *Puebla Conference,* no. 1134.

30. Quoted in Crossan, *El nacimiento del cristianismo,* 469.

31. Schmidt-Leukel, *Las religiones y la comida,* 18.

Chapter 14

POPULAR CATHOLICISM
AND THE POOR

LUIS MALDONADO

In this essay I look at the option for the poor in Christian theology with respect to liturgy and more specifically to popular Catholicism. I identify and clarify some of the key terms that are used in this discussion and then look at particular faith expressions of the poor in the way they depict Christ. Since I have lived and worked in Spain most of my life, I focus in particular on some of the Christological expressions in the towns, villages, and cities of my country that come out of the suffering of the people and have become a tradition all their own. In doing so, I bring out the integral relationship between community and Christology and bring out how the God of the poor is a God of hope because God is revealed as one who suffers with them. Last, I comment on how our increasing awareness of Latin American popular religiosity has enhanced our developmental understanding of the life of the poor and these rich spiritual expressions.

POPULAR RELIGION AND POPULAR CATHOLICISM: SOME KEY DISTINCTIONS

The publications that have appeared over the past few years on liturgy and justice show a clear oscillation in terminology regarding how the poor pray and worship. Some refer to *popular religiosity* and others to *popular Catholicism.* The terms are not synonymous but rather are separate categories with entirely different meanings. *Popular religiosity,* as distinct from *popular Catholicism,* refers to the participation in certain celebrations, or the practice of certain rites, by which people experience and express a sense of God's mystery and transcendence. As such, the sacraments and the celebrations of the liturgical year are celebrated as "rites of transition" that help those who participate in them pass from one situation in life to another or from one stage to another in the solar or lunar cycles of cosmic time. Participants feel that God is the fountain of life and fertility, the provident Lord and Father, and also the source of order and of morality.

Popular Catholicism, on the other hand, refers not only to participation in the sacred mystery of the Spirit but also to the expression of the particularity of the Spirit of Jesus Christ, who reveals the love of God the Father. In this Spirit participants experience the history of salvation in its various stages, a sacramental sense of responsibility to one's brother or sister in need, a love of one's neighbor, an ecclesial communion, a closeness of Mary, and other such dimensions that shape popular Catholicism.

To this Catholicism we must add the qualifier *popular* to differentiate it from official Catholicism. Official Catholicism follows hierarchical norms, revealed truths, dogmas, academic theology, moral precepts, and the regulated rubrics and rites of the church. *Popular* means something more here, namely that the subjects of all of these acts are communities that are simple, humble, and poor, without a great deal of catechetical formation but with a series of traditions and with a genuine culture.

POPULAR DEVOTIONS AND POPULAR PIETY: SOME CLARIFICATIONS

According to some, popular devotion is the religious activity that unfolds in a series of nonliturgical acts that, in contrast to liturgical acts, are individual and private. While there is truth to this perception, much more is involved in popular devotions or popular piety.

Some of these acts are not simply private but have a communal and even liturgical dimension. Some devotional acts can be perfectly liturgical when celebrated in community and in accordance with (explicitly or implicitly) the Word of God. Such forms include practices like the Stations of the Cross *(Via crucis)* and the rosary. We can call something liturgical not simply when it takes place in a church but because it is an act of the community, the "People of God" gathered "in the name of the Lord" (Matt. 18:20). That an act does not adhere to certain official rubrics does not deprive it of its fundamentally liturgical character. I make these clarifications so that we may carefully distinguish between the popular and the official and between popular liturgy and official liturgy.[1]

Devotion and *piety,* however, may also have other meanings. They allude to liturgical acts, including official acts, lived in a very experiential and emotional way. These are certain celebrations that, by their texts, songs, and rites, mobilize the sentiments of the faithful. Celebrants' whole affective world is awakened and stimulated so that they participate with their total being.

By contrast, many of us are familiar with the cold, dry, abstract liturgy, which can be particularly alienating when a liturgy in different cultures uses prayer texts composed in ancient or foreign cultural contexts. In the past some believed that such forms of celebration inspired devotion and piety, but today there is much more emphasis on engaging believers holistically and not just in terms of their inner, private lives.

The Different Expressions of
Christ in Popular Catholicism

Although some may dismiss the value of popular Catholicism, it is worth taking the time to examine some of its core evangelical values. We have already hinted at a few of them, but one of the most important comes out of the Christological depictions of the people (*Cristos Populares,* Popular Christs or Christs of the People), the Christology created by the community. These expressions of Christ, in many ways, manifest the people's trust in the suffering God who always accompanies those who, abandoned by society, find themselves on the margins and in the hells of existence.

In Spain in particular, the context with which I am most familiar, there is a long Christological tradition of the Nazarenes, the suffering Christs whose hands are tied, who are flagellated, and who are tied to columns. We also see Christs carrying the cross, being crucified, agonizing, lying in the hands of the Sorrowful Mother. These Christologies reveal Jesus as a man of suffering, the servant of Yahweh, who emptied himself in a real *kenosis* so that we might be reconciled to God. They actualize the mystery of the Incarnation, lived fully, without any kind of Docetic evasion.

Many of these depictions of Christ mirror and capture, in their features, the faces of those who suffer today, like those in the community who are imprisoned or assassinated unjustly. These Christological expressions, however, the most famous of which is the "Cachorro" of Triana in Seville, portray the suffering of life so realistically that some feel they snuff out any hint of resurrection and fall into an extreme form of fatalism. Because they so graphically highlight Christ's pain and agony, some feel the integrity of the paschal mystery is compromised. There is some truth to this charge, but this same community celebrates, on the same day, not only the passion and death of Jesus but also his resurrection. We can see similar examples in other places in Spain like Priego, Córdoba. In many respects, these Christological expressions, resembling the practices of the early church, express the unity of the paschal mystery through a single celebration during the Easter Vigil.

One of the core values of popular Catholicism is that it enables people to live an authentic faith in the resurrected Lord without falling into dualistic triumphalism, which is characteristic of many celebrations today. For the community, the resurrected Christ is not one who now lives in the best of all possible worlds, disconnected from the suffering of his followers here on earth. The resurrected Christ is one who lives in the company of his poor and suffering people, participating in their suffering, even while living in his glory with the Father. And in this sense, as Pascal said, Jesus "is in agony until the end of history." Jesus continues to live in solidarity with the poor because millions of his brothers and sisters continue to suffer the burden of poverty and exploitation.

For those who are poor, the suffering Christ and the resurrected Christ are not mutually exclusive. The Resurrection does not mean distancing oneself from this world full of pain and injustice; on the contrary, it means moving closer to it, surpassing the limitations of the earthly Jesus. The resurrected Jesus exceeds and transcends the limitations of time and space, making himself the contemporary of any age and companion of any place.

Although the Second Vatican Council has largely forgotten this Christology, patristic authors like Origen continually reiterated the God who suffers with us:

> My Savior remains in mourning; he still mourns because of my sins. My Savior cannot be happy as long as I remain off the path. He cannot drink the wine of celebration alone. He must wait until all arrive in the Kingdom. He who carried, with all of our injuries, and suffered for us, will he stay indifferent of all of the injuries and of so many people? The Savior cannot be happy while I am lost in my life. He waits for our conversion to rejoice in our company. The Lord and Savior will not have the fullness of joy as long as one member of the Body is missing. We are speaking here of the One Body, although with many members. . . . The Lord will not receive his full glory without you, without his people.[2]

In another passage, Origen adds: "God in his mercy suffers with us. He is not impassible. He does not lack a heart. What is the nature of the suffering he endures for us? The suffering is love. He endures the suffering of love."[3] And in another text from the seventh century, Maximus the Confessor states, "God suffers mystically because of his love until the end of time to the degree which each person who suffers, suffers."[4]

J. Jimenez Lozano, a contemporary writer, well versed in the history and art of the church in Spain, has described why and how the resurrected Christ is venerated by the popular Catholicism of Castille. The Christ of Diego de la Cruz, venerated in Cobarrubias (Burgos), Spain, is a Christ that appears as a poor man, crushed by suffering, flattened in pain, with sunken eyes and bruised cheeks, yet he is called the resurrected Christ. But his anguish is more intense than that of the Christ on the cross.[5]

The communities perceive the double nearness of the Son and of the Father. The Father and the Son are so united for them that they even speak of "Our Father Jesus" because the Father suffers in the Son. The Christian God is a crucified God, a "patient" or "compassionate" God who dies on the cross, who suffers with others who are crucified, beaten, and whipped because of the sin of the world and evil that others inflict on them.[6] The communities sense a God who is near to them, who is close at hand in their sufferings. They express this spirituality in their sculptures, images, paintings, and plastic figures of the suffering Christ, and as they venerate them in sincere and heartfelt devotion.

THE INTEGRAL RELATIONSHIP BETWEEN COMMUNITY AND CHRISTOLOGY

The Christs of popular Catholicism are in a certain way the creation of the religiosity and faith of the Christian community. They emerge from a community that has been poor throughout its history and has suffered injustice and exploitation. They are called the poor Christs precisely because of their suffering. To make this point even more precise, the communities project onto these Christs their problems and their suffering. Thus this image of Jesus is a reflection of the community's poverty and suffering. But does that mean that it is then only a projection, a mere mirage?

Beyond such psychological considerations, there is an objective biblical foundation to the relationship between the community and its Christological expressions. We read in Matthew 25: "Whatever you do to the least of these you do to me" (v. 40). In this passage, Christ identifies himself with the poor and affirms that he shares the poverty and pain of the community, making himself one with the poor.

As we look at these Scriptures in light of the suffering of the community, we see the beaten Christ in those who are tortured, the naked Christ in those who are homeless, the flagellated Christ in those who are imprisoned, the manacled Christ in those who are enslaved, the crucified Christ in the suffering of the innocent. In all of these, we see a reciprocal relationship between those who suffer and the Christ who reaches out to them in their pain. What is done to the least of these is done to the Lord. The different faces of Christ in the Christ of Medinaceli, the "Cachorro" of Seville, the "Greñuo" of Cadiz, and many others like them give expression to the God who suffers with suffering humanity.

Because of this relationship between the suffering of Christ and the pain of the community, the people have a profound devotion to Christ, who they feel accompanies them in their daily struggles. The people similarly read and interpret the narrative of the Passion on Good Friday. This communion with Christ inspires a deep hope in them. In Jesus they see their own hope of rising again. Because he triumphed over injustice, they too hope to overcome injustice; because he proclaimed the reign of God here on earth, they hope to experience some share of that kingdom, not only when they die but here and now.

A GOD OF SUFFERING, A GOD OF HOPE

A few days before being executed by Hitler, the great German theologian Dietrich Bonhoeffer wrote: "Only a God who suffers can help us." The community has always had this intuition, knowing that only a God who shares in human suffering can help them in their pain. Only a God that really accompanies the poor and walks with them can help and ultimately save them. Only a God in solidarity with those who struggle can transmit encouragement, trust, and faith to confront pain and injustice. Only the crucified God that is born and dies outside the city limits (Luke 2:7; Heb. 13:12) can understand and save those who are rejected. Only a God who has been marginalized can identify with those who live on the fringes of society. Only a God who has become vulnerable can offer a saving hope to others who are unprotected and in need.

According to the rabbinic tradition, when the Messiah comes he will appear among the beggars that sleep outside the walls of the city of Rome. We likewise could say that when the Messiah returns he will be mixed in with the shipwrecked refugees who arrive on the beaches of Europe or live in jail with the undocumented immigrants who seek protective asylum.

Jürgen Moltmann lucidly described this recurring phenomenon of the relation between the popular Christs and the poor:

> What does Jesus's healing power consist of? The answer can be found in Matthew 8:16–17, where we are told that Jesus fulfills the prophecy of Isaiah 53:5, where he announces that he assumed our weakness and carried our infirmities. The healing power of Jesus is rooted, then, in his capacity for suffering. He heals by his wounds. His healing consists in communion, participation, and sharing of all. God heals us by taking part in our sufferings in such a way that these are converted into part of his eternal love. I am reminded here of the crucified Christ on the Isenheim altarpiece. The author is Mathias Grünewald, of the sixteenth century. This Christ is not only twisted and disfigured by the pain but also completely covered in

boils from the plague. What this image is telling us is what Isaiah affirms—He has borne our suffering. And this is what the image said to the thousands of plague-ridden victims who were taken to that church and who recognized themselves in that suffering man because he was turned into someone just like them. Upon looking at that image, they felt the eternal and indestructible communion with the crucified God. And through this communion, which even the plague could not impede, many of them experienced healing.[7]

In a similar example, I recall the image of a Christ in Spain that deeply moves me, an image of the Christ of humility and patience. He wears a torn tunic, he is crowned with thorns, and he is seated on a rock along a path, tired and exhausted. His face reveals the face of a person that cannot continue. Is this not the image of so many of the poor and dejected at certain moments of their lives? In their imagery, their carvings, their footsteps, the community rediscovers and expresses the deepest intuitions of their faith; in some ways, these Christological images confess the faith of a people, a faith that is full of trust, hope, and love in the midst of the adversities of their lives.

THE CONTRIBUTION OF LATIN AMERICAN THEOLOGIANS TO POPULAR CATHOLICISM

While much of our reflection above has focused on Spain as a social context for understanding popular Catholicism, Latin American theologians as well have contributed much to our understanding of these faith expressions of the poor within their respective contexts. The author who best sums up this Latin American contribution is Diego Irarrázaval, who speaks of the importance of inculturation and the humble and loving science of poor people.[8] He describes how this "science" captures the essence of the salvific event through several crucial themes such as gratitude, human solidarity, celebration, community, the condemnation of evil, and trust in a God who loves us.

Here, he adds, lies the human wisdom of the community, as well as a theological knowledge through which the seeds and fruit of the Word are manifested.[9] Irarrázaval also refers to the symbol of the cross, which has now become the sign of protection for the poor. He highlights, more importantly, the numerous devotions to Mary that have been creating Catholic communities throughout history. In many of these, the marginalized people make an alliance with the Mother of Christ. In this way, they secure their own identity and energy. Marian devotion contributes solid theological concepts such as "Goodness saves," "God gives life," "Faith is joyful," "Pain goes along with courage," and "Strength goes with Spirit." Marian wisdom has decisively helped the effort to unite the dynamics of liberation with the process of inculturation.

It is also important to affirm that the community of the poor perceives God as a fountain of communal joy. This is why they understand salvation as originating from God through play, dance, blessing, and human love, which all converge toward one goal: celebrating *fiesta*. But above all this community lives for God with a great sense of familiarity. They find God to be proximate to them through the pain of the crucified. This is why they call him *diosito,* our *papa.* The poor often create rites, actions, or gestures that help them to move, symbolically, from a bad situation *(malestar)* to a good one *(bienestar).* The diverse ritual processes, which are rooted in the notions of promise, offering, sacrifice, reconciliation, thanksgiving, and the holding of goods in common, have their own particular logic according to the life of the people. With these ritual processes, communities of the poor develop a symbolic language that is to a large extent their own. By means of this language, they celebrate life, they enjoy the loving presence of God, and, from the perspective of *fiesta,* they project a new vision of reality that transforms them. It can be said that these rites and festive symbol systems are the most important "theological text" of the Latin American continent.[10]

Along these lines, we can also affirm that the common denominator, or the logic of the diverse celebrations of the community, is the existing reciprocity between suffering lack and knowing how to sustain joy rooted in faith in a God who suffers with the community. This reciprocity implies a convergence between the joyful faith of those who enact the rites and divine mercy. Its logic expressed in the ritual festivity transforms the conditions of impoverishment in which the poor live, infusing a genuine hope.

Last, we should highlight that habitual phrases in the conversations of the community like "God willing" *(si Dios quiere)* and "Thanks be to God" *(Gracias a Dios)* manifest a relationship between the poor and God that rests on the gift of the Spirit and a more or less conscious realization that God is the center of their lives. This Spirit is always intimately tied to the incarnate Son, to the crucified Christ who emptied himself, to the patient and humble Jesus, and to the suffering servant of Yahweh.

Notes

1. I have developed this point in Luis Maldonado, "Devociones y liturgies," in *Para comprender el catolicismo popular* (Estella: Verbo Divino, 1990), 117–25. There I show that this interpretation has also been advanced by scholars like J. A. Jungmann and S. Marill.

2. Origen, *On Leviticus,* Hom. 7.2 (ed. J.-P. Migne, PG 12.405).

3. Origen, *On Ezekiel,* c. 16. (ed. J.-P. Migne, PG 13.812A).

4. Maximus the Confessor, *Mystagogia* 24 (ed. J.-P. Migne, PG 91.713).

5. J. Jiménez Lozano, *Guía espiritual de Castilla* (Valladolid: Universidad de Valladolid, 1984), 214.

6. In his now-classic book *The Crucified God: The Cross of Christ as the Foundation and Criticism of Christian Theology* (London: SCM Press, 1974), Jürgen Moltmann articulates this theology more systematically.

7. Jürgen Moltmann, *Diaconía* (Santander: Sal Terrae, 1987), 77–79.

8. Diego Irarrázaval, "Otro modo de pensar," *Alternativas* 8, nos. 20–21 (2001): 113–36.

9. See Luke 10:21 and Matt. 11:25, also Paul VI, "Lumen gentium," November 21, 1964, no. 12, www.vatican.va/archive/hist_councils/ii_vatican_council/documents/vat-ii_const_19641121_lumen-gentium_en.html, and "Ad gentes," no. 22, www.vatican.va/archive/hist_councils/ii_vatican_council/documents/vat-ii_decree_19651207_ad-gentes_en.html (both accessed August 9, 2006). J. C. Scannone, *Evangelización, cultura y teología* (Buenos Aires: Guadalupe, 1990), 268.

10. F. Taborda, *Sacramento, praxis, y fiesta* (Madrid: Ediciones Paulinas, 1987).

Part Eight

POVERTY, RELIGIONS,

AND IDENTITY

Chapter 15

THE OPTION FOR THE POOR AND THE RECOVERY OF CHRISTIAN IDENTITY

Toward an Asian Theology of Religions Dictated by the Poor

ALOYSIUS PIERIS

The Early Beginnings of Christianity's Identity Crisis

It is common knowledge that the transition from the evangelical simplicity of the nascent church to the pyramidal structure of Romanized Christianity began not long after the birth of the Christian community. The first signs of a loss of Christian identity can be detected already in the New Testament period. The pastoral letters indicate that the previous generation's ideal of equality in class, race, and gender (Gal. 3:28), a distinguishing mark of a Jesus community, had faded away into the Greek and Roman social mores of women and slaves living in submission to advisedly benign masters and husbands.[1] "For the householder in the church of the pastorals is rewarded for being male, prosperous, respectable, and a competent household manager."[2] Therefore, "The equality and mutuality of his followers which Jesus taught and encouraged and which was amply evidenced in the gospel narratives was by this time a dim memory and a discarded reality."[3]

There is a reason for this evolution. Despite Paul's remark that most of the early converts did not come from the wise, powerful, and noble strata of society (1 Cor. 1:26), by which he might *not* have meant that only menial slaves constituted the communities he speaks of,[4] there is evidence of an unhealthy influence of the social elite (1 Cor. 11:20–22, 33–34) or perhaps even of aristocrats.[5] As the numbers of converts increased, first among the Jews and then among the Gentiles, the inevitable reliance on the rich, who not only financed the first missions but also allowed the use of their spatial mansions for liturgical gatherings, must have had its impact on the selection and quality of church leaders and consequently also on the social relationships forged among Christians. Were even some of the women who exercised leadership accepted as women (which would be commendable), or were they accepted only because they were rich and powerful persons? Undoubtedly, the rich were bound by the Gospel to share their resources with the community to relieve the poor and, by extension, to support the missions that brought good news to the poor; however, they would not be sharing a gift but only buying position and power within the believing community if thereby a class division set in. Did the advice given in 1 Timothy 6:17 presuppose such a situation?

This is a problem endemic to the church then and now. It seems to have started with the apostles, who certainly gave up all things to follow the Gospel but continued to hanker after power and position already during the earthly life of Jesus (Matt. 9:33–35). The Gospels make it clear that here we are dealing with the sin that even Jesus had to struggle against (Matt. 4:1–11). The thirst for power that the Servant-Messiah renounced became the temptation of the nascent church. The picture that Matthew draws of his church is not flattering. The parable of the wicked tenants (Matt. 21:43) warns that authority will be transferred from a sterile leadership to one that bears fruit; the Parable Discourse (Matt. 13) speaks of a mixture of the good and the bad among the disciples, and the Community Discourse (Matt. 18), addressed to the leaders of the community, speaks of "little ones," precious to the Father in heaven, who need to be protected from the scandals of the bigger people, such as perhaps the high-ranking money-handling official who was unmerciful toward an erring brother of a lower rank.[6] The leadership, which was called upon to serve as the *stable rock* on which the community was to rest (Matt. 16:18) became a *stumbling block* (scandal) when it opted for a Christ without a cross (Matt. 16:23),— that is, for a power-wielding messianism.[7]

How the guiding principle of equality, once an identifying feature of the church, disappeared had everything to do with the way the church handled the rich and their riches—or was it also the way the rich and their riches handled the church? Apart from the changes that took place in the late New Testament period of the pastorals, the post–New Testament era saw Christianity gaining an elevated social standing in an increasingly decadent empire, thanks especially to mixed marriages between the pagan elite and Christian women.[8] Christianity's respectability, enhanced especially after the persecutions, was merely recognized, not created, by the Imperial Edict of Constantine. In these circumstances, a Christianized empire could not avoid being a social embodiment of an imperialized Christianity. Yesterday's colonization and today's globalization, in which this species of Christianity serves rather than challenges the empire of Mammon, is a monumental witness to a loss of Christian identity.

If this is the information derived from the Scriptures and from the early history of the church, our response to the similar identity crisis of the church in our own time will not be a naïve regression to the Church's *beata infantia* (blessed infancy) with Spirit possessions and mass conversions, as some zealous Christian sects maintain on the basis of Acts 2, but something less triumphalistic and more challenging: a profound reflection over the nascent church's struggles and failures to remain faithful to the spirit of the Gospel, as well as a sincere effort at learning how to regulate the role of the rich and their riches in the day-to-day life of a Jesus community, a community whose essence is the discipleship of equals.

No community can claim itself to be Christian unless it is animated by the Spirit of Christ dwelling in the little ones. These little ones are not only those who become one family with him by their obedience to the Word (Matt. 12:49) but also the victims of human neglect, who by that very fact become Christ's own presence (Matt. 25:36ff). These two categories of the poor (mentioned also in Matthew's and Luke's beatitudes respectively) are citizens of God's reign and therefore members of Christ's body, the dwelling place of the Spirit. All claims to be possessed by the Spirit, as well as the appeal to mass manifestations of mystical outpourings as divine authentication of such claims, must be tested by the infallible criterion given by the end-time judge whose presence is revealed in the victims of nations (Matt. 25:36ff). Solidarity with the poor is fidelity to the Spirit.

Our task, as mentioned above, is to learn from the earliest Christian experiment the art of resisting the reign of Mammon. Even if that experiment seemed to have failed, it was an experiment worth failing; therefore it is an experiment worth repeating until it bears the fruit that the Johannine Jesus would expect. I allude to the effort of early Christians to transform or leaven the imperial society by means of powerful symbolic gestures, sacraments of social transformation, acted out with a persistent regularity. There are two well-known examples: the Christian Sabbath and the Covenant Meal.

Ever faithful to the ancient covenant of Israel, the early Christians turned Sunday into their Sabbath. It was as much a holiday from work as a holy day for divine worship, combining worship with a general strike from all labor, even for slaves. Worship was rendered to the "God of Slaves" through Jesus, the "Slave of God" *(ebed Yahweh),* who, under the imperial law of Caesar *(sub Pontio Pilato),* had succumbed to a cruel death penalty meted out only to the slaves, the lowest stratum *(humiliores)* of the empire. Jesus was celebrated as the hope of the slaves, those deemed to have been condemned to a life of dehumanizing indebtedness.

On such weekly holidays, these Christians indulged in another similar act of silent protest against slavery, the economic base of the empire. While the Romans were kneeling before an altar in the temple where a leisure class of priests offered sacrificial victims to the gods of the powerful, the gods whose "mediator with humans" *(Pontifex Maximus)* was the emperor himself, the followers of Jesus did the exact opposite: masters and slaves, males and females, Jews and Gentiles sat round a table in their homes as a community of equals, not only sharing the life of their God at a covenant meal but also exercising their royal and priestly co-victimhood in, with, and through Christ. The table challenged the altar; the meal defied the cult; the home dwarfed the temple; the fellowship of equals questioned the pyramid of power; the solidarity with the co-victims of Christ expressed in self-oblation undermined the cultic priesthood of the leisure class placating gods with ritual sacrifices; and finally, the God who had pitched God's tent among the slaves belied the gods created by the slave-owning empire.

These simple acts performed week after week were the gentle but consistently regular strokes of a hammer that, with time, could have crumbled an empire thriving on slavery. They were like David's sling, capable of pelting down a gigantic power. This was the only way, Christ's own way, of converting people from the attractions of the Roman empire: the constant and consistent witnessing to a contrasting model of society where life and worship, with no show of pomp and power, anticipated the new age promised to humankind. Such *ecclesiolae,* or what we could call "little flocks of Christ" (or anachronistically, basic ecclesial communities), proliferating in the empire, seemed to have been invested with the holiness of Christ as long as they retained their identity as the little ones *(microi).* To these our God revealed all things; he remained ever at home among the lowly ones *(tapeinoi),* with whom Christ identified himself. For holiness has been recognized as a distinguishing mark of the true church from ancient times and is derived from the church being poor and being with the poor.[9]

It follows, then, that the reclaiming of our original charisma—that is, our Christian uniqueness—is the task of the poor and the powerless, who have God as their covenant partner in the mission of redemption. We are here dealing with the essence of biblical Christianity, namely God's covenant with Egypt's slaves at Sinai in the First Testament, which was upheld, confirmed, and sealed anew by Jesus on Calvary, where he revealed himself as God's new covenant with the victims of Mammon-worshippers. Jesus's scandalous predilection for the despised, which seemed exaggerated in the eyes of the privileged class,[10] was the way he lived out his unique mission of uniting in his own person God and the poor to form one covenanted salvific reality. In Jesus, therefore, both partners of this covenant, Yahweh and the slaves of all times, can be encountered. Hence any community that claims to believe in Christ will show signs of allegiance to both signatories of the covenant. Association with the lowly ones, recommended by Paul to his more privileged Christians (Rom. 16:20), is the surest way to be associated with God in Jesus. The option for the poor is the mark of the church's divine origin.

THE RECOVERY OF CHRISTIAN IDENTITY IN (SOUTH) ASIA TODAY

An "Operation Identity" that consisted of realigning the church with God's poor was certainly in the air in various parts of the church and began to assume concrete expression in the 1970s. A movement for a Christian socialism that assimilated the social doctrine and praxis of other religions had already been launched in Sri Lanka in the 1950s with the formation of the Christian Workers' Fellowship only a few years before the emergence of the Latin American counterpart. It seemed that the Spirit was blowing particularly, though not exclusively, in the most non-Christian continent as well as in the most Christian: Asia and South America, respectively. Certain theologians were beginning to reach out to Yahweh's suffering servants in India (the Dalits) and Korea (the Minjung) as their mentors and partners in the task of restoring to the church its lost identity. And Christian identity seekers in Asia (where they constituted a minority among the Christian minority) were beginning to hear about the small efforts of small people in Latin America to accomplish the same task there. The news of the rise of basic ecclesial communities (reminiscent of the above mentioned *ecclesiolae* in the Roman Empire) in this region, where so many poor people and so many Christians were concentrated,[11] accompanied by Gustavo Gutiérrez's *Theology of Liberation,* fueled the enthusiasm of Asian Christians who had already begun a similar journey.[12] Some Asian Christians who were skeptical about their own colleagues' involvement in this enterprise were awakened from their dogmatic slumber by Gutiérrez's epoch-making thesis.

This was the most creative phase of theological thinking in our continent in recent times. For the age-old missionary enthusiasm for preaching Christianity and making converts had by then reached an all-time low except in tribal areas. Some blamed Vatican II for this crisis. Whatever the cause of that discouragement, there was an unsettling feeling that we Christians had lost our way. Anything good we had said and done seemed, at best, a duplication of whatever good had been said and done by other religionists. On the other hand, whatever looked new that distinguished us from them was, in their eyes, our organizational skills and material resources, which linked us with the colonial and neocolonial powers. This association with and reliance on foreign sources of wealth and power seemed unique to Christianity, a sort of a mark of the church that allegedly revealed its true identity.

This was precisely the critical diagnosis that had been made available to the church since the early nineteenth century by certain non-Christian reformers of South Asia (such as Raja Ram Mohun Roy, Sir Syed Ahmed, Swami Vivekananda, and most of all Mahatma Gandhi, all of them admirers of Jesus and some of them even self-proclaimed "followers" of Jesus):

they lamented that the church's concern for the poor was motivated not by the love of the poor in themselves but by the allegedly sinister goal of rescuing souls from Hinduism by incorporating them into the church, thus using the poor and their poverty as an alibi for foreign-financed proselytism.[13]

This harsh criticism took a new meaning in the 1970s when the aforementioned theologians began to realize that the church's lost identity could be regained only by an "option for the poor" *regarded as a mission in itself,* in contrast with the previous era's policy of an "option for the church" *motivating service to the poor.* There was a crucial demand for a paradigm shift, a new way of thinking about the Christian mission that was not easily understood by church officials of the time.[14]

The new missionary policy, that the church is for the poor rather than the other way around, promised a recovery of Christianity's lost identity. This policy consisted of a response to a twofold vocation, the struggle to be poor and the struggle for the poor. This double calling seemed to demand that the poor be recognized as the true body of Christ rather than as potential converts to be added onto the ecclesial body. The conflict between the church's claim to be Christ's body and Christ's claim that the poor are his body could be resolved only when church not only became "poor in Spirit" by the humble obedience to the Word that ensures membership in Christ's family but also identified itself with the "poor by circumstances," those who judge the nations as Christ, the end-time judge. It is these two categories of the poor that give the church its identity.

In the light of this new awareness, all Christian attempts at indigenization or inculturation, as processes by which the church tried to be like other religions without making the option for the poor, seemed no more than a camouflage used by beasts of prey, to borrow a metaphor used in a Buddhist critique of these efforts.[15] Besides, the earliest instance of indigenization in Asia, which resulted in an apostolic community of Jesus followers in Kerala (India) in the first century CE under the patronage of the Persian (East Syrian/Nestorian) Church, had unfortunately assimilated what was and still is a regrettable weakness of the Hindu tradition, namely the religiously justified practice of caste discrimination. It took a millennium and a half before the victims of this nefarious caste system could receive baptism at the hands of a Francis Xavier, though the species of Christianity that brought about this change remained culturally European. Later efforts to indigenize this same Christianity (first in the sixteenth century by De Nobili and then in the nineteenth century by Gnostic Christians) are seen by Dalit theologians as a mere replacement of the European theology of domination with a Brahmanic theology of the same kind. Thus the option for the poor, rather than zeal for church expansion, began to emerge as the authentic form of evangelization.

Here, then, is the dilemma of the seekers of a Christian identity in South Asia. What kind of witness *(martyrion)* would guarantee that the proclamation *(kerygma)* of the good news *(euangelion)* to the poor would inspire the conversion *(metanoia)* of both the oppressor and the oppressed, the rich and the poor, the elite and the marginalized, in such a way that the victims of injustice would be neither proselytized into the church nor abandoned to the sinful structures associated with socioreligious traditions? The resolution of this dilemma became possible as various political theologies of liberation began to emerge during the critical decades mentioned above[16] and, concomitantly, as the contours of a liberation theology of religions inspired by the poor became better defined.

The Asian Way of Doing Theology of Religions as if the Poor Mattered

An Asian Perspective on the Vatican's Apprehensions

After issuing admonitions about Latin American liberation theology, the Congregation for the Doctrine of the Faith (CDF) and its president, Josef Ratzinger, began to show concern about Asian Christians and their theological approach to other religions. John Allen of the *National Catholic Reporter* has listed twelve such documents appearing within a span of twelve years (1989–2000), climaxing in *Dominus Jesus.*[17] The Christological content and the ecclesiological presuppositions of these documents, including certain misapprehensions of what the Asian theologians are actually saying,[18] provide the key to a correct understanding of the paradigm shift that Rome has failed to recognize and that some Asians may have failed to articulate.

Once liberation theology associated with Latin America had been dealt with, it was obvious that Asia's inculturation theology had to be called back to the twofold truth it had allegedly diluted: that Christ is the only universal agent of salvation and that the (Roman) Church is the absolutely essential means of salvation. My surmise is that the CDF's non-Asian advisers and Asian informants were unaware of the inculturation liberation debate that polarized the Asian theologians in the late 1970s and early 1980s. For there is still a strand of inculturationist theology that has not assimilated the struggle *to be* the poor and the struggle *for* the poor as its essential ingredients and has therefore ignored Christ's uniqueness and Christianity's identity.

It is common knowledge that some confusion arose around inculturation and liberation at the Asian Theological Consultation in 1979— ironically, after my presentation of a paper in which I deliberately avoided the theme of inculturation, which was a nonissue for me, and proposed a paradigm in which religiousness and poverty, each in its *liberating* as well as *enslaving* dimension, would serve as the two poles of a tension constituting the dynamics of an Asian theology of liberation. Later, some theologians read "religiousness" and "poverty" as their accustomed poles of inculturation and liberation, thus missing the new paradigm and its implications.[19]

The dust settled within a couple of years, and the Asian theologies of liberation, and they alone, moved forward along the binary track of religiousness and poverty with greater clarity. Their focus, in other words, was not on culture as such but on the liberative dimension of its religious core and was less on the metacosmic religiosity of the so-called higher (scriptural) religions of Asia than on the localized cosmic religiosity of the poor. I introduced the use of the word *cosmic* to designate the this-worldly religiosity of the Asian poor, as contrasted to the "secular" viewpoint— that is, the nonreligious this-worldliness of Western liberals.[20] The term embraces the sacred worldliness of tribal and clan cultures as well as popular interpretations and practices of scriptural religions at the grassroots level in Asian societies. As the history of Asia's various revolutionary struggles has amply demonstrated, the cosmic religiosity of the poor conceals an explosive potential for sociospiritual liberation.[21] The Dalit, Minjung, and feminist theologies of Asia, all categorized under the rubric of liberation, definitely lean toward the cosmic.

Thus every effort at inculturation in Asia that tended to assimilate only the metacosmic religiosity of the elites without integrating the cosmic spirituality of the poor seemed to have ignored what ultimately spells out Christ's uniqueness as well as Christianity's identity. Furthermore, such attempts seemed to many of us a mere duplication in Asia of what had regrettably happened in Europe since the Hellenization of Christianity. Asian inculturationists and the *defensores fidei* (defenders of the faith) of the Western patriarchate who are now censoring them actually think along the same theological lines. In other words, the traditional Western theology that serves as the norm of orthodoxy is no different from any Asian theology that does not have the struggle of the poor in its agenda, for they all have begun as a process of inculturation minus liberation and therefore harbor a Christology without a soteriology. They have failed to articulate the uniqueness of Christ and consequently the true identity of Christianity.

Christianity's *caesura,* Karl Rahner's preferred term for the "neat break" from the cultural constraints of the Jewish tradition, thanks to the decision of the apostles at the so-called Council of Jerusalem (Acts 15:1–29), prevented the Jesus community from remaining a mere sect of Judaism like the Essenes. Perhaps this was essential at the time, and it guaranteed Christianity's inculturation among non-Jews. The result was that the new religion took root among the cosmopolitan and even racially hybrid communities of Greek-educated Jews and Gentiles living in the urban centers of the Roman Empire.[22] Christianity was thus released from the Semitic culture only to be buried in a Hellenistic one. More significantly, the Christianity of the relatively poor class of people in Palestine, for whom Paul organized financial assistance from the richer Greek-speaking churches, evolved into a sophisticated brand of doctrinaire religiosity elaborated by the social elite. Paul's failure to communicate the core of Christian soteriology, the death and the resurrection of Jesus, to the sophisticated Greeks of Athens in their own philosophical idiom (Acts 17:16–34) and the lesson Luke tried to teach the nascent church by narrating it (or inventing it?) seemed to have been forgotten by this time.[23]

This is most evident from Aloys Grillmeier's analysis of the way Christological controversies cropped up in the context of what he calls "pagan philosophy" and even more the way they were finally resolved by a resort to dogmatic formulas that smacked of Greek "metaphysics."[24] Elaborate speculations about the Incarnation replaced the main soteriological theme of the Christ-event. The fact that Nestorius's early Christology tended to be more soteriological, while his later work *Liber Heraclidis,* which was so orthodox as to approximate the future Chalcedonian definitions, was more ontological,[25] surely indicates that as we move further away from the Semitic idiom of the Bible toward the Hellenistic ethos of the first councils the theological language becomes less soteriological and more ontological. The thoroughly European idiom of these councils, *pace* (with due deference to) Norman Tanner,[26] failed, unfortunately, to conserve the biblical doctrine of salvation.[27] Grillmeier, the authority on this matter, has complained that in the traditional Christology emanating from these first councils "a development was at hand which is still a burden to Christology, the divorce between the person and the work of Jesus, between Christology and soteriology."[28]

Thus the inculturation of Christianity in the elitist culture of the Hellenistic world resulted in an eclipse of soteriology: it neglected the message of liberation proclaimed through the life, work, death, and resurrection of Jesus. This traditional Christology missed what constitutes the uniqueness of Christ. The "God-man concept" lying behind the doctrine of the Incarnation eclipsed the "God-poor covenant" sealed on the cross. The theology that the CDF employs as the norm of orthodoxy, derived from this same Christology, and the theology that the same CDF has censored in Asia have both failed to address the question of Christ's uniqueness and Christianity's identity. The reason is that they both originated as a process of inculturation that did not take into account the liberation of the oppressed and oppressors. Therefore, any Asian theology of religion that is dictated by the poor not only is innocent of the charge of diluting the uniqueness of Christ but throws it back on the censors.

The Option for the Poor and the Asian Method of Doing Theology

Asian theologies of religion that are dictated by the poor show a two-pronged methodology. First, they seek a fresh understanding of the Scriptures in their Semitic/Asian idiom in order to prevent the justice dimension of biblical faith from being drowned in philosophical speculations, Asian or otherwise. Second, they vernacularize theological education in the context of Asia's poverty, with a concomitant assimilation of the soteriological thrust of Asian cultures.[29]

The first strategy imposes on us a long-overdue caesura or rupture from the European particularity of the church's traditional theology so that we may reread the biblical message of liberation in its Asian/Semitic idiom, unhampered by the Hellenism of the Christological councils. This is an extended version of the strong plea made by the late Stanislao Lyonnet, S.J., that when we read the Bible, even the Septuagint and the New

Testament, which are in Greek, "we must not have recourse to the [thought patterns of the] Greeks" *(non dobbiamo recorrere ai Greci),* lest we grossly misinterpret the message of revelation, as has happened so often in current theology.[30]

We are convinced that the Chalcedonian Christology, circumscribed as it is in the philosophical language of the Greeks, not only presents a rather diminished figure of Christ compared to that of the scriptural Christ but also poses a serious obstacle to our proclamation of Christ in Asia because it either makes no sense at all when transposed into certain Asian languages, assuming that a translation is possible,[31] or makes him one of the many incarnations *(avatars)* of god-men in the Hindu tradition,[32] or, as in a Buddhist context, reduces Christ to one of the many nontranscendent and nonsalvific cosmic forces *(devas),* contrary to the intentions of Chalcedon.[33] Asian theologians can fall into this same rut if they too are contented with speculating about Christ in terms of the many Asian philosophies that have been manufactured by the leisure class instead of trying to recapture the biblical message of liberation in the context of the soteriological aspirations of Asia's religious poor.

This is what has made me plead for a covenant Christology, according to which Jesus, as the crucified, risen Christ or the life-giving Spirit, is the new covenant between God and the powerless, or the new law of love. In proposing this approach, I have responded to an ancient Asian (Judaic) impulse that Grillmeier himself mentions in passing: the identification of Jesus as the covenant *(diatheke)* and as the law *(nomos).*[34] With this approach, we can spell out the uniqueness of Christ, which Chalcedon's God-man concept fails to articulate, in terms of Christ's universality, neither underestimating the soteriological role of other religions nor ignoring, as Chalcedon was doing, the clamor of God's poor for justice and freedom.[35] Since I have elaborated this vision in the many sources quoted above, all I shall do here is articulate a few aspects of it.

In the first place, the justice dimension of the biblical faith, mentioned above as the first prong of our strategy, requires a clarification because, ever since the Roman Synod of 1971, the inseparable link between the preaching of the Gospel and the liberation of the poor has been expressed as a combination of "[the proclamation of] faith and [the promotion of] justice" in an explicitly antibiblical sense. The confusion originated from our traditional theology, where justice is a merely human virtue, which therefore is not salvific unless informed by the infused divine virtue of faith. Apart from the Chalcedonian mentality that is operative here, a Roman juridical notion of justice is involved.[36] No wonder that a complaint was persistently heard in the postsynodal era that the struggle for justice, understood in this scholastic sense, had eclipsed the faith dimension of our mission. This seems to have compelled John Paul II to issue the encyclical *Dives in misercordia* to show how God mitigates justice with forgiving love and saving mercy.

Let us, therefore, turn once more to Lyonnet. Contrary to the current theological understanding of justice, he insists, the biblical notion of justice is not to be confused with the end-time judgment (condemnation) of the unjust, for which the appropriate biblical term is God's wrath *(orge tou theou);* therefore, the biblical notion of justice does not need to be mitigated by God's redeeming and forgiving love, as presupposed in the current theological parlance. Rather, justice in the Bible is always an expression of God's mercy and love, which forgives and saves rather than judges and condemns. It is none other than God's own fidelity to the covenant[37]—that is, God's partiality to the powerless who are God's covenant partners, summoning the oppressors to repentance and conversion. Even the end-time judgment, God's wrath, can be avoided by partaking in God's justice to the poor. We are dealing with the covenant spirituality in which God's love is extended both to sinners and to those who are sinned against, a spirituality that must pervade the church's entire lifestyle, liturgy, and pastorate.

This spirituality, therefore, is our faith-response to that covenant, our participation in the justice of the covenant. Our faith is not merely our trust in the One whose justice never fails the little ones who are his covenant partners but also our own unfailing fidelity to that same covenant—that is, our solidarity with the poor. What is even more significant, the Just One's end-time judgment *(orge)* (Matt. 25:36 ff.) is passed by the little ones of today who are covenanted with him. Therefore our faith expresses the covenantal justice to the oppressed in view of the eschatological judgment that the victim judge of nations would pass on the oppressors who fail to repent and cooperate with that same divine justice. Our faith, therefore, impels us to seek the conversion of the unjust.

Since the justice dimension of biblical faith is thus traced back to the covenant between God and the poor, enfleshed as Jesus the Christ, every kind of God-talk (theology) must invariably revolve around the poor: It must be a Christology in which the Asian poor as well as the Asian religions are taken in their dialectical relationship, as befits the soteriological thrust of Asian cultures. This means that Christ, in whom "the God of the violated" is also "the violated God" prophesied in the servant songs of Isaiah and thematized in the Passion narratives of the Gospels, can only be good news, and no threat to the Asian poor or to the Asian religions and their founders.

God's Reign for God's Poor

When Jesus refers to the poor as part of God's realm of the saved, he does so without attaching any religious label to them. Blessed are the poor, not because they are potential converts to the church but because they are poor. Not only the poor in spirit (Matt. 5:3), or the "detached ones" associated with Asia's metacosmic religiosity, but also the socially poor (Luke 6:20) and the "dispossessed ones" with their cosmic spirituality are the stuff that the reign of God is made of. The church, being the servant and sacrament of God's reign, is defined by its identification with these two categories of the poor, who therefore give Christianity its identity. Christ is one body with them already; they do not have to be converted to the church. For the radical conversion *(shub, metanoia)* he demands as a condition for salvation is not a change of one's religion (or proselytism, which he ridiculed in Matt. 23:15) but a change of one's life—that is, the acceptance of the beatitudinal spirituality (greedless or nonidolatrous living), which happens to be the common soteriological thrust of all Asian cultures.

This means that God's enemies are not other religionists, as the evangelical Christians believe, but the Mammon-worshippers who create poverty. To them the church must dauntlessly proclaim the need for conversion from housetops and public places. This is true evangelism. Our mission to them is to demonstrate that God's wrathful judgment and God's merciful justice are both mediated by the poor themselves. For the Christ whom we believe in and proclaim to the world is not merely a divine person or substance assuming human nature but a corporate person in whom God is one body with the victims of human greed. It is in terms of this Christology that we claim that the option for the poor constitutes *our service to Christ in the poor* whereas the administration of word and sacraments in the church represents *Christ's service to us through his ministers.* The former (corporal works of mercy) is in the order of salvation, whereas the latter (spiritual works of mercy) is in the order of sanctification and fortification. Baptism and the Eucharist are in the second order as sacramental expressions of the salvific event that happens in the first order.

If this is the Christological understanding of the sacraments, then surely Christ's mission command to baptize and make disciples of all nations is a command to continue his own mission, the mission for which he was anointed by the Spirit at Nazareth (Luke 4:17–21): to liberate the victims of oppression, the poor, the captives, those in pain of heart and body, and to declare the Jubilee year, which grants end-time amnesty to the oppressors so that they might be reconciled with their victims by submitting to the covenantal stipulations. It was to achieve this mission that Jesus received his own baptism on the cross (for this is what Jesus always meant by his baptism), in solidarity with his co-victims of all ages in the end-time today of Calvary.

Those who impose this cross on the masses, then and now, are not necessarily atheists, but they are idolaters. The baptism of a nation and its conversion to the discipleship of the beatitudes consists of a death-bringing struggle to break down the vicious idols that enslave that nation: religious bigotry, national pride, racial prejudice, class elitism, military superiority, gender discrimination, color consciousness, and language domination. The social conflict (i.e., the "cross") that the church and the nation face in this anti-idolatrous mission is also their share in the saving baptism of Christ.

That this missiology meets strong and fierce resistance from fundamentalist groups both Catholic and otherwise here in Asia is very well known.[38] In their view, Christ is involved in a conversion race with the founders of other religions rather than being persecuted in his members by the worshipers of the money demon. They have not identified the real enemy, the attractive beast that brands its worshipers with its ugly identity mark (Rev. 16:2; 19:20) and that can rob the church of its identity if it does not live its option for the poor. They have not discovered that if we were as self-effacingly humble as our Master was, other religionists would join us as partners in a common mission, the mission of baptizing nations into beatitudinal living, as has happened in many parts of Asia through basic human communities. Nor do these Christian zealots believe that Christ's uniqueness is revealed only when he draws all hearts to himself from the cross (John 12:32–33), where he is being baptized, and that our own identity as Christians lies precisely in following that ideal rather than in elating our collective ego by advertising a mass-mesmerizing Messiah. The basic human communities acting like leaven in human society on the one hand and the colorful mass rallies of evangelicals on the other witness to two conflicting images of Christ and Christianity in Asia today.

Roman as well as non-Roman evangelicals have expressed their strong reservations with regard to our missionary approach. "How can your understanding of baptism and discipleship of nations be reconciled with the mass conversions to the church that the apostles encouraged immediately after Pentecost under the impulse of the Holy Spirit (Acts 2)?" In response to this objection, we draw their attention to what the Spirit is saying to the churches today and how we ought to respond to that Word by following another precedent recorded in the same book of the Acts.

First, the situation of the Mediterranean region during the time of Acts 2 radically differs from what we experience in South Asia today. In the post-Pentecostal decades, the religion of the Romans and the Greeks was on the wane and there was a spiritual vacuum that, providentially, served as the entry point for Christ's message of liberation into what was then the known civilized world. Our situation here in South Asia is quite the opposite. Precisely that same Christianity is now in crisis, while, on the contrary, the non-Christian religions are not on the decline but very much self-assertive and capable of inculcating anti-idolatrous beatitudinal spirituality, notwithstanding the persistence of many negative elements, which are not absent in Christianity either. Our own solidarity with them in the anti-idolatrous spirituality common to all religions can ensure our own renewal as well as their perseverance in the path of covenantal justice.

Moreover, and more significantly, the five-hundred-year-old failure of Christianity to effect mass conversions in this part of the globe, in contrast with its almost total success in Latin America, the Philippines, and Oceania, is a phenomenon that must serve as a sign of the time revealing what the Spirit is saying to the churches in South Asia.[39] To read God's design through this remarkable datum of history, and also to act according to that reading, we could follow another precedent mentioned in Acts 15: the radically revolutionary decision to exempt the Gentiles from the divinely ordained initiation rite of Israel, something that parallels the ritual baptism in the church. By whose authority did the apostles change this sacrosanct obligation of ritual circumcision issuing from the revealed law of God?

It was indeed a synergistic decision made by the Spirit and the Apostles in the light of new evidence brought from the frontiers of the church (Antioch). The power of binding and loosing, which Israel's leaders claimed to have received from God, was, to use a later Jewish expression, the authority to determine *halakkah,* to decide what practices should be followed by the community,[40] rather than what new dogmas should be imposed on the believers. This very same authority of binding and loosing was given by Christ to his disciples, obviously as the power of discretion in the matter of making policy changes in the praxis of the church. The apostles, guided by the Spirit, exercised this authority under pressure from frontier ministers such as Paul and Barnabas in changing the pristine practice of circumcision sanctioned by Scripture and the sacred tradition. So do the frontier ministers working in South Asia, today, press on the church to promulgate the nonritual but more radical form of baptism and conversion to discipleship that our option for Christ and his co-victims has disclosed to us.

NOTES

1. F. J. Cwiekowski, *The Beginnings of the Church* (New York: Paulist Press, 1988), 140–42.

2. H. Hendrickx, *The Household of God* (Quezon City: Claretian Publications, 1992), 119.

3. Ibid., 120.

4. Cwiekowski, *Beginnings of the Church*, 119–20.

5. R. E. Brown, *An Introduction to the New Testament* (New York: Doubleday, 1997), 68.

6. H. Hendrickx, "Image of the Church in the New Testament," *Japanese Missionary Bulletin* 8 (1978): 413–14.

7. H. Hendrickx, "Matthew and the Church, Then and Now," *Japanese Missionary Bulletin* 8 (1978): 535–36.

8. See Ann Yarbrough, "Christianization in the Fourth Century: The Example of Roman Women," *Church History* 45 (June 1976): 149 ff.

9. For how this "mark of holiness" is derived from the church's option for the poor, see Jürgen Moltmann, *Church in the Power of the Holy Spirit* (London: SCM Press, 1977), 352–55; Aloysius Pieris, "Ecumenism in the Churches and the Unfinished Agenda of the Holy Spirit," *Spiritus* 3 (Spring 2003): 54–56, 65.

10. W. G. Kummel, *Introduction to the New Testament*, rev. ed. (London: SCM Press, 1975), 139.

11. M. de C. Azevedo, S.J., *The Basic Ecclesial Communities in Brazil: The Challenge of a New Way of Being the Church* (Washington, DC: Georgetown University Press, 1987), 177–244.

12. See the observations of Asians (Preman Niles and Tissa Balasuriya, both from Sri Lanka) at the International Ecumenical Congress of Theology, February 20–March 2, Sao Paolo, Brazil, in *The Challenge of Basic Christian Communities*, ed. S. Torres and John Eagleson (Maryknoll, NY: Orbis Books, 1981), 253–54, 259–62.

13. See M. V. Nadkarni, "Ethics and Relevance of Conversion: A Critical Assessment of Religious and Social Dimensions in Gandhian Perspective," *Economic and Political Weekly* 38 (January 18–24, 2003): 227–41. The author, however, exempts Mother Teresa from this accusation.

14. The Vatican's CDF (Congregation for Doctrine of Faith, then under Cardinal Seper), exchanged letters with my provincial expressing concern about my paper "Towards an Asian Theology of Liberation," read at this Asian Theological Consultation of the Ecumenical Association of Third World Theologians in 1979. This paper has been published in Aloysius Pieris, *An Asian Theology of Liberation* (Maryknoll, NY: Orbis Books, 1988), 69–86.

15. G. Vithanage, "The New Look with a Note: A Comment on Fr. Mervyn Fernando's Article on 'Is Adaptation Outmoded?'" *Quest* (Colombo) 4 (1969): 80–81.

16. See Aloysius Pieris, "Political Theologies of Asia," in *Blackwell Companion to Political Theology,* ed. Peter Scott and William T. Cavanaugh (Oxford: Blackwell, 2004), 256–70.

17. John L. Allen, "Perils of Pluralism," *National Catholic Reporter,* September 15, 2000, www.natcath.com/NCR_Online/archives/091500/091500e.htm (accessed August 10, 2006).

18. See Aloysius Pieris, "The Roman Catholic Perception of Other Religions and Other Churches after the Vatican's *Dominus Jesus,*" *East Asian Pastoral Review* 38 (2001): 1, 207–30.

19. For notes on this controversy, see Pieris, *Asian Theology of Liberation,* 88, 133 nn. 3 and 4.

20. See my entry in Virginia Fabella and R. S. Sgirtharajah, eds., *Dictionary of the Third World* (Maryknoll, NY: Orbis Books, 2000), s.v. "cosmic/metacosmic religions" (where, regrettably, *this-worldly* has been misspelled *third-worldly*). See also Aloysius Pieris, *Fire and Water: Basic Issues in Asian Buddhism and Christianity* (Maryknoll, NY: Orbis Books, 1996), 15–26.

21. Pieris, *Asian Theology of Liberation,* esp. 98–108.

22. Brown, *Introduction to the New Testament,* 63–64.

23. According to current scholarly opinion, Luke's story is not historical; rather, it reflects his desire to show that Athens, the center of Hellenism, was also evangelized (Cwiekowski, *Beginnings of the Church,* 103).

24. Aloys Grillmeier, *Christ in Christian Tradition,* vol. 1, *From the Apostolic Age to Chalcedon (AD 451)* (London: Mowbrays, 1975), 36–37.

25. Ibid., 44.

26. Norman Tanner, *Is the Church Too Asian? Reflections on the Ecumenical Council* (Bangalore: Dharmaram Publications, 2002).

27. As I have argued in my review of Tanner's thesis in *Vidyajyoti: Journal of Theological Reflection* 67 (September 2003): 782–92, and in the ensuing discussion between us: his response in *Vidyajyoti* 67 (November 2003): 948–54; my reflection on his response in *Vidyajyoti* 68 (April 2004): 301; his counter-reply in *Vidya-*

jyoti 68 (April 2004): 302–4; and my concluding comment in *Vidyajyoti* 68 (September 2004): 702–3.

28. Aloys Grillmeier, *Christ in Christian Tradition,* vol. 2, *From the Council of Chalcedon to Gregory the Great (590–604)* (London: Mowbrays, 1987), pt. 1, 5.

29. The Savana (Asian Institute of Missiology), directed by the Scripture scholar Dr. Shirley Lal Wijeysingha and the ecclesiologist Rev. Dr. Hilarion Dissanayaka, O. M. I., in Sri Lanka, follows this methodology, as do a few of the Jesuit Regional Theologates in India.

30. Stanislao Lyonnet, *Il Nuovo Testamento alla luce dell'Antico,* Studi Biblici Pastorali 3 (1968; reprint, Brescia: Paideia, 1972), 36–37.

31. I am supported in this by J. Neuner, S.J., "Mission Theology after Vatican II," *Vidyajyoti: Journal of Theological Reflection* 58 (April 1994): 213.

32. For a thorough discussion of this topic, see J. Neuner, "Das Christus-Mysterium und die indische Lehre von den Avataras," in *Das Konsil von Chalcedon und Gegenwart* (Wuerzburg: Echter, 1954), 786–824.

33. Aloysius Pieris, "Christologies in Asia: A Reply to Felipe Gomez," *Voices from the Third World* 11 (1989): 155–72.

34. Grillmeier, *Christ in Christian Tradition,* 1:44.

35. Aloysius Pieris, "Christ beyond Dogma: Doing Christology in the Context of the Religions and the Poor," *Louvain Studies* 25 (2000): 187–231.

36. As substantiated in Pieris, *God's Reign for God's Poor,* 19–24 and esp. 48–51.

37. Lyonnet, *Il Nuovo Testamento,* 49ff, esp. 61–64.

38. A few random examples: in Sri Lanka a Catholic bishop tried hard to use the resources of the heavily funded "Holy Childhood" to disestablish the interreligious and locally self-reliant children's movement called *lakrivi,* spread across the country by the Oblates of Mary Immaculate, who had subscribed to the new missiology. Evangelistic pastors from Korea who were influenced by the U.S.-based fundamentalist sects (which undermined the struggles of Minjung Christians and Minjung theologians) opened missions in Sri Lanka polarizing a particular denomination that had, till recently, many advocates of the new missiology even among its leadership. Other evangelists, financially backed by rich Christian organizations in the West, have infuriated the Buddhists by their fanatical acts of breaking Buddha statues and burning sacred objects as part of their policy of proselytism, interpreting the Buddhist reactions to their insensitivity as persecutions. This is a repetition of what Portuguese missionaries did in the sixteenth century.

39. For a sociohistorical analysis of this situation, see Aloysius Pieris, "Does Christ Have a Place in Asia," *Concilium* 2 (1993): 33–47, reprinted as ch. 7 in Pieris, *Fire and Water,* 65–70.

40. David H. Stern, introduction to *Jewish New Testament,* ed. David H. Stern (Jerusalem: Jewish New Testament Publications, 1994), xxiii.

Chapter 16

SOCIAL JUSTICE IN JUDAISM

MICHAEL A. SIGNER

One of the most profound developments in Jewish-Catholic relations in recent times came with the publication of *Nostra aetate* on October 28, 1965. This document set in motion new opportunities for Jews and Christians to come to know one another not as adversaries arguing over the future of who would inherit the kingdom but as companions working toward the reign of God on earth.[1] In *Nostra aetate,* the council fathers wanted to "foster and recommend that mutual understanding and respect which is the fruit above all of biblical and theological studies, and of brotherly dialogues." The first document issued by the Commission on Interreligious Relations with the Jews in 1979 sought to implement the ideas of *Nostra aetate* and called for chairs of Jewish studies in Catholic institutions of higher learning and collaboration with Jewish scholars.[2] Nearly forty years separate us from those initial efforts. We have made some progress here in America on mutual understanding of our respective traditions. However, activity in our dialogue ebbs and flows. In some countries there is no significant Jewish demographic presence with whom the church might engage in dialogue. Yet a knowledge of the Jewish tradition and those who still bear witness to its teachings might be a blessing for Christians.

The preferential option for the poor evokes a future that, in the words of Pope John Paul II, has called us as Jews and Catholics to be a blessing to one another so that we can be a blessing to the world.[3] Jews and Catholics will continue their relationship of yes and no to one another, and, while respecting these differences, they can come to a deeper understanding of God's mystery in what is required of us as religious human beings as we continue to embody, each of us in our traditions, the words of the Scripture that we still hold in common.[4]

To turn our thoughts to the poor forces us to look hard at the reality of our times. It can be stipulated that the word *poverty* means the presence of a hunger and a sense that something is missing from the lives of human beings. We can then surely acknowledge that there are many types of poverty around the globe. There is hunger for bread, but there is also hunger for love and for comfort, and there is hunger for an understanding of how the Word of God can heal shattered lives in America, in Asia, in Africa, and indeed all around the world. We may seek global solutions, but ultimately this hunger must be fed differently within each country and within each culture. Simple food may fulfill the basic needs of those who are hungry, but they will soon again lack food. They need more than food; they need ways to produce food in a social structure that will make them feel valued as human beings. A story may not feed the bellies of the hungry, but it can give hope to those who feel that friends, family, and indeed their society have abandoned them.

Throughout their history the Jewish people have wandered through many lands and lived in many cultures. Material prosperity has not always been their companion. In their movement between expulsions and persecutions, the harmony of their households and communities has often been plagued by social inequities. The stability of the Jewish community has been nurtured by the study of Torah, which derives from the Hebrew word meaning "instruction." For generations of Jews, *Torah* meant both the written and the oral Torah. These somewhat confusing terms refer to the canon of scriptural books and the traditions of the Rabbis, which reached written form for the first time in the third century in a collection called Mishnah, which means "teaching," and continued with the Talmud and in continuous commentaries and legal literatures down through the centuries.[5] Other literary discourses have enriched the Jewish tradition, such as philosophy, philology, and esoteric teachings called Kabbalah or mysticism. However, these genres have, in many ways, always been linked to the constant study of the rabbinic literature known as Talmud. Therefore, in searching for the Jewish roots of social justice, one must always go back and forth between the Tanakh, the Jewish Scriptures, what Christians call the Old Testament or Hebrew Scriptures, and the teachings of the Rabbis, as well as between these texts and the immediate praxis or situation of life. The relationship between the study of texts and the experience of life has been at the heart of Judaism for nearly two millennia.[6]

The locus for the study and absorption of both of these literatures was the Beit Midrash, the house of study, which stood in close proximity to, and many times may have been the same building as, the synagogue.[7] The liturgy, the developing literature of Jewish public prayers, contains many citations from these rabbinic texts. It was in the context of the liturgy that these texts were quoted and served as the object of meditation and indeed the framework for pedagogy and lessons in life. In this manner, in Judaism, the text of prayer became the guide for life.[8]

In this essay, I would like to trace the path of a text from the daily Jewish liturgy back to its biblical sources. Since this text is from the Mishnah, it will demonstrate how that legal document, the foundational text of rabbinic Judaism, can serve as a meditative guide and text for daily conduct. We know that the text of the Mishnah described the idealized contours of Jewish life in the community. Once we have explicated the Mishnah text within its liturgical context, we will move on to two sections from the Pentateuch, Exodus 21 and 24 and Leviticus 19, as the foundational texts that constitute the Jewish roots of social justice. In conclusion, I will briefly examine the relationship between the legal discourse of these texts and the place where each appears in the narrative of the Torah. These three parts form the embodiment of my basic thesis, that any phenomenon in the life of the Jewish community and its religious faith is grounded in a dialogue between the praxis of life and the texts of the tradition throughout the generations.

Mishnah *Peah,* Morning Prayer, and Social Justice

Upon awakening in the morning, Jews prepare for the morning prayer. The first rubric of these prayers is called *Birkhot HaShahar,* the morning benedictions.[9] According to the twelfth-century legal authority and philosopher Maimonides, these blessings were originally said at home and corresponded to the activities connected with awakening in the morning and acknowledging the divine presence.[10] Later these blessings, as well as readings from Scripture, were transferred to the synagogue, where they remain part of the morning prayers to the present day.[11]

Among these blessings is a section called *Birkhot Torah* (blessings of Torah). Jews acknowledge God for the gift of revelation and pray that they may be granted the privilege of studying it and living by its word.[12] Within these prayers is a section from the second tractate of the Mishnah *Seder Zeraim* called *Peah,* the gleanings left at the corners of the field at harvest time. The text reads as follows, with my own commentary in brackets:

> These are the things that have no measure. [In other words, there is no limit on precisely how much one can leave, and indeed it is praiseworthy to do this in excess.] And these are they, the produce at the corner of the field, and the first fruits [that the Israelites are required to bring to the sanctuary in Jerusalem], and the number of sacrifices one brings to the Temple in Jerusalem at the time of the pilgrimage festival, and *Gemilut Hasadim,* acts of loving-kindness, and Talmud Torah, the study of Torah.[13]

In this passage, we observe the Mishnah's unique literary quality of juxtaposing elements of past and present. By the time the Mishnah was composed in the third century the temple was no longer in existence, but since the Rabbis hoped for its restoration and maintained this hope as a central tenet of their faith, they maintained the memory and embedded it in their text. In this manner, one can understand that the first fruits and sacrifices for the pilgrimage festival could no longer be brought to be offered in the Temple, but the memory of those biblical commandments engendered a significant hope for their future restoration. However, even in early times and up to the present day for those Jews who continue to live in the geographic boundaries of the land of Israel, it has been a continuing obligation to leave the corners of the field for the poor to harvest. Moreover, the Rabbis add topics to the biblical agrarian duties of gleaning, first fruits, and sacrifice (Lev. 19:16–18 and Deut. 26:1–11), namely *Gemilut Hasadim* (acts of loving-kindness) and *Talmud Torah* (the study of Torah). Their addition of the acts of loving-kindness and study of Torah becomes immediately clear as the Mishnah continues with "These are the things whose fruit a man enjoys in this world and whose capital is set aside for him in the world to come: honoring one's father and mother, performing deeds of loving-kindness, and bringing peace between human beings." The Mishnah then concludes with a broad statement: "And the study of Torah is considered equal to them all." The Rabbis seldom make statements about eschatology or life in the next world, but they assert in this Mishnah both that certain commandments will produce rewards in this lifetime and that the merit from their praxis will sustain the individual in the next world.

The first action described in this Mishnah is obedience to the biblical commandment to honor one's father and mother. This commandment, in its formulation in Exodus 20:11, indicates that honoring parents will give the individual length of days. I want to emphasize that the commandment in Exodus 20 to honor father and mother is repeated, with slightly different wording, in Leviticus 19:3, the holiness code. The repeated mention of acts of loving-kindness in both parts of the Mishnah appears to lack any biblical warrant beyond the appearance of both terms in Proverbs 21:21, "The one who pursues righteousness and good deeds will find a life of righteousness and honor." In any case, deeds of loving-kindness are linked to the bringing of peace between human beings. In this manner, the rabbinic sages of the Mishnah set forth an agenda for a just society. It would be a society where parents were honored, where deeds of loving-kindness and active financial support for those who were less fortunate were mandated, and where individuals made peace where there was strife. We can then conclude that family, economic justice, and peace are at the heart of the Jewish perspective on social justice.

However, this portrait of a just society concludes with the rabbinic statement that the study of Torah is equal to or corresponds to all the other commandments. One modern prayer book translator adds the phrase "because it leads to them all."[14] This added gloss on the words of the Rabbis seems to be justified. The study of Torah is at the center of Jewish life. Without its narratives and its legal passages, the Jewish community would be deprived of its precious source for discerning the divine will regarding its praxis in the contemporary world.

From this Mishnah text, embedded within the context of morning prayer, we can extrapolate the broad outlines of social justice for the Jewish community. Social justice is realized in a society where the elders are honored and the physical sustenance of unfortunate members is a response to a divine commandment. Ultimately, the underlying motivation for social justice is the constant study of and devotion to the word of God as embedded in the Scripture and the teachings of the Rabbis.

Space limitations on this essay proscribe a lengthy description of the premodern Jewish *Kehillah* or community. However, any investigation into the medieval Jewish community in Europe would discern that its primary identity was expressed in the Hebrew phrase *Kehillat Kodesh* (the holy community) because it actually had juridical power in courts. The community was empowered to bring justice between its own members. It was possible even to interrupt the required prayers, a divine commandment, if one of the members felt that the court had denied him justice. The unfortunate and the poor thus had the same access to the place of prayer as those who had material sustenance and could deny the entire community their ability to fulfill the divine will if justice was denied them.[15]

Prayer and study created the framework for individual participation in a life working toward social justice. This imperative to provide for the physical sustenance of the poor and those who were deprived of material elements of life applied to both the Jewish and the non-Jewish community. For the Talmud requires, and later Jewish codes enshrined, that Jews give financial sustenance to the non-Jewish nations of the world as well as to the Jews in order to promote the paths of peace.[16] The Mishnah passage from *Peah* is our portal to understanding the Jewish roots of social justice. I would like to underscore the importance of the biblical allusions within this Mishnah. which point to the Pentateuch rather than to the prophetic books of Hebrew Scripture.

One could surely demonstrate that the concern for social justice within the Jewish community originates in the literature of the Hebrew prophets. Their explicit cry for justice to the poor and the widow is at the heart of any vision for peace and justice that turns to the Hebrew Scriptures for inspiration.[17] Indeed, my own branch of the Jewish community, the Reform movement, described the prophetic literature of the Hebrew canon as the hermeneutical center of the Hebrew Bible. All other parts of the Bible were read through the lens of the prophetic books. Abraham Geiger, a brilliant rabbi in Berlin during the nineteenth century, formulated a vision of Judaism as ethical monotheism and shaped his notion on Jewish practice, centered on the mission of Israel as a light unto the nations.[18] However, in this essay I want to draw attention not to those well-known passages in the prophetic literature but more directly to the five books of Moses, which stand at the center of Jewish formulations of community and identity.

FROM THE PRAYER BOOK TO SCRIPTURE

The Mishnah read in the morning service is a portal to two sections of the Pentateuch: the legal formulations that follow upon the theophany at Sinai (Exod. 21–23) and the holiness code in Leviticus 19. We discern elements of caring for the poor and those who are deprived in both of these sections of Scripture. Exodus 21–24 is known as *Sefer Habrit,* the Book of the Covenant. It focuses on elements of inequity and injustice such as the treatment of slaves, the treatment of grave offenses such as murder, parental abuse, kidnapping, infliction of body harm, and damages caused by animals. The Book of the Covenant also speaks of the treatment of the stranger, widows, and orphans. Exodus 22:21 states, "You shall not ill treat any widow or orphan. If you do mistreat them, I will hear their outcry as soon as they cry out to me." The intertextual relatedness of these chapters in the book of Exodus with the earlier story of God's hearing the cry of the Israelites when they were in slavery is undeniable (Exod. 3:7).

The holiness code in Leviticus 19 also provides an outline for a just society within the framework that those commandments make Israel a holy people. "You shall be holy for I the Lord your God am a Holy God" (Lev. 19:2). However, the first two commandments to constitute that holiness are "You shall, every one of you, honor your father and mother and you shall keep my Sabbaths" (Lev. 19:3). The conjunction of honoring one's parents and keeping the Sabbath is in our modern discourse a juxtaposition of the social and the ritual. These two elements form the heart of the holiness code that is articulated in Leviticus 19. There is an intertwining of these demands as directions are set forth regarding the treatment of the poor and the stranger. The commandment about leaving the corners of the field for the poor is as much a part of the embodiment of holiness as the establishment of courts and the supervision of weights and measures in the marketplace.

While it may be argued that many elements in each of these passages from the Pentateuch may be unjust from our modern perspective, when we look at the overall structure of them we discern that they provide an overarching framework for a society that had the potential and indeed the commandment to create equity. To put it in other words, if there is no acknowledgment of slavery, there can be no knowledge or hope for freedom. If slavery means that the chattel is only an object at the whim of the master, there is no hope that there can even be proposed limits on the master's conduct. In each case, the Pentateuch provides a framework that can lead to a praxis of justice and peace. Indeed, we can observe that the deeper the study of Torah, the greater the opportunity for justice.

NOMOS AND NARRATIVE

The Book of the Covenant, Exodus 20:1–23, is juxtaposed to the theophany at Sinai in Exodus 19 and the revelation at Sinai, the Decalogue, in Exodus 20.[19] Immediately after the account of how the Israelites experienced the vision of thunder and lightning atop the mountain and stood in the presence of the Deity, the Pentateuch provides a section of what appear to be desiccated legal passages. The holiness code, in all its complexity, appears in narrative juxtaposition to the death of the two sons of Aaron, who offered strange fire upon the altar. Once again, after the story of that event of divine punishment, the Pentateuch provides numerous sections of legal discourse. The first modern critical biblical scholars developed a method that cut the ties between these two forms of discourse, pronouncing them to be separable and indeed desiring their separation, asserting that story enlivens but legal discourse destroys the spirit. Justice was to be pursued beyond the minutiae of ritual law.[20]

The ancient Rabbis were aware of the jarring disjunction between these two literary forms as well. But perhaps, as we search for the Jewish roots of social discourse, rabbinic wisdom points to another way to handle the juxtapositions that have so offended modern thinkers. Here I quote the Rabbis, who begin by quoting the words of Scripture:

> *These are the statutes:* Just as it is written in the book of Exodus above this in a previous portion, "They shall judge the people at all times," and Scripture says, "These are the statutes and the commandments are in the middle. This juxtaposition may be compared to the noble woman who goes forth with an armed guard on one side and an armed guard on another side." So it is with Torah. The law stands before her and after her while she is in the middle. So Scripture states in Proverbs 0.20, "Your attempt is a path of righteousness." The Torah says, "In what path shall I walk? I shall walk in the paths of the one who *does* righteousness and in the midst of the pathways, in the midst of the law, in the midst of the statutes."[21]

Here we can observe an embodiment of Torah as a woman who is identified with wisdom. Torah is identified with the narrative, and standing as guardians of its preciousness are the laws and statutes. Torah itself walks the path of righteousness because the ability to judge or to establish judgment (*Mishpat* in Hebrew) indicates the clear path.

Another passage from the Rabbis restates this important theme, "*These are the statutes.*" Isaiah 5:16 states, "The Lord of Hosts is exalted in justice and the holy God is sanctified by righteousness." The Rabbis comment, "Great is justice, for the holy one has multiplied meritorious character traits in his world." These character traits are peace and truth, deeds of loving-kindness, humility, faith, and blessing. Out of all of these character traits, God linked only one with the divine name: *Mishpat,* or justice.

We know this because Scripture says in Malachi 2:17, "Where is the God of justice?"[22] The endless discussions of the nature of divine attributes in rabbinic literature and medieval Jewish philosophical discourse are epitomized in the rabbinic passage that ends with this question and are expressed there with great rhetorical power. This essay has, I hope, demonstrated that the answer lies between *nomos* (law) and narrative. For the Jewish community, the question of praxis always lies at the center of the search for God. Jews, Christians, and indeed other religions in the world continually ask themselves the question posed by the prophet Malachi, "Where is the God of justice?" The answer for Jews is that the God of justice may be found in our stories, but these stories must be protected again and again by justice and laws.

A final passage from the Rabbis, "*These are the statutes,*" is addressed directly to judges of future generations. "The holy one said to the judges who sit in the courts, Be cautious in judgment, for I sit among you." As Scripture states in Psalm 92:1, "God sits in the congregation of the Lord." The Rabbis further comment, "Be cautious about widows and orphans because I am their father." As Scripture states in Psalm 68:7, "God is the father of orphans and the advocate, the judge, of widows." Furthermore, Jerusalem was destroyed only because judges perverted justice. As the prophet Isaiah said, "Your rulers are rogues and cronies of thieves; every one of them is avid for presents and greedy for gifts. They do not judge the case of the orphan and the widow's cause never reaches them" (Isa. 1:23).[23]

We see here that we have come full circle—from the idea of the Mishnah text and its description of what brings reward in this world of praxis and carries on into the next world, through the juxtaposition of *nomos* and narrative in Scripture, to the idea that even the judge's court of law is to be held up to the standard of justice. Not only are judges to dispense justice, but it is to be not their justice but God's justice, the justice of caring for orphans and widows. Indeed, if judges are greedy and the widow's cause never reaches them, then there may be courts but they are not courts of justice.

I close with a quote from Abraham Joshua Heschel, the great teacher of Jewish spirituality and Jewish intellectual life. He wrote to President John F. Kennedy in 1962, "The hour calls for high moral grandeur and spiritual audacity."[24] In calling the world to the preferential option for the poor, Christianity and Catholicism awaken within each tradition its own reflection and its own unique contribution to making this world a place of greater justice. The Jewish tradition, through reading its daily prayers, the Hebrew Bible, and the Rabbis, gives the Jewish people a vision of moral grandeur that requires each generation to be linked to courage and audacity of spirit.

NOTES

1. For the text of *Nostra aetate* and its significance, see Roger Brooks, ed., *Unanswered Questions: Theological Views of Jewish-Catholic Relations* (Notre Dame: University of Notre Dame Press, 1988), 17–22.

2. Commission on Interreligious Relations with the Jews, "Guidelines and Suggestions for Jewish-Christian Relations," in ibid., 29.

3. The most significant statements by John Paul II can be found in *Spiritual Pilgrimage: Texts on Jews and Judaism 1979–1995,* ed. Eugene J. Fisher and Leon Klenicki (New York: Crossroad, 1979). Statements since 1995 are available at www.vatican.va.

4. The possibilities for the future of Jewish-Christian dialogue are explicated in Tikva Frymer-Kensky et al., eds., *Christianity in Jewish Terms* (Boulder, CO: Westview Press, 2000), 366–73. *Dabru Emet: A Jewish Statement on Christians and Christianity,* issued in September 2000 by the Jewish Scholars Group on Christianity, is the first theological statement of response to the profound changes in Christian theologies of Judaism during the past forty years. See the response to *Dabru Emet* by the Christian Scholars Group, "A Sacred Obligation: Rethinking Christian Faith in Relation to Judaism and the Jewish People" (2002), www.bc.edu/research/cjl/meta-elements/partners/CSG/Sacred_Obligation.htm (accessed May 24, 2006).

5. H. L. Strack and Gunther Stemberger, *Introduction to Talmud and Midrash* (Minneapolis: Fortress Press, 1992), provides a survey of the genres in rabbinic

literature. A sensitive and subtle analysis of how the Rabbis built their authority structure can be found in Hindy Najman, *Seconding Sinai: The Development of Mosaic Discourse in Second Temple Judaism* (Boston: Brill, 2003).

6. Michael A. Signer, "Searching the Scriptures: Jews, Christians, and the Book," in *Christianity in Jewish Terms* (Boulder, CO: Westview Press, 2000), 85–99, describes the link between Tanakh and Torah study in Judaism and parallels in the Christian tradition.

7. Lee I. Levine, *The Ancient Synagogue: The First Thousand Years* (New Haven: Yale University Press, 2000), 124–60, describes the functions of the synagogue.

8. The history of Jewish liturgy is presented in Ismar Elbogen, *Jewish Liturgy: A Comprehensive History,* trans. Raymond P. Scheindlin (Philadelphia: Jewish Publication Society of America, 1993). Jewish liturgy and its theological implications are explored by Adin Steinsaltz, *A Guide to Jewish Prayer* (New York: Schocken Books, 2000).

9. All references and citations of the *Birkhot HaShahar* will be from Joseph H. Hertz, ed., *The Authorized Daily Prayerbook,* rev. ed. (New York: Bloch, 1957), 12–32.

10. Moses Maimonides, "Laws of Prayers," in *Mishneh Torah* (Jerusalem: Makor, 1975), ch. 1.

11. Elbogen, *Jewish Liturgy,* 57.

12. Hertz, *Authorized Daily Prayerbook,* 4–16.

13. *Peah* 1:1 (Mishnah). The translation is my own.

14. Chaim Stern, ed., *Gates of Prayer: The New Union Prayer Book* (New York: Central Conference of American Rabbis, 1983), 53.

15. Salo W. Baron, *The Jewish Community,* 3 vols. (Philadelphia: Jewish Publication Society of America, 1942); Louis Finkelstein, *Jewish Self-Government in the Middle Ages* (New York: P. Feldheim, 1964).

16. Babylonian Talmud, *Tractate Gittin* 61a, is the primary statement of this principle of Jewish law. It appears also in Moses Maimonides, "Law of Gifts to the Poor," in *Mishneh Torah* (Jerusalem: Makor, 1975), ch. 7, halakhah 7, and in the Northern European law code *Kol Bo,* par. 97.

17. See the beautiful formulations of social justice in Sheldon Blank, *Prophetic Faith in Isaiah* (Detroit: Wayne State University Press, 1967), and Abraham Joshua Heschel, *The Prophets* (New York: Harper and Row, 1969–72).

18. On Abraham Geiger's influence on Reform Judaism, see *Abraham Geiger and Liberal Judaism: The Challenge of the Nineteenth Century,* comp. Max Wiener (Cincinnati: Hebrew Union College Press, 1981), and Ludwig Geiger, ed., *Abraham Geiger: Leben und Werk für ein Judentum in der Moderne* (1910; reprint, Berlin: Jüdische Verlagsanstalt, 2000), 295–300.

19. The rubric that serves as the title of this section is taken from Robert M. Cover, "Foreword: Nomos and Narrative," *Harvard Law Review* 97 (November 1983): 4.

20. Jewish theologians Michael Wyschogrod and Jacob Neusner, "The Torah as Law in Judaism" and "Talmudic Law and Criticism," both in *Seeds of Reconcili-*

ation: Essays on Jewish-Christian Understanding, ed. Katharine T. Hargrove (Berkeley, CA: Bibal Press, 1996), 117–28 and 139–53 respectively, describe the relationship of law and narrative.

21. Menachem Kasher, *Torah Shelemah,* Exod. 21:2.

22. Ibid.

23. Ibid.

24. Abraham Joshua Heschel, *Moral Grandeur and Spiritual Audacity,* ed. Susannah Heschel (New York: Farrar, Straus, Giroux, 1996), vii.

CONTRIBUTORS

MARÍA PILAR AQUINO is a Professor of Theology and Religious Studies and Associate Director of the Center for the Study of Latino/a Catholicism at the University of San Diego. She is the author of many articles and books, including *Our Cry for Life: Feminist Theology from Latin America* (1993) and *A Reader in Latina Feminist Theology: Religion and Justice* (2002).

J. MATTHEW ASHLEY is an Associate Professor of Systematic Theology at the University of Notre Dame. He is the author of *Interruptions: Mysticism, Politics and Theology in the Work of Johann Baptist Metz* (1998) and the translator of Johann B. Metz's *A Passion for God: The Mystical-Political Dimension of Christianity* (1998). He is also author of a forthcoming book on Ignatian spirituality and twentieth-century academic theology called *Ignatius and the Theologians*.

M. SHAWN COPELAND is an Associate Professor of Theology at Boston College; an Associate Professor of Systematic Theology at the Institute for Black Catholic Studies, Xavier University of Louisiana, New Orleans; and a past president of the Catholic Theological Society of America. She is the author of over seventy articles and book chapters, including "Disturbing Aesthetics of Race," in the *Journal of Catholic Social Thought* (2006), and "Body, Race, and Being: Theological Anthropology in the Context of Performing and Subverting Eucharist," in *Constructive Theology: A Contemporary Approach to Classical Themes* (2005).

BRIAN E. DALEY, S.J., is the Catherine F. Huisking Professor of Theology at the University of Notre Dame. He has published many monographs, articles, and reviews on patristic and historical theology. Among his latest books are *The Dormition of Mary: Early Greek Homilies* (1998), *The Hope of the Early Church: A Handbook of Patristic Eschatology* (rev. ed. 2003), and *Gregory of Nazianzus* (2006).

VIRGILIO ELIZONDO holds the chair of the Notre Dame Professor of Pastoral and Hispanic Theology at the University of Notre Dame. The university also awarded him its highest honor, the Laetare Medal, in 1997, and *Time* has recognized him as one of the top spiritual innovators of this century. Among his many books are *Galilean Journey* (1983, 2000), *Guadalupe: Mother of the New Creation* (1997), *Beyond Borders* (2000), and *God of Incredible Surprises* (2004).

THE LATE CASIANO FLORISTÁN was Professor of Pastoral Theology at the Pontifical University of Salamanca. He served as an advisor to the Spanish bishops at Vatican II and was a member of the Board of Directors of the international journal *Concilium*. He is the author of, among many books, *The Parish: Eucharistic Community* (1964) and *Teología práctica: Teoría y praxis de la acción pastoral* (2002).

DANIEL G. GROODY, C.S.C., is an Assistant Professor of Theology and Director of the Center for Latino Spirituality and Culture at the University of Notre Dame's Institute for Latino Studies. He is the author of *Border of Death, Valley of Life: An Immigrant Journey of Heart and Spirit* (2002), *Globalization, Spirituality and Social Justice* (2007), other edited books, and many articles. He has directed numerous international conferences, including "The Option for the Poor in Christian Theology" (2002) and "Migration and Theology" (2004), and has produced numerous videos, including the documentary *Dying to Live: A Migrant's Journey* (2005), which has aired on PBS and other television stations.

GUSTAVO GUTIÉRREZ, O.P., is the John Cardinal O'Hara Professor of Theology at the University of Notre Dame. He is best known for his groundbreaking book *A Theology of Liberation: History, Politics, and Salvation* (1971), *On Job: God-Talk and the Suffering of the Innocent* (1987), and *We Drink from Our Own Wells* (1984). Among his many other books are numerous publications on issues of liberation theology, spirituality, and the preferential option for the poor.

MARY CATHERINE HILKERT, O.P., is a Professor of Systematic Theology at the University of Notre Dame and a past president of the Catholic Theological Society of America. Her publications include *The Praxis of the Reign of God: An Introduction to the Theology of Edward Schillebeeckx,* with Robert J. Schreiter (2002); *Speaking with Authority: Catherine of Siena and the Voices of Women Today* (2001); and *Naming Grace: Preaching and the Sacramental Imagination* (1997).

BISHOP PATRICK A. KALILOMBE is the Executive Director of the Centre for Black and White Christian Partnership at Selly Oak Colleges, Birmingham, England. From 1972 to 1976 he served as Roman Catholic Bishop of the Diocese of Lilongwe, Malawi, in Africa. He has founded various African religious centers, and his publications include *The Theology of Communications from an African Point of View* (1993) and *Doing Theology at the Grassroots: Theological Essays from Malawi* (2000).

LUIS MALDONADO is Professor Emeritus of Pastoral Theology at the Pontifical University of Salamanca. He is a priest of the Archdiocese of Madrid and advisor to the Special Movements of Catholic Action in Spain. He is a specialist in liturgy and popular religion, studies that he has disseminated through numerous books, including *Experiencia religiosa y lenguaje de Santa Teresa* (1982) and *Génesis del catolicismo popular: El inconsciente colectivo de un proceso histórico* (1979).

HUGH R. PAGE JR. is an Associate Professor of Hebrew Scriptures and the Walter Chair in Theology at the University of Notre Dame. His publications include *The Myth of Cosmic Rebellion: A Study of Its Reflexes in Ugaritic and Biblical Literature* (1996), *Exploring New Paradigms in Biblical and Cognate Studies* (1996), and many articles, reviews, reference works, bulletins, and monographs.

ALOYSIUS PIERIS, S.J., the founder-director of the Tulana Research Center, Kelaniya, Sri Lanka, is an Indologist specializing in Buddhist philosophy and ancient Pali literature as well as a theologian who has worked out an Asian model of Christian thought and practice. He has held chairs of theology in many universities and has been a guest lecturer on many theological and Buddhist faculties. He has authored several books and several hundred research papers in both fields. He is also the editor of *Dialogue,* an international review for Buddhists and Christians, which he co-founded with the Methodist theologian Dr. Lynn A. de Silva in 1974.

MICHAEL A. SIGNER is Abrams Professor in the Department of Theology at the University of Notre Dame. He is Director of the Notre Dame Holocaust Project, an interdisciplinary faculty group that designs educational opportunities for students to engage in the study of the Shoah. Since 1998 he has been Co-chair of the Joint Commission on Interreligious Affairs of the Reform movement. Rabbi Signer is the author and editor of five books, including *Memory and History in Judaism and Christianity* (2001), *Jews and Christians in Twelfth-Century Europe* (2001), and *Humanity at the Limit: The Impact of the Holocaust Experience on Jews and Christians* (2000), as well as various articles.

JON SOBRINO, S.J., is a Professor of Theology at the University of Central America. He has been living in El Salvador for more than forty years and is the author of many books, including *Christology at the Crossroads* (1978), *Jesus the Liberator: The Principle of Mercy* (1994), *Where Is God? Earthquake, Terrorism, Barbarity, and Hope* (2004), and, with Ignacio Ellacuría, *Mysterium Liberationis: Fundamental Concepts of Liberation Theology* (1993).

ELSA TAMEZ is Professor of Biblical Studies at the Latin American Biblical University. She has written several books and many articles. Among her books translated into English are *Bible of the Oppressed* (1982), *The Scandalous Message of James* (1989), *Amnesty of Grace* (1993), *When the Horizons Close: Rereading Ecclesiastes* (2000), and *Jesus and Courageous Women* (2001).

DAVID TRACY is Andrew Thomas Greeley and Grace McNichols Greeley Distinguished Service Professor of Catholic Studies and a Professor of Theology and of the Philosophy of Religion in the Divinity School of the University of Chicago. Among his major publications are *Blessed Rage for Order: The New Pluralism in Theology* (1975) and *On Naming the Present: Reflections on God, Hermeneutics, and Church* (1994). He has also edited a number of issues of the international journal *Concilium*. Professor Tracy is currently working on a three-volume work on the doctrine of God.

GENERAL INDEX

agape, 239–42, 247–50, 252, 255, 256
Aguirre, R., 248
Ahmed, Sir Syed, 276
Albright, William F., 60
Allen, John, 278
"already," 138–39
Amnesty International, 208
Anderson, Rufus, 174
Angela of Foligno, 144
apocalyptic, 124–25, 129–30, 132,
    135–39, 142, 144, 146–48.
    See also "already"; "not yet";
    "soon"
apocalypticism, Second Temple
    Jewish, 135
apophasis, 132, 145–46
Aquino, María Pilar, 228–30, 232
Aristophanes, *Ecclesiazusae,* 254
Ashley, J. Matthew, 120
Asian Theological Consultation
    (1979), 279
Augustine, 19, 101, 124–25, 149

baptism, 165–66, 170, 244, 284–87
Barnabas, 287
Barth, Karl, 24, 150
Basil of Caesarea, 78–80
Beit Midrash (house of study), 292

Benjamin, Walter, 30, 119, 133, 144
Bernstein, Richard, 119
Birkhot HaShahar (morning
    benedictions), 292
Birkhot Torah (blessings of the Torah),
    293
Bloch, Ernst, 135, 137
Boff, Leonardo, 48
Bonhoeffer, Dietrich, 107, 265
Book of the Covenant (*Sefer Habrit,*
    Exodus 21–24), 296–97
brother, 244–45, 248
Buddhism, 126, 282
Bultmann, Rudolf, 125, 130, 136–37

"Cachorro," 262, 264
Camdessus, 51–52
Cassidy, Richard, 221
caste discrimination, 277
Castillo, J. M., 242
cataphasis, 145–46
Catherine of Siena, 233
Catholicism: official, 260; popular,
    260–64, 266
Centesimus annus, 56, 58
Chalcedon, Council of, 96, 280, 282
Chenu, Marie-Dominique, 33
Christian Workers' Fellowship, 276

INDEX OF SCRIPTURE REFERENCES

DANIEL G. GROODY

is assistant professor of theology
and director of the Center for Latino Spirituality and Culture
at the University of Notre Dame.
He is the author and editor of a number of books,
including *Border of Death, Valley of Life:*
An Immmigrant Journey of Heart and Spirit.